Organ Transplants
from Executed Prisoners
revised edition

ALSO BY LOUIS J. PALMER, JR.,
AND FROM MCFARLAND

*The Death Penalty in the United States:
A Complete Guide to Federal and State Laws,*
second edition (2014)

*Encyclopedia of DNA and the United States
Criminal Justice System* (2004; paperback 2013)

*Encyclopedia of Capital Punishment
in the United States,* second edition (2008)

———————————

BY LOUIS J. PALMER, JR.,
AND XUEYAN Z. PALMER

Encyclopedia of Abortion in the United States,
second edition (2009)

Organ Transplants from Executed Prisoners

An Argument for Death Sentence Organ Removal Statutes

Louis J. Palmer, Jr.

REVISED EDITION

McFarland & Company, Inc., Publishers
Jefferson, North Carolina

LIBRARY OF CONGRESS CATALOGUING-IN-PUBLICATION DATA

Palmer, Louis J., Jr., 1956– author.
    Organ transplants from executed prisoners ; an argument for death sentence organ removal statutes / Louis J. Palmer, Jr. — Revised edition.
       p.   cm.
    Includes bibliographical references and index.

    ISBN 978-0-7864-7990-0 (softcover : acid free paper) ∞
    ISBN 978-1-4766-1636-0 (ebook)

    1. Donation of organs, tissues, etc.—Law and legislation—United States. 2. Capital punishment—United States.
3. Dead bodies (Law)—United States. I. Title.
KF3827.D66P35 2014
344.7304'194—dc23   2014012482

BRITISH LIBRARY CATALOGUING DATA ARE AVAILABLE

© 2014 Louis J. Palmer, Jr. All rights reserved

No part of this book may be reproduced or transmitted in any form or by any means, electronic or mechanical, including photocopying or recording, or by any information storage and retrieval system, without permission in writing from the publisher.

Front cover images © 2014 TongRo Images, iStock/Thinkstock

Printed in the United States of America

McFarland & Company, Inc., Publishers
  Box 611, Jefferson, North Carolina 28640
    www.mcfarlandpub.com

To the memory of past,
present and future victims
of capital murder

Table of Contents

Introduction	1
1. Creation of Rights in a Corpse	5
Origin and Meaning of Common Law	5
Common Law No-Property Rule	7
Initial Use of No-Property Rule in America	20
American Courts Develop Quasi-Property Rule	24
2. The Market for Human Body Parts	43
Medical Science Breakthrough	44
Unfulfilled Demand for Body Parts	45
Sale of Body Parts Prohibited	47
Current Method of Obtaining Body Parts	52
Proposals for Commercializing the Body-Part Market	53
Presumed Consent	57
The Israeli Organ-for-Organ Law	59
Mandated Choice	60
3. Removing Transplantable Organs of Capital Felons	62
Statutory Disposal of Corpses	63
Removing Organs as Part of the Death Sentence	64
Justification for Removing Organs	71
4. Organ-Removal Statutes and the United States Constitution	85
Free Exercise Clause	86
Establishment Clause	90
Involuntary Servitude Clause	94
Slavery Clause	95
Takings Clause	96

Table of Contents

Seizure Clause	98
Equal Protection Clause	99
Due Process Clause	104
Cruel and Unusual Punishment Clause	107
5. The Need for a New Method of Execution	115
Current Methods of Execution	115
Inefficiency of Present Execution Methods	138
Utilizing an Efficient Method of Execution	141
6. Other Necessary Changes in Capital Punishment Laws	142
Minimizing Discrimination in Capital Punishment	143
Expediting Capital Punishment	155
7. Practical Considerations	161
Ownership of Body Parts	161
Anonymity Issues	162
Appendix: Model Death Sentence Organ Removal Statute	163
Chapter Notes	167
Index	181

INTRODUCTION

In 1999 the first edition of this book made a controversial proposal: utilize the transplantable organs of executed felons to save countless American lives. The proposal made in the first edition has been cited in numerous publications including: Ruth Richardson, *Death, Dissection and the Destitute*, second edition (University of Chicago Press, 2001); Donny J. Perales, "Rethinking the Prohibition of Death Row Prisoners as Organ Donors: A Possible Lifeline to Those on Organ Donor Waiting Lists," 34 *St. Mary's Law Journal* 687 (2002); Pat M. McCarrick and Martina Darragh, "Incentives for Providing Organs," 13 *Kennedy Institute of Ethics Journal* 53 (2003); Kathryn Staiano-Ross, "Losing Myself: Body as Icon/Body as Object(s)," 154 *Semiotica* 57 (2005); David I. Flamholz, "A Penny for Your Organs: Revising New York's Policy on Offering Financial Incentives for Organ Donation," 14 *Journal of Law & Policy* 329 (2006); Tracie M. Kester, "Can the Dead Hand Control the Dead Body? The Case for a Uniform Bodily Remains Law," 29 *Western New England Law Review* 571 (2007); Brandi L. Kellam, "A Life for a Life: Why Death Row Inmates Should Be Allowed to Donate Their Organs Following Execution," 81 *UMKC Law Review* 461 (2012). In his article, "Transplantation and the Trolley Case: Why Not Confiscate Cadaveric Organs?," available from the Social Science Review Network (SSRN 2030011, 2012), Professor Pablo De Lora of the Universidad Autónoma de Madrid wrote the following:

> [T]here is a legitimate concern that a confiscatory policy of cadaveric organs could have the undesirable side effect of reinforcing death penalty or even establishing it. Arguably, the U.S. public might compel the authorities to prioritize death row inmates for organ confiscation after their execution. This policy has been defended, among others, by Louis Palmer, Jr.

Introduction

... Palmer is not alone; he has been joined even by some of the potential "donors": the Oregon death row inmate Christian Longo has launched the organization GAVE (Gifts of Anatomical Value from Everyone) which advocates that prisoners sentenced to death should be authorized to "donate" [*Id.* at 45–46, http://blogs.law.harvard.edu/billofhealth/files/2012/09/Transplantation-and-the-Trolley-Case-long-version.pdf].

The revised edition of this book continues the debate on whether transplantable organs of executed capital felons should be used to save American lives. The revised edition provides the general public with the relevant data and information that is necessary for making an informed and intelligent decision on this crucial matter.

The majority of American states have decided that criminals who commit capital murder do not have a right to life and must be executed. It is my position that transplantable organs of capital murderers should be removed at the time of execution, and made available without charge to citizens in need of transplantable organs. It is patently illogical to argue that capital murderers have no right to life, and in the same breath proclaim that capital murderers have a right to have their transplantable organs buried with their cadavers. Mercy should flourish for the living, not the decomposing remains of executed individuals. In the final analysis, if confronted with the choice, capital murderers would let society have their transplantable organs upon dying of old age, in exchange for the right to die of old age.

If society must execute capital murderers, then society must approach the issue wearing the lenses of the twenty-first century. Medical advancements permit the callous vision of past centuries to be discarded while holding out a guarantee of extending the life of those who need healthy transplantable organs—if such organs can be made available. It is imperative that society embrace the outstretched promises of tomorrow by grasping the promises of today. The execution of capital murderers must no longer be an end in itself; it must be a beginning for those who will benefit from the healthy transplantable organs of those who brutally took the lives of others.

Death is inevitable. This daunting truth, however, must never be a platform for accepting resignations to life. The will of the living, though torn and tattered by the march toward inevitability, must cling to the

Introduction

genius of its imagination and wring life out of death. This is the clarion call of the proposal to utilize the healthy transplantable organs of those executed for the senseless murder of others. We must make the unforgivable capital murderer a tree of life.

Of course, much work must be done to set in motion the forces that will bring about the ultimate necessary changes to death-sentence laws. The debate raging in the legal community is currently being won by those who would deny extending life through utilization of the transplantable organs of executed capital felons. The intellectual voice of reason must and will beat back those who fear not simply the future, but the possibilities of the present.

The emotionally propelled obstacles of a surging minority in the legal community will be quickly overcome. This is not the main battlefront. The trench warfare that must be waged to implement statutes for death-sentence organ removal resides outside the legal community. Death-sentence organ-removal statutes will become commonplace in the nation once individual citizens intelligently weigh the benefits reaped from such statutes versus the loss occasioned by traditional death sentence statutes. The scales of justice tilt overwhelmingly in favor of statutes for death-sentence organ removal.

The following chapters provide a blueprint for the future of capital punishment in the United States. Chapter 1 outlines the legal history of the human corpse as that history unfolded in England under the common law. The chapter traces early U.S. legal curiosity over human cadavers and follows that curiosity to the present legal status of cadavers. Chapter 2 shifts the focus by setting out the broad contours of the modern-day market for transplantable human organs. The material in Chapter 3 presents legal justifications for permitting courts to impose, as part of a capital felon's death sentence, the removal of all healthy transplantable organs. Chapter 4 examines in detail the federal constitutional arguments that will be made by capital felons attempting to challenge the removal of their transplantable organs. In Chapter 5 a brief examination of current methods of execution is provided, along with some discussion of the need to implement a new method of execution that will allow harvesting the healthy transplantable organs of capital felons. Chapter 6 reviews other changes that must occur in prosecuting

Introduction

capital murderers. The additional changes include expediting executions and minimizing ethnic, racial, gender, and economic discrimination in the determination of who will be prosecuted for capital murder. Chapter 7 looks at some of the practical issues, such as ownership and anonymity, involved in harvesting the organs of capital felons. An appendix provides a model for legislatures to consider in creating statutes for death-sentence organ removal.

1

CREATION OF RIGHTS IN A CORPSE

An American court at the turn of the century stated, "A corpse in some respects is the strangest thing on earth."[1] The intent of this chapter is to retrace the legal steps of the "strangest thing on earth," that is, the human corpse. This journey will necessarily have as its starting point the shores of England, since the jurisprudential richness that engulfs American law is indebted to English jurisprudence.

In setting out the review of the legal development of a human corpse, the chapter has been divided into four major parts. In the first part some discussion is devoted to understanding the origin and meaning of the multipurpose phrase *common law*. The second part presents a discussion of the common law's treatment of a corpse. In the third part an examination of how a corpse was viewed by early American law is provided. The final part of the chapter narrows the discussion to the abrupt shift in the manner in which American courts treat a corpse.

Origin and Meaning of Common Law

It is important to understand at the outset that two dichotomous types of legal systems existed in the early history of England. The island nation had a temporal legal system and an ecclesiastical legal system. The common-law legal principles that will be introduced in this chapter were developed in the temporal courts. It will be shown shortly that England's dual legal system played a significant role in causing the human corpse to be treated as a worthless object by the temporal courts.

Organ Transplants from Executed Prisoners

ORIGIN OF COMMON LAW

A good summary of the earliest beginnings of the dual judicial system of England was provided by an American court in the case *Beard v. Worrell*.[2] The court in *Beard* said the following:

> England in the reign of Henry II (1154–1189) was a feudal domain in which the king's courts were struggling to establish a national system of law (i.e., a law "common" to all parts of England) in the face of competition from traditional local centers of judicial power. Among the strongest competitors for judicial power were the manorial courts of local magnates who held courts for their vassals in furtherance of their authority as landlords, and the ecclesiastical courts which claimed jurisdiction with regard to all matters touching faith and morals. The claims of the ecclesiastical courts presented a monumental problem for the king's jurisdiction because in the middle ages almost everything touched faith and morals, including testamentary disposition of personal property, obligations involving an oath, and all matters concerning the family.
>
> Resistance from the manorial courts did not present a major political problem, but rather a problem more akin to the resistance which a modern leader experiences in attempting to innovate in the face of an entrenched bureaucracy.
>
> However, the struggle against the courts Christian was another matter, involving as it did a general power struggle throughout Europe between temporal and ecclesiastical authorities. The struggle between Thomas Becket and Henry II was basically a struggle concerning the proper domain of ecclesiastical jurisdiction. In 1164 the Constitutions of Clarendon attempted to resolve the conflict by establishing the respective areas of jurisdiction of the temporal and ecclesiastical courts and by providing that royal justices would decide which tribunal had jurisdiction.[3]

The temporal courts of England developed what came to be known as the common law. It has been documented that the "[t]he term 'common law' came into use in England during the reign of Edward I (1272–1307)[.]"[4] The origin of the phrase *common law* is intertwined with the various meanings that it conveys.

THE MEANING OF COMMON LAW

Several issues are at play in looking at the meaning of the phrase *common law*. It is appropriate, therefore, to start out by examining the terms *common* and *law* separately. With reference to the term *common*,

1. Creation of Rights in a Corpse

an American court stated, "In the context of English law, use of the word 'common' ... does not mean 'ordinary' or 'vulgar,' but rather 'uniform.'"[5] That is, legal principles that derived from England's temporal courts were perceived as customs or beliefs that were *commonly* or *uniformly* recognized and accepted on the English isle, before being embraced by its temporal courts.

The term *law* is generally associated with statutes and ordinances that are enacted by legislative bodies. For example, the U.S. Congress and the British Parliament are legislative bodies that enact laws. The creation of a law, however, is not restricted to legislative bodies. Judges in the temporal courts of England began a practice, adopted by American judges, of creating what are referred to euphemistically as unenacted laws (for constitutional reasons, it is taboo in the United States to refer to judicial pronouncements as laws).

A contemporary example of the creation of an unenacted law is found in the famous case of *Miranda v. Arizona*.[6] In *Miranda* the U.S. Supreme Court created a legal principle, that is, an unenacted law, that required the police to inform apprehended criminal suspects of certain constitutional rights before attempting to interrogate them. Although the American system of government does not permit calling the *Miranda* warning a law, in the final analysis its application and effect are identical to that of a legislatively enacted law.

One of the meanings conveyed by joining the terms *common* and *law* is the reference to legal principles that have the force and effect of law but were developed by judges in England's temporal courts. In the specific context of this chapter and throughout the book, the breadth of common law is restricted to laws made in temporal courts by English judges before the twentieth century.

Another meaning attached to the phrase *common law* is the reference to England's temporal courts. That is, traditionally England's temporal courts are called common-law courts.

Common Law No-Property Rule

In reducing the description of a human corpse to its analytical essence, we may say that the corpse is nothing more than an inanimate object—like a chair or shoe. But even though a corpse may be described as an inanimate object, the common law did not attach to a corpse a specific term commonly associated with inanimate objects. The common law grouped inanimate (as well as animate) objects under the term property and gave citizens rights to whatever was deemed property. However, there was one exception. The common law refused to recognize a human corpse as property and did not permit others to claim rights in a corpse. In this regard, the common law developed the human corpse no-property rule. To understand the significance of the no-property rule, we will examine the earliest recorded pronouncements of the rule.

A Corpse Is a Lump of Earth

In 1614 a judicial opinion, *Haynes' Case,* was decided in England.[7] *Haynes* was a criminal case involving the larceny of sheets. The defendant in the case had dug up four human bodies and stole the sheets that were used to wrap the bodies. Eventually the defendant was apprehended and indicted for larceny in stealing the sheets.

The defense raised by the defendant was that larceny could not be committed against a corpse. The *Haynes* court essentially agreed with the defendant and stated that "a dead body, being but a lump of earth, has no capacity" to possess anything.[8] This description of a dead body by the *Haynes* court became the foundation for what would later become the common law's human corpse no-property rule. Ultimately, however, the *Haynes* court was able to uphold the larceny charge against the defendant. It did so by determining that ownership to the sheets remained to those who had wrapped the sheets around the dead bodies.

Haynes' pronouncement that a dead body was "a lump of earth" was an infantile principle of law searching for an identity. Two observations need to be made regarding this undeveloped common-law principle.

First, the principle derived from *Haynes* indicates that during the period in which the case was decided, the common law did not know how to address a human corpse. The common law was fully able to address sheets because sheets were recognized as property. The fact that sheets were property meant that they were the subject of ownership.

1. Creation of Rights in a Corpse

Anything that was the subject of ownership was protected by the common-law crime of larceny.

Second, the real question confronting the *Haynes* court was whether a corpse had protectable rights. This issue was not analyzed by the court. Instead of presenting a well-reasoned analysis of the nature of a corpse and its relationship to the living, the court sidestepped the matter and pronounced that a corpse was merely a lump of earth. The terse treatment was not wholly unexpected. The jurisdiction over dead bodies rested in England's ecclesiastical courts. Therefore, the common law did not feel there was an urgency to grapple with an ecclesiastical issue. Consequently, *Haynes* set a precedent that would not permit the common law to properly analyze the nature of a corpse *vis-à-vis* the living.

BIRTH OF THE NO-PROPERTY RULE

Haynes' undeveloped precedent hovered over the common law in a shapeless form until the 1749 case of *Exelby v. Handyside*.[9] *Exelby* was a civil case. The facts in the case reveal that a woman gave birth to Siamese twins who were joined at the torso. The infants apparently died shortly after birth. A local doctor became intrigued by the joined bodies of the two infants (no doubt for experimental purposes). Therefore, during the night, the doctor ventured onto the parents' property and dug up the bodies of the two infants. The couple learned of the doctor's actions and filed a civil suit against him for wrongfully taking the bodies of their dead infant twins.

The *Exelby* court looked on the lawsuit filed by the couple as a curious and unrecognizable civil claim. The only guide or legal precedent available to the court was the terse and unartful legal principle announced in *Haynes*: a corpse was a lump of earth. The court in *Exelby* concluded that the principle set out in *Haynes* was insufficient as a legal doctrine. A more definitive principle was needed to address the claim raised by the couple. In short order, the *Exelby* court latched on to the essence of what it was being asked to do by the couple. That is, the parents were asking the court to acknowledge that they had a right to their twins' cadavers and that any interference with that right was grounds for a civil lawsuit.

The *Exelby* court rejected the couple's argument. The court understood the argument as requiring it to recognize that a human corpse was property and that others could have rights to such property. The argument made by the parents was too radical and revolutionary for the court. Therefore, the court ruled, in succinct and everlasting form, that there existed no property rights in dead bodies. Thus, the common-law corpse no-property rule was born.[10]

The court in *Exelby* did not leave the couple empty-handed. It concluded that even though they could not sue for the nonconsented removal of the twins' cadavers, the parents could sue the doctor for trespassing on their land when he dug up the grave. The record in the case shows that the doctor entered into a settlement with the couple in order to avoid a trespassing lawsuit.

GROWTH OF THE NO-PROPERTY RULE

Exelby's transformation of *Haynes*' crude lump-of-earth doctrine into the no-property rule was a dramatic legal step. By distinguishing a corpse from property, *Exelby* enabled the common law to conceptualize and pigeonhole a corpse. That is, the phrase "lump of earth" had no legal significance. It was, in a sense, a fugitive doctrine in search of a legal home. *Exelby*'s pronouncement of the no-property rule rescued the lump-of-earth doctrine and placed a corpse in legal perspective. By disassociating a corpse from property, the court made it quite easy for the common law thereafter to form logically consistent and sound judgments pertaining to cadavers.

Evidence of the legal posture in which *Exelby* placed a corpse was fully apparent in the next major common-law civil case to address an issue concerning a corpse. In 1882 an English court was asked to decide the case of *Williams v. Williams*.[11] The underlying facts of *Williams* involved the last will and testament of a deceased man. In the will the decedent left instructions that his mistress, as executrix of his estate, cremate his body. However, after the man died, his family buried his corpse whole. The decedent's mistress later had his body exhumed and cremated. She then filed a civil suit against the deceased man's family, seeking reimbursement for the costs incurred in exhuming and cremating his corpse.

1. Creation of Rights in a Corpse

The court in *Williams* noted at the outset, "[T]he law of this country recognizes no property in a corpse."[12] This statement, of course, was the principle set down by *Exelby*. The court then observed, "[T]he law in this country is clear, that after the death of a man, his executors have a right to the custody and possession of his body (although they have no property in it) until it is properly buried."[13] The court's latter observation was a slight rebuke of the position taken by the *Haynes* court, insofar as it recognized that designated persons had a duty to at least bury the dead. This acknowledgment was a concession to a duty that was actually imposed and enforced by ecclesiastical courts.

After making the above two quoted observations, the *Williams* court addressed the specific issue presented to it. That is, if the mistress was allowed to recover a monetary sum, it would mean that a person had a right to dispose of his or her corpse by will. This issue was earthshaking for the court. The mistress, in effect, was asking the court to recognize a corpse as property in a narrow way and to allow each person to have a limited right in his or her corpse. The spirit of legal revolution was not churning in the *Williams* court. With logical consistency the court concluded: "[A] man cannot by will dispose of his dead body. If there be no property in a dead body it is impossible that by will or any other instrument the body can be disposed of."[14] The court denied the mistress a monetary compensation and dismissed her case. Thus, *Williams* laid down the rule that a living person could not by will dictate the disposition of his or her corpse.

JUSTIFICATION FOR THE NO-PROPERTY RULE

Combining the principles set out in *Exelby* and *Williams*, the common-law no-property rule held that neither a decedent (by will) nor the relatives of a decedent had legal standing to dictate the disposition of a corpse. The common-law no-property rule was justified on two grounds.

First, the common law took the position that a corpse was a valueless object that belonged to no one, except perhaps to God. A corpse was deemed valueless because, in the eyes of the common law, it could not impart any legally cognizant benefit to anyone. Since no benefit was derived from a corpse, it could not constitute property. Therefore, the common law had no basis to provide protectionist principles for a corpse.

The second justification for the no-property rule involved the existence of ecclesiastical courts in England. Although common-law courts had jurisdiction to resolve matters related to burial sites and monuments, which constituted property, ecclesiastical courts had jurisdiction over the actual corpse and its burial. An American court made the following observations regarding this issue:

> It is said that burial in churchyards was introduced into England by Cuthbert, Archbishop of Canterbury, in the year AD 750. At an early date the church began to take jurisdiction in regard to places of burial and the sepulture of the dead. This jurisdiction gradually became more enlarged and more firmly fixed, until the ecclesiastical courts left little for the common law courts to decide upon those subjects.[15]

Further comments on common-law and ecclesiastical courts were provided in the case *In re Beekman Street*[16]:

> An attentive examination of the progress and the proceedings of the Ecclesiastical tribunals, will show that the ancient civil [common-law] courts of England gradually lost their original, legitimate authority, over places of interment ... and their proper and necessary control over the repose of the dead. The clergy, monopolizing the judicial power over the subject, [held that] burial was committed solely to ecclesiastical cognizance; while the secular courts, stripped of all authority over the dead, were left to confine themselves to the protection of the monument and other external emblems of grief erected by the living....
> The reverent regard of the common law for these memorials is curiously manifested by Coke in the *Third Institute,* where he expatiates upon a monumental stone ... inscribed with the name of a Jewish rabbi, and inlaid in the ancient wall of London; as if to intimate, that the law would protect from injury that venerable piece of antiquity.
> But at this point the courts of the common law stopped; and held, in deference to the ecclesiastical tribunals, that the heir could maintain no civil action for indecently, or even impiously, disturbing the remains of his buried ancestor[.][17]

In 1788 a common law court in the case *Rex v. Lynn*[18] succinctly addressed the second justification for the no-property rule. The *Lynn* court quoted Lord Coke as saying: "It is to be observed that in every

1. Creation of Rights in a Corpse

sepulcher, that hath a monument, two things are to be considered ... [:] the burial of the cadaver ... belongs to ecclesiastical cognizance; but as to the monument, action is given at the common law for defacing thereof."[19]

The mere fact that common-law courts did not have jurisdiction over cadavers does not tell the full story. The common law went out of its way to formulate negative legal principles regarding dead bodies, that is, the no-property rule. The better course for the common law was to merely pronounce that it lacked jurisdiction to resolve matters pertaining directly to cadavers. By creating the no-property rule, the common law, as will be seen later, created major problems for American jurisprudence.

OTHER COMMON-LAW CADAVER CASES

The no-property rule was not ironclad. Loopholes in the rule permitted temporal courts, particularly in criminal cases, to recognize certain matters involving cadavers. A review of some of the exceptions to the rule follows.

Arresting a Dead Body. The essence of the no-property rule is the legal conclusion that a corpse does not have any value. One of the exceptions to this principle involved the cadaver of a debtor. For reasons unknown, the common law permitted a creditor to hold the corpse of a debtor hostage until payment of the debt by the decedent's loved ones.

Two incidents involving the arrest of cadavers for debts involved notable people. In 1700 the body of the poet John Dryden was arrested pending payment of his debts.[20] In 1784 the corpse of Sir Barnard Turner was apprehended until his friends arranged to pay his debts.[21] It was not until 1804, in the case *Jones v. Ashburnham*,[22] that the common law overruled precedent and prohibited arresting cadavers for the payment of debts. Lord Ellenborough, writing for the court in *Jones*, stated: "To seize a dead body upon any such pretense [of a debt] would be *contra bonos mores*, and an extortion on the relations. It is contrary to every principle of law and moral feeling. Such an act is revolting to humanity, and illegal, and, therefore, any promise extorted by it could never be valid law."[23]

An 1841 case, *Regina v. Fox*,[24] involved holding hostage the corpse of a man named Henry Foster until payment of a debt. The twist in *Fox* was that a local jailkeeper was the person holding Foster's cadaver hostage. The case record indicates that Foster had died while in jail. During his stay in jail Foster had incurred a debt to the jailer for various articles supplied to him by the jailer. When Foster died, the jailer refused to turn the corpse over to Foster's loved ones until they paid his debt. The court in *Fox* ordered the jailer to release Foster's corpse to his family.

The *Fox* case did not end with the release of Foster's body. Shortly after Foster's body was released, the jailer was indicted for unlawfully using Foster's corpse as a bargaining chip for the payment of a debt. The indictment came in 1842, in the case *Regina v. Scott*.[25] The court in *Scott* stated "that the notion of a [jailer] being authorized to detain a dead body on account of pecuniary claims was a mistake, and that a [jailer] doing so was guilty of a misconduct in his public character, for which he was liable to prosecution."[26] The jailer eventually entered a plea of guilty to the indictment.

By initially sanctioning the arrest of cadavers for debts, the common law was being inconsistent with its no-property rule. Implicit in the act of holding a cadaver hostage was a recognition that the cadaver held some value to others. This implicit acknowledgment, however, ran counter to the no-property rule. The common law never explained this inconsistency. Moreover, *Jones'* eventual prohibition of arresting cadavers for debts was justified by Lord Ellenborough on grounds that implicitly imparted value to cadavers—again, such reasoning was contrary to the no-property rule.

Libeling a Dead Body. Defaming a person's character through writings was criminally punished under the common law. Imposing criminal sanctions for libel was deemed necessary to prevent the libelee from resorting to violent actions against the libeler. This rationale is sound in the context of a living libelee. However, in the context of libeling a corpse, the rationale breaks down. Nonetheless, as was pointed out in the case *Rex v. Topham*,[27] the common law made it a crime to libel a corpse.

No real justification undergirded imposition of criminal sanctions for libeling a cadaver. True, the feelings of a decedent's loved ones may

1. Creation of Rights in a Corpse

have been harmed by libeling a corpse, but recognition of this was contrary to the no-property rule. No adequate explanation was ever given by the common law for permitting criminal punishments to be inflicted on anyone who libeled a corpse.

Duty to Bury a Corpse. Nature has cleverly designed all flesh so that it will give off pungently foul odors at death and decomposition. There is no great mystery behind this. The stench of any kind of cadaver attracts carnivorous animals—thereby providing food for them once the location of the odor is found. In former times human cadavers made a hefty meal for many animals.

Although it may be true that the spiritual march of Christianity caused Englanders to begin the practice of burying human cadavers, a case can be made that the brutal force of the stench from decaying flesh also played a role in this matter. From the perspective of the common law, it was the *nuisance* caused by the odor of rotting flesh that demanded the imposition of a duty to bury human cadavers.

The case *Regina v. Stewart*[28] addressed the issue of burying the corpse of a pauper. The court in *Stewart* noted at the outset, "[T]he common law casts on some one the duty of carrying to the grave, decently covered, the dead body of any person dying in such a state of indigence as to leave no funds for that purpose."[29] The court then provided a rough sketch of circumstances attendant to the duty to bury the corpse of a pauper:

> [T]he individual under whose roof a poor person dies is bound to carry the body decently covered to the place of burial[;] he cannot keep him unburied, nor do any thing which prevents Christian burial[;] he cannot therefore cast him out, so as to expose the body to violation ... or endanger the health of the living[;] and, for the same reason, he cannot carry him uncovered to the grave.... [T]herefore ... where a pauper dies in any parish house, poor house, or union house, that circumstance casts on the parish or union [the duty] to bury the body; not by virtue of the Statute of Elizabeth, but on the principles of the common law.[30]

Another common law case, *Regina v. Vann*,[31] involved the criminal prosecution of a pauper, William Vann, for failing to provide for the burial of his deceased child. The indictment charged Vann "for a nuisance in having refused and neglected to bury the dead body of his deceased child, whereby and by reason of the decomposition whereof various stenches arose, and the air was thereby greatly infected and rendered unwholesome[.]"[32] The issue confronting the court was whether Vann had a duty to incur a debt, which he could never pay, in order to provide for the burial of his child. The court resolved the matter as follows:

> It is true, that a man is bound to give Christian burial to his deceased child, if he has the means of doing so; but he is not liable to be indicted for a nuisance, if he has not the means of providing burial for it. He cannot sell the body, put it into a hole, or throw it into the river ... even though a nuisance may be occasioned by leaving the body unburied, for which the parish officer would probably be liable.... We are all of opinion that he was not bound ... to contract a debt which would render him liable to be proceeded against, and to lose his liberty.[33]

The case *Regina v. Price*[34] involved the criminal prosecution of a man who attempted to burn the body of his deceased child rather than having it buried. The issue raised by the *Price* decision was whether the common-law duty to provide a "Christian burial" for dead bodies precluded all other methods of disposition. The *Price* court reasoned, "'Christian burial' ... is obviously inapplicable to persons who are not Christians, Jews for instance, Mahommedans [sic], or Hindoos [sic]."[35] In recognizing that other religious faiths existed, the *Price* court acknowledged that a Christian burial was not the only acceptable method of disposing of a dead body. The court then made the following observations:

> Whether decay or fire consumes corpses matters not. The difference between the two processes is only that one is quick, the other slow. Each is so horrible that every healthy imagination would turn away from its details; but one or the other is inevitable.... There are, no doubt, religious convictions and feelings connected with the subject which every one would wish to treat with respect and tenderness.... [H]owever, ... it can[not] be said that every practice which startles and jars upon the religious sentiments of the majority of the population is for that reason a misdemeanor at common law.[36]

The court concluded "[A] person who burns instead of burying a dead body does not commit a criminal act, unless he does it in such a manner as to amount to a public nuisance at common law."[37]

1. Creation of Rights in a Corpse

A final case that wrestled with the duty to bury a corpse was *Ambrose v. Kerrison*.[38] In this civil case, a husband refused to pay the expenses incurred in providing for the interment of his estranged wife. The *Ambrose* court had little difficulty in finding that the husband, who was not indigent, had a duty to pay for the burial even though he was separated from his wife at the time of her death. The decision in *Ambrose* was consistent with the common-law rule that "[a] husband is bound to bury his deceased wife, and a wife must bury her deceased husband."[39]

The burial duty imposed by the common law was not inconsistent with the no-property rule. The duty to bury was based on the stench of a corpse, not on any rights to the corpse. Further, the duty to bury did not usurp the jurisdiction of ecclesiastical courts. The imposition of the duty was premised on the nuisance caused by the stench of a dead body. Enforcement of the law of nuisance was vested in common-law courts.

Digging Up the Dead. The previously discussed case of *Exelby v. Handyside* was a civil case involving disinterment of the cadavers of Siamese twins. *Exelby* should not be interpreted as precluding criminal prosecution for the unauthorized disinterment of dead bodies. Digging up a dead body without authorization was criminally punished by the common law. The first case to hold that it was a criminal offense to disinter a corpse without authorization appears to be the 1788 case *Rex v. Lynn*.[40]

The defendant in *Lynn* was convicted of disinterring a dead body without authorization. In determining whether such conduct constituted an offense, the *Lynn* court reviewed prior cases and legal writings to determine if anyone had ever been criminally prosecuted for such conduct. The court made the following observations:

> [I]t was also the opinion of Lord Coke that the present charge is not the subject of an indictment in a Criminal Court. There is an instance ... of a person being [arrested] with the head and face of a dead man, with a book of sorcery, and was brought into the King's Bench, but no indictment was preferred against him; and the only crime imputed to him was that of being a sorcerer. And all the writers on this subject have ... tak[en] it for granted that the act of carrying away a dead body was not criminal.[41]

The *Lynn* court rejected the historical acceptance of digging up and carting off dead bodies, and held "that common decency required that the practice should be put a stop to."[42] The court affirmed the defendant's conviction and, in doing so, made it a common-law crime to disinter a corpse without authorization.

Another leading common-law case involving the unauthorized disinterment of a corpse is *Regina v. Sharpe*.[43] "The defendant in *Sharpe* was convicted of the common law crime of removing 'without lawful authority a corpse from a grave in a burying ground belonging to a congregation of Protestant dissenters[.]'"[44] The defendant dug up his mother's body for the purpose of reinterring her at the grave site of his father. In spite of the familial gesture of the defendant, his conviction was affirmed. The court in *Sharpe* stated: "[O]ur law [does not] recognize the right of any one child to the corpse of its parent as claimed by the defendant. Our law recognizes no property in a corpse."[45]

The ruling in *Sharpe* was amplified in *dicta* by the court in *Regina v. Price*. The *Price* court stated, "[T]o open a grave and disinter a dead body without authority is a misdemeanor, even if it is done for a laudable purpose."[46] The court in *Gilbert v. Buzzard*[47] put into perspective the reasoning of the common law with respect to a buried corpse. The *Gilbert* court held, "[T]he ground once given to the body is appropriated to it for ever—it is literally in mortmain unalienably—it is not only the *domus ultima*, but the *domus aeterna* of that tenant, who is never to be disturbed[.]"[48]

The common law's general rule prohibiting disinterment of a corpse is consistent with the duty to bury a corpse. That is, the duty to bury a corpse would be meaningless if the law allowed dead bodies to be dug up.

Permitting Dissection of a Corpse. The court in *Price* pointed out a qualification to the common-law duty to bury a corpse. *Price* noted that there was not "an absolute duty on the part of persons in charge of dead bodies to bury them[.]"[49] The qualification to this duty involved turning over cadavers for dissection and experimentation. The court in *Price* addressed this issue as follows:

> Anatomy was practiced in England at least as far back as the very beginning of the seventeenth century. It continued to be practiced without ... any interference on the part of the legislature down to the year 1832, in which [year] was passed the [Anatomy] Act for regulating schools of

1. Creation of Rights in a Corpse

anatomy. This act recites the importance of anatomy, and that "the legal supply of human bodies for such anatomical examination is insufficient fully to provide the means of such knowledge." It then makes provision for the supply of such bodies by enabling "any executor or other party having lawful possession of the body of any deceased person," to permit the body to be dissected[.] The effect of this has been that the bodies of persons dying in various public institutions whose relations are unknown are so dissected.[50]

The Anatomy Act of 1832 was the focus in the criminal case *Regina v. Feist*.[51] The defendant in *Feist* was convicted of 64 charges of selling dead bodies for the purpose of dissection. On appeal, the defendant contended that his actions were legal under the Anatomy Act. The court in *Feist* observed, "[A]t common law it is a misdemeanor to take up a corpse out of a burial ground and sell it even for the purpose of dissection[.]"[52] This common-law proscription was at odds with the Anatomy Act. One of the appellate jurists in *Feist*, Lord Willes, articulated the direction the common law had to take in the face of the Anatomy Act. Lord Willes stated, "[I]n modern times the requirements of science are larger than formerly, and when they are so extensive it seems to me that we ought not to entertain any prejudice against the obtaining of dead bodies for the laudable purposes of dissection, but we ought rather to look at the matter with a view to utility[.]"[53]

Ultimately the court in *Feist* reversed the defendant's convictions and dismissed the charges against him. In doing so, the court held, "[T]he Anatomy Act has altered the common law, and has rendered the selling of a dead body for the purpose of dissection lawful under certain circumstances."[54]

Two other points should be underscored concerning dissection. First, the crudest of all forms of dissection was actually a common-law punishment for treason. A defendant convicted of treason was "hanged by the neck and then cut down alive, and his entrails [were] taken out and burned while he [was] yet alive, and ... his head [was] cut off and his body divided into four parts[.]"[55] Second, in addition to the authorization of dissection under the Anatomy Act, the court in *Rex v. Cundick*[56] pointed out that under the common law, dissection (at anatomy schools) could be imposed as part of a capital felon's death sentence.[57]

Initial Use of No-Property Rule in America

A legal commentator correctly observed in 1798, "[O]ur ancestors, who emigrated from England, were possessed of the knowledge of the laws and jurisprudence of that country[.]"[58] The birth of American law descended from the womb of, and was umbilically connected to, English jurisprudence. A significant distinction existed, however, between the English and the American legal systems.

Unlike England, America did not have an ecclesiastical legal system. This fact would logically lead one to the believe that, at the outset, American courts did not follow the common-law no-property rule. Unfortunately, this was not what happened. In 1891 an American court addressed this issue:

> The repudiation of the ecclesiastical law and of ecclesiastical courts by the American colonies left the temporal courts the sole protector of the dead and of the [interest] of the living in their dead. Inclined to follow the precedents of the English common law, these courts were at first slow to realize the changed condition of things, and the consequent necessity that they should take cognizance of these matters and administer remedies as in other analogous cases.[59]

In general, early American courts followed the common-law no-property rule.

LEADING AMERICAN NO-PROPERTY RULE CASES

As might be expected, early American courts did not have an overwhelming number of cases involving corpses. However, a significant number of cases were brought into court. Listed below are four issues involving corpses and the leading cases that addressed those issues.

Mutilation of a Corpse. One of the leading early American cases involving the mutilation of a corpse was *Griffith v. Charlotte, Columbia & Augusta R'd Co.*[60] The facts of *Griffith* reveal that the body of a deceased man was run over several times by the train cars of a railroad company. The administrator of the decedent's estate sued the railroad company to recover a monetary sum for the mutilation of the corpse.

1. Creation of Rights in a Corpse

Additionally, the administrator sought to recover the cost of the decedent's clothing and a silver watch that he had worn.

As to the claim for mutilation of the corpse, the administrator argued that the corpse should be looked on as property. The court in *Griffith* initially responded by noting that the common law did not acknowledge a corpse as property. The court then denied the relief for mutilation of the corpse:

> The term property may be defined to be the interest which can be acquired in external objects or things.... Now to entitle one to bring an action for injury to any specific object or thing, he must have a property [interest] therein.... If he has no such property [interest], he can have no cause of action however flagrant or reprehensible the act complained of may be....
>
> ... [W]hile it is natural that we should all feel that the remains of ancestors and loved ones should be tenderly watched ... and the mutilation of their dead bodies ... severely punished, and while all laws necessary to that end should be passed and strictly and sternly enforced, yet even for this purpose, to make such venerated remains the ... property of any one ... would be abhorrent to every impulse and feeling of our natures.... [R]everence for the dead has become a universal and most sacred sentiment, one which would revolt at the idea of their remains becoming property....
>
> ... [W]e are constrained to the conclusion that so far as this [case] is founded upon the mutilation of the deceased by the defendant company, whether accidental, willful, or negligent, it cannot be sustained by the plaintiff[.][61]

Although the *Griffith* court rejected the administrator's claim for a monetary award due to the mutilation of the decedent's body, it held differently on the issue of the destruction of the decedent's clothing and silver watch. The court indicated that its application of the no-property rule to the corpse did "not apply to the clothes in which the body was clad, and the silver watch upon the person.... As to these, then, the action was maintainable[.]"[62]

The case *Long v. Chicago, Rock Island & Pacific R'y Co.*[63] involved the unintended mutilation of a corpse. The parents of a deceased boy had made arrangements with a railway company to have the child's corpse transported from Oklahoma to Indiana. In carrying out this task for the parents, the railway company negligently handled the child's casket, thereby causing it to break open "and mutilat[e] and disfigur[e] the body of their dead son[.]"[64]

Organ Transplants from Executed Prisoners

The parents of the deceased child sued the railway company in order to recover the cost of replacing the casket. They also sought to recover a monetary sum for the pain and anguish they endured because of the mutilation of their son's corpse. The railway company agreed to pay the cost of replacing the casket but refused to compensate the parents for pain and anguish. The court in *Long* agreed with the position of the railway company:

> Where a corpse is mutilated before or after burial, in such a way as to render necessary the expenditure of extra money or labor in caring for it, or where injury is done to the coffin or clothes, the actual damages sustained may be recovered ...; but, after carefully considering [the matter], we are firmly convinced that no recovery can be [obtained] for mental pain and anguish caused by the negligent mutilation of such body.[65]

In rendering its decision to deny recovery for pain and anguish, the *Long* court justified its position by holding: "Since at common law there can be no such thing as property in human remains, no [lawsuit] for civil damages will lie for an injury to a dead body[.]"[66]

Digging Up a Corpse. The leading early American case involving digging up a corpse was *Meagher v. Driscoll*.[67] *Meagher* involved the unauthorized disinterment of the corpse of a child. The body was buried on the property of the deceased child's father. When the father learned that the body of the child had been dug up and removed, he filed a civil suit against the person responsible. The court in *Meagher* held that a corpse was not property and that, therefore, the father could not receive compensation in a court of law for matters attendant to its removal. The court did, however, rule that the father could sue the defendant for trespassing on his land.

In fairness to early American courts, the decision in *Meagher* must be viewed in its proper context. *Meagher* did not approve of unauthorized disinterment of corpses. The decision held only that the law would not provide monetary compensation for the mere act of digging up and removing a corpse without having the authority to do so.

Early American courts did intervene, when requested, to prevent buried corpses from being disinterred. A line of cases illustrates this point. In *Secord v. Secord*[68] the court held that a widow could obtain an injunction to prevent the removal of her deceased husband's corpse from

1. Creation of Rights in a Corpse

his grave. The court in *State v. Wilson*[69] ruled that a landowner who consented to the interment of dead bodies on his land had no right to have them removed. In the case of *Peters v. Peters*[70] an injunction was issued to prevent a widow from removing her spouse's corpse from a grave that the father of the deceased had purchased. In a similar case, *Hackett v. Hackett*,[71] a widow was restrained by the court from moving the corpse of her spouse from the burial ground purchased by the deceased spouse. The court in *Thompson v. Deeds*[72] prevented a widow from removing her spouse's corpse from a burial plot where the deceased spouse had expressed the desire to be buried. Finally, in *Choppin v. Labranche*[73] the court held that a tomb owner could not remove bodies he had permitted to be placed in the tomb with the assurance that the bodies would never be removed.

Holding a Corpse for Payment of Debt. It was mentioned earlier in the chapter that the common law permitted a corpse to be arrested when it was shown that the decedent left behind an unpaid debt (the practice was eventually repudiated by the common law). It does not appear that any early American court permitted a corpse to be formally arrested in a debt dispute. However, precedent was established by an American court for permitting a corpse to be kept by the person to whom the decedent owed a debt.

The case of *Keyes v. Konkel*[74] involved a debt incurred by a man after he died. The man had died in a hospital, and the hospital turned his body over to an undertaker. The undertaker performed unrequested services on the decedent's body in preparation for burial. The brother of the decedent eventually demanded the body from the undertaker. The undertaker refused to turn over the body until he was paid for the services performed on the body. The decedent's brother refused to provide payment on the grounds that the services performed were not requested.

The decedent's brother filed a lawsuit asking the court to order the undertaker to give him the corpse. The court refused to order the undertaker to turn over the body. In doing so, the court observed that under the common law there was "no property in a human [corpse]."[75] Therefore the court concluded, "It is apparent that no return of the [corpse] can be ordered ... and it is equally true that its value in money can neither be appraised nor ascertained by a jury."[76]

Organ Transplants from Executed Prisoners

Disposing of a Corpse by Will. The leading early American case addressing the issue of disposal of a corpse by will was the decision in *Enos v. Snyder*.[77] The decedent was married but had lived with another woman for several years before his death. While still living, he made out a will in which he left specific instructions that his mistress was to provide for the burial of his corpse. After the man's death, his wife sought possession of the body. The mistress refused to relinquish the corpse.

The decedent's wife filed a lawsuit seeking to have his body turned over to her. The mistress argued that she was in lawful custody of the body and had the legal right to bury it, based on the wishes expressed by the decedent in his last will and testament. The court in *Enos* disagreed with the mistress: "It is quite well established … that … there is no property in a dead body; that it is not part of the estate of the deceased person; and that a man cannot by will dispose of that which after his death will be his corpse."[78] The mistress was required to relinquish the corpse.

American Courts Develop Quasi-Property Rule

The common-law no-property rule created a ghastly and unworkable situation in America. Without legal protection, a human corpse was the same as the rotted carcass of an animal. With ever-increasing horror stories about human corpses and the uncompensated emotional pain of bereaved loved ones, it became imperative that American courts repudiate the common-law no-property rule. This issue was succinctly addressed by the court in *Hockenhammer v. Lexington & Eastern R'y Co*[79]:

> The English common-law authorities [on corpses cannot be] applicable in America, for the reason that the ecclesiastical courts in England exercised exclusive jurisdiction as to the burial of the dead, and the common-law courts treated such matters as being exclusively to the church. But as we have no ecclesiastical courts in this country exercising the jurisdiction conferred on such courts in England, rights in the bodies of the dead must be protected by the civil courts [of this country].[80]

1. Creation of Rights in a Corpse

BIRTH OF QUASI-PROPERTY THEORY

To protect the integrity of corpses and the emotional sentiment of surviving relatives, American courts had to devise a theory of law that associated a corpse with property. With the passage of time, courts slowly carved out a legal theory that would eventually bury the common-law no-property rule.

The legal theory developed by American courts to protect corpses was called the *quasi-property theory*. The court in *Pierce v. Proprietors of Swan Point Cemetery*[81] said the following regarding the theory of quasi-property rights in a corpse:

> That there is no right of property in a dead body, using the word in its ordinary sense, may well be admitted. Yet the burial of the dead is a subject which interests the feelings of mankind to a much greater degree than many matters of actual property. There is a duty imposed by the universal feelings of mankind to be discharged by some one toward the dead, a duty, and we may also say a right, to protect from violation, and a duty on the part of others to abstain from violation; it may therefore be considered as a sort of quasi property, and it would be discreditable to any system of law not to provide a remedy in such a case.[82]

Listed below are cases that will illustrate the development of quasi-property rights in a corpse.

Compensation for Disinterment. The first American case to challenge the no-property rule was *In re Beekman Street*.[83] This case involved the removal of nearly 100 corpses from their graves in order to widen a New York City street. The daughter of one of the decedents asked the court to allow her compensation for the disinterment of her father so that she could reinter his corpse in a grave site of her choice. In wrestling with the daughter's request and the dictates of the common-law no-property rule, the *Beekman* court made the following observation:

> If no one has any legal interest in a corpse, no one can legally determine the place of its interment, nor exclusively retain its custody. A son will have no legal right to retain the remains of his father, nor husband of his wife, one moment after death. A father cannot legally protect his daughter's remains from exposure or insult, however indecent or outrageous, nor demand their reburial, if dragged from the grave.[84]

The *Beekman* court turned next to setting out its rationale for departing from the common-law no-property rule:

> The things which may ... be exclusively appropriated, and thereby made "private property," are not confined to tangible or visible objects; for light and air are "property," and belong exclusively to the occupant, so long as he has possession. The right to the mere repose of a grave, although intangible or invisible, may none the less be property. The dividing line between "property" as a thing objectively appropriated by a person, and a "personal right" as subjectively belonging to a person, is not entirely distinct. The proprietary right to a grave-stone, and the personal right to its undisturbed repose, may measurably partake of both. In a certain sense, even a purely personal right may be said to be appropriated. Nor is the distinction very essential; for if there be a right in a grave, or its contents or appendages, which the law will recognize, it matters little whether the right is appropriated by, or belongs to its possessor.[85]

The final task undertaken by the court in *Beekman* was that of setting out four propositions, which ultimately became the foundation of the quasi-property theory:

> 1. That the right to bury a corpse and to preserve its remains, is a legal right, which the courts of law will recognize and protect.
> 2. That such right, in the absence of any testamentary disposition, belongs exclusively to the next of kin.
> 3. That the right to protect the remains includes the right to preserve them by separate burial, to select the place of sepulture, and to change it at pleasure.
> 4. That if the place of burial be taken for public use, the next of kin may claim to be indemnified for the expense of removing and suitably re-interring their remains.[86]

The decision in *Beekman* laid down broad principles, but it addressed only one issue: compensation for the cost of reinterring a corpse that was wrongfully disinterred. The decision did not address the issue of compensation for the emotional anguish caused by the wrongful disinterment of a corpse. The latter issue was squarely tackled after the decision in *Beekman*.

In two cases, *Bessemer Land & Improvement v. Jenkins*[87] and *Jacobus v. Congregation of Children of Israel*,[88] courts were asked to abandon the no-property rule and permit monetary awards for the mental anguish caused by the wrongful disinterment of corpses. The court in *Jenkins*

1. Creation of Rights in a Corpse

tersely but unequivocally held, "In an action for unlawful removal of the body of plaintiff's child from its burying place, injury to the feelings is an element of damages."[89] The court in *Jacobus* was less terse:

> In a suit for damages for wrongfully disinterring a dead body, if the [act] has been wanton and malicious, or is the result of gross negligence or a reckless disregard of the rights of others, equivalent to an intentional violation of them, exemplary damages may be awarded, [and] in estimating [the award] the injury to the natural feelings of the plaintiff may be taken into consideration.[90]

Compensation for Mutilation. The leading precedent for allowing surviving relatives compensation for the emotional trauma caused by the mutilation of a corpse is *Kyles v. Southern Railway Co.*[91] The decedent in *Kyles* was struck and instantly killed by a train while trying to cross several railroad tracks. The events of the ensuing 24 hours was described by the court in *Kyles*:

> The body was found on the defendant's track—head, pool of blood, hair, eyeballs, etc., near the four mile post from Salisbury.... The body was stripped of its head, legs, and arms, and all clothing.... That the body was further mutilated is shown by the fact that the headless body was 250 or more yards east of the four-mile post; the [underwear was] found 1¼ miles west; a part of the overcoat a mile east; pocket of overcoat 27 miles west; arms 75 yards east, and on the north side of track; legs still further east and on the south side of track; head near the four-mile post, and hair all along down the track on angle bars; trunk all rolled up in cinders and dirt, and mangled and mutilated beyond recognition. A dozen or more trains passed over the body.... The evidence indicates ... that the body was stricken after death by different trains going east and west, and that it, and parts thereof, were thrown hither and thither, backwards, and forwards, by the passing trains, going in opposite directions.[92]

The issue confronting the court was whether the wife of the decedent had a right to receive his corpse in the condition it was in when he was initially struck and killed or whether the common-law no-property rule allowed her to receive it in the mutilated condition caused by being run over by an additional 11 or more trains. The court compassionately observed: "The deceased may have moved in the humbler walks of life[,] but to the plaintiff he was husband and the father of her children. It was her right, old as time, as broad as humanity, and as deep as the heart of man, that his mortal remains should be treated with due respect."[93] In its rejection of the common-law no-property rule, the court in *Kyles* held:

> While the common law does not recognize dead bodies as property, the courts of America and other Christian and civilized countries hold that they are quasi property, and that any mutilation thereof is actionable.... Where the rights of one legally entitled to the custody of a dead body are violated by mutilation of the body ... the party injured may in an action for damages recover for the mental suffering caused by the injury.[94]

Compensation for Unauthorized Autopsy. Two American courts got an early opportunity to apply the developing quasi-property theory to cases involving unauthorized autopsies. In the first case, *Foley v. Phelps*,[95] the decedent fell through an elevator shaft and died several hours after being rushed to a hospital. The decedent's widow "applied to the hospital for his body, and begged and implored those who were in charge of it not to allow or permit an autopsy to be performed[.]"[96] In spite of the widow's "request and protestations, the defendant, without her knowledge [performed] an autopsy on her husband's body, which autopsy was performed without any authority of law[.]"[97]

The widow asked the court in *Foley* to abandon the common-law no-property rule so that she could seek to recover a monetary award for the anguish she endured over the unauthorized autopsy of her husband. The court responded:

> In more recent times the obdurate common-law rule has been very much relaxed ... and the necessity for enforcing that protection which is due to the dead, ha[s] induced courts to re-examine the grounds upon which the common-law rule reposed, and have led to modifications of its stringency....
>
> ... Irrespective of any claim of property, the right which inhered in the [widow] ... was a right to the possession of the body for the purpose of burying it.... The right is to the possession of the corpse in the same condition it was in when the breath leaves the body, and not merely to such a hacked, hewed, and mutilated corpse as some stranger ... may choose to turn over to an afflicted relative. If this right exists, as we think it clearly does, the invasion or violation of it furnishes a ground for a civil action for damages.[98]

Another early autopsy case was *Larson v. Chase*.[99] The facts of the case were not adequately set out in the opinion. All that is factually revealed is that a widow filed a lawsuit over "the unlawful mutilation and dissection of the body of [her] deceased husband."¹⁰⁰ The *Larson* court explicitly rejected application of the no-property rule to the case and held:

> The right to the possession of a dead body for the purposes of preservation and burial belongs, in the absence of any testamentary disposition, to the surviving husband or wife or next of kin, and the right of the surviving wife is paramount to that of the next of kin.
>
> This right is one which the law recognizes and will protect, and for any infraction of it,—such as an unlawful mutilation of the remains,—an action for damages will lie. In such an action a recovery may be had for injury to the feelings and mental suffering resulting directly and proximately from the wrongful act, although no actual pecuniary damage is alleged or proven.¹⁰¹

Compensation for Unauthorized Removal of a Body Part. In the case of *Koerber v. Patek*,¹⁰² the son of a deceased woman acquiesced to a physician's request to merely examine the decedent's stomach before interment. However, the physician "willfully, maliciously, fraudulently ... and without any authority ... cut out, removed, and carried away the stomach of said body, and refused to return the same on request[.]"¹⁰³ The decedent's son was forced to bury her without a stomach. The son subsequently filed a civil lawsuit to recover a monetary award for the emotional anguish caused by the removal and retention of his mother's stomach.

During the case the physician strenuously argued that the lawsuit could not proceed "because there can be no property in a dead body."¹⁰⁴ The court in *Koerber* rejected the no-property rule argument and cited several cases from other courts that had adopted the corpse quasi-property theory. The opinion in the case held:

> From the authorities ... cited, and from original reason, the conclusion seems to us irresistible that in the nearest relative of one [deceased], so situated as to be able and willing to perform the duty of ceremonious burial, there vests the right to perform it, and that this is a legal right, which, as said in some of the cases, it is wrong to violate, and which, therefore, courts can and should protect and vindicate....
>
> ... We can imagine no clearer or dearer right in the gamut of civil liberty and security than to bury our dead in peace and unobstructed....

... The right to entomb the remains of his deceased mother in their integrity and without mutilation ... must be recognized as a legal one.[105]

Compensation for Failing to Turn Over a Corpse. The case of *Renihan v. Wright*[106] presented the issue of recovery of a monetary sum for the emotional anguish caused by the loss of a corpse. A couple engaged caretakers "to take charge of, and safely keep, in a secure vault, the body of [their] deceased daughter ... until such time as they might be prepared and ready to inter the [body]."[107] However, when the parents eventually came for their daughter's corpse, they learned that the caretakers had "carelessly and negligently ... allowed the [corpse] to be taken and buried, or otherwise disposed of, and [the caretakers] wrongfully refused ... to inform the [couple] where [the] remains ha[d] been removed to[.]"[108]

The *Renihan* court rebuffed the caretakers' argument that, under the common law, the parents had no property rights to their daughter's corpse. In making the rebuff, the court stated:

> The real question is not of the disposable, marketable value of a corpse, or its remains, as an article of traffic; but it is of the sacred and inherent right to its custody, in order to bury it, and secure its undisturbed repose.... Our courts of justice should place [this right] at once where it would fundamentally rest forever, on the deepest and most unerring instincts of human nature, and hold it to be a self-evident right of humanity, entitled to legal protection by every consideration of feeling, decency, and Christian duty.[109]

The court concluded that the no-property rule could not be used to prevent the parents from seeking to recover a monetary award for the loss of their daughter's corpse. The court ruled: "The courts of this state, in our opinion, possess the power to enforce the rights of the [parents] to the body of their deceased daughter ... and the right to give it decent burial; and they also possess the power to assess such damages as may accrue to them on account of being deprived of such right."[110]

JUSTIFICATION AND GROWTH OF QUASI-PROPERTY THEORY

In the final analysis, necessity demanded that American courts abandon the common-law no-property rule and develop a theory that

1. Creation of Rights in a Corpse

would afford respect and protection for human corpses. A recent commentary succinctly articulated the justification for the quasi-property theory:

> The recognition of a corpse as quasi-property, or the object of rights, developed in Anglo-American jurisprudence to alleviate the emotional hardship caused to the bereaved by the harsh consequences of the common law no-property rule. The justification for designating a corpse quasi-property was grounded on two basic propositions. First, it allowed the law to be consistent. That is, by attaching the term *property* to a corpse, the law could then apply pre-existing legal principles to afford it protection. Second, it was necessary to label a corpse *quasi-property* in order to establish that not all legal principles attendant to *pure property* were applicable to a corpse.[111]

The quasi-property theory has traveled a case-by-case evolutionary growth. Rights attendant to a corpse as quasi-property include the following:

1. The right to dispose of one's corpse by will[112]
2. The right of relatives to have possession of the corpse[113]
3. The right of relatives to bury the corpse[114]
4. The right of relatives to have a corpse removed to a different grave[115]
5. The provision of criminal sanctions for disinterring a corpse without authority or proper relationship[116]
6. The right of relatives to prevent the removal of body parts[117]
7. The right of a decedent to determine by will the disposition of his or her body parts[118]
8. The right to prevent an autopsy[119]
9. The right to burial where the closest relative desires[120]
10. The right to sue over a delay in the delivery of a corpse[121]
11. The right to file suit for exposing a corpse to bad weather[122]
12. The right to a monetary award for an outrage or indignity done to a corpse[123]

In 2001, the Florida Supreme Court was called upon in *Crocker v. Pleasant*[124] to decide whether parents had a constitutionally protected property interest in the body of their son and a right to procedural due process under the Fourteenth Amendment of the United States Constitution prior to the deprivation of their property interest in the body. The facts in *Crocker* revealed that the parents' twenty-three year old son was found dead by the West Palm Beach police. Although the police became aware of the address of the decedent's parents, the parents did not receive notification that the police had found his body. Even though the parents had filed a missing person's report with the police, their son's body was turned over to the county for burial. Six months after their son's burial the parents learned of what happened to his body. Thereafter the parents sued the police and county under 42 U.S.C. § 1983, for failure to use reasonable efforts to notify them of their son's death before his burial.[125] The Supreme Court held that the parents could bring a cause of action under § 1983:

> Broadly speaking, claims against the State under section 1983 have been grouped into three general categories. First, a person may bring an action under section 1983 for a state official's deprivation of that individual's fundamental rights guaranteed by the Bill of Rights, such as freedom of speech or freedom from unreasonable searches and seizures. Second, a person may bring a section 1983 action for a violation of substantive due process that amounts to arbitrary, wrongful government actions regardless of the fairness of the procedures used to implement them....
>
> Lastly, and important for our analysis in this case, a person also may bring a section 1983 action for the deprivation of procedural due process under the Fourteenth Amendment of the United States Constitution. To maintain a claim under this third type of section 1983 action, the individual bringing an action for deprivation of procedural due process must first establish the existence of a constitutionally protected property or liberty interest that has been interfered with by the State.... Accordingly, the threshold question presented in this case is whether the Crockers have a constitutionally protected property interest, "quasi-property right," or "legitimate claim of entitlement" to possess their son's remains for burial so as to give rise to procedural due process protection.
>
> ***
>
> ... Florida recognizes a limited right to possession of the body for burial, sepulture or other lawful disposition. This conclusion is consistent with the approach of other courts that have found that this right constitutes a legitimate claim of entitlement or a quasi-property interest.
>
> ***
>
> Thus, Florida cases have recognized causes of action based upon interference with a dead relative's body in a variety of circumstances where the underlying conduct alleged rises to the level of intentional misconduct or malice.

1. Creation of Rights in a Corpse

Based upon these statutory rights of the next of kin in their dead relatives' bodies, along with the case law on this issue, we conclude that in Florida there is a legitimate claim of entitlement by the next of kin to possession of the remains of a decedent for burial or other lawful disposition. We also find that referring to the interest as a "legitimate claim of entitlement" most accurately describes the nature of the interest. Accordingly, [our precedent] does not preclude all section 1983 claims grounded on interference with an interest in a dead body.[126]

LIMITATIONS ON QUASI-PROPERTY THEORY

It should be clearly understood that courts have not opened all legal doors to protect the integrity of a corpse. For example, in 2012 the Tennessee Supreme Court was asked in *Akers v. Prime Succession of Tennessee, Inc.*,[127] to decide whether parents could sue the owner of a crematorium under the state's Consumer Protection Act and under the common law doctrine of bailment. The parents in *Akers* had the deceased body of their adult son sent to a crematorium in Georgia. They eventually received back what they thought were the cremated remains of their son. However, the parents learned that the owner of the crematorium was facing criminal charges for operating a fraudulent crematorium. The criminal investigation revealed the following:

> [A]uthorities recovered bodies and body parts of over 320 persons, in widely varying stages of decay. Some were buried in shallow graves. Some had been dumped in surface trash pits. Human remains and bodies were found in virtually every building on the property. A body was found in a hearse, another in a van, and a partially mummified corpse of a man in a suit was discovered in a box. Some of the bodies recovered had been partially cremated, some were without arms and legs, and some had their extremities burned away. An unburned corpse was laying in the crematory's retort [oven].[128]

The parents in *Akers* sued the crematorium owner for improperly disposing of their son's body. Two of the legal theories the parents wanted to rely upon for monetary compensation involved Tennessee's Consumer Protection Act (TCPA) and the doctrine of bailment (the parents were successful in recovering money for intentional infliction of emotional distress). The Supreme Court held that the parents could not sue under those legal theories. The opinion in the case addressed the matter as follows:

> The TCPA does not provide a cause of action for purely emotional loss....
>
> The [parents] have stated a claim for emotional loss and have not demonstrated that they have suffered an ascertainable loss of money, property, or any other article, commodity or tangible thing of value. Although a person's cremains have significant emotional and sentimental value, they do not have tangible economic value as required by the TCPA. Consequently, by the plain and unambiguous terms of the TCPA, that statute does not provide a cause of action for their recovery.
>
> ***
>
> This Court has defined a bailment as a delivery of personalty for a particular purpose or on mere deposit, on a contract express or implied; that after the purpose has been fulfilled, it shall be redelivered to the person who delivered it, or otherwise dealt with according to his direction or kept until he reclaims it.... Although there was no express agreement between the [parents] and [the defendant], there existed a constructive or involuntary bailment on which a bailment claim could be made.
>
> The bailment claim fails, however, because a corpse is not "personalty" for bailment purposes.[129]

The question of whether the estate of a deceased person and the decedent's daughter had rights in tissues from the decedent's body was addressed in 2012, by the Texas Supreme Court in the case of *Evanston Ins. Co. v. Legacy of Life, Inc.*[130] In *Evanston* the daughter of the decedent sued an organ donation charity. Prior to the lawsuit the daughter consented to letting the charity harvest some of her terminally ill mother's tissues after she died. The daughter agreed to this because the charity represented the tissues would be distributed on a nonprofit basis. However, the charity transferred the tissues to companies that sold them for a profit. The daughter's lawsuit alleged the charity had caused her mental anguish and deprived her and her mother's estate of the use of property through wrongfully profiting from the sale of her deceased mother's tissues. After the lawsuit was filed the insurance company that issued a policy to the charity, asked the trial court to declare that the policy did not provide coverage for the claims asserted by the daughter. The issue of insurance coverage was brought to the Texas Supreme Court. The Supreme Court was asked to answer questions which, in effect, would decide whether the daughter or her mother's estate had any rights in the tissues. The Supreme Court found that neither the daughter nor her mother's estate had any rights in the tissues:

1. Creation of Rights in a Corpse

[W]e first assess whether Alvarez's mother's tissues are Alvarez's property. The common law gives Alvarez the right to direct the burial, which we have called a quasi-property right. The common law also allows next of kin to sue for mental anguish damages when acts are performed on a decedent's body or tissues without the next of kin's consent in certain circumstances. In recognition of the many advances in medical science … and the ability to transplant tissues, the Anatomical Gift Act also gives next of kin the right to gift tissues.

Despite these rights Alvarez has in her deceased mother's tissues, there are many rights Alvarez does not have. Some of the key rights that make up the bundle of property rights include the rights to possess, use, transfer, and exclude others. Next of kin have no right to possess a body other than for burial or final disposition. Next of kin have no right to use tissues unless they have been designated by the individual as a transplant recipient. Next of kin have no right to transfer tissues other than as set forth in the Anatomical Gift Act. And next of kin have no right to exclude, other than to seek damages in certain circumstances for acts done beyond their consent. In light of these limited rights, we cannot say that tissues have attained the status of property of the next of kin.

***

We next decide whether the mother's tissues are the property of her estate. The Anatomical Gift Act gives an individual the right to designate a recipient of their tissues while they are alive and gives their agent at the time of death the right to designate a recipient immediately before their death. The Anatomical Gift Act does not give the estate the right to designate a recipient once the individual dies. Nor can the estate be compensated financially for the individual's tissues. The Anatomical Gift Act only allows a person to charge a reasonable amount for certain services rendered (such as removal and processing). The Act does not allow for compensation for the tissue itself. In sum, the individual can designate a recipient for their tissues before their death, but once they die, their estate cannot designate a recipient or receive compensation for the tissues. The estate therefore has fewer rights in tissues than next of kin, who may designate a recipient once the individual dies. Because we have held that tissues are not the property of next of kin, we necessarily conclude that tissues are also not the property of the estate.[131]

In *Board of Regents v. Oglesby*[132] the Court of Appeals of Georgia was asked in 2003, to decide whether Francis Oglesby waited too long to sue the Medical College of Georgia for its use of her mother's deceased body. The facts of the case show that in 1949, Francis' mother, Bessie Wilborn, died in part as a result of a disease called Paget's disease. Francis was seven years old at the time of her mother's death. Under circumstances that were unknown, the Medical College took possession of Bessie's body. In 1951, a doctor on the staff at the Medical College published a paper that discussed the Paget's disease and Bessie's affliction with the disease. The article and the disposition of Bessie's body was set out by the Court of Appeals as follows:

> In the article, Dr.[Peter B.] Wright gave detailed information about [Bessie], including her medical and other history. The article also states that after her death, her body was "obtained for autopsy and physical study." The article has photographs showing that [Bessie's] skin was removed, that her skull cavity separated, and that her entire skeletal remains were placed in a glass case for display. A card in the glass case states that her skeletal remains were "presented as an exhibit at the 1950 New York meeting of the American Academy of Orthopedic Surgery and received the Gold Medal Award." [Bessie's] remains are maintained by the [Medical College's] Department of Anatomy and are used in the education of medical students. Her remains have been on display for a number of years in the glass case in an anatomy laboratory at the [Medical College].[133]

Francis learned of the disposition of her mother's remains in 1987. However, Francis did not file a lawsuit until 2001. The lawsuit "alleged causes of action for trespass and interference with [Francis'] quasi-property rights, mutilation of [Bessie's] remains, and intentional infliction of emotional distress."[134] The Court of Appeals found that Francis' lawsuit was barred by the statute of limitations as follows[135]:

> A cause of action in negligence accrues ... when there is a negligent act coupled with a proximately resulting injury.... Consequently, any cause of action arising from the treatment of [Bessie's] body accrued in 1949.
> In this case, even if we were authorized to apply the discovery rule, [Francis'] claims still are barred because the record shows that [Francis] was aware that [the Medical College] had possession of her mother's remains in 1987. Even under the "discovery rule," the right of action accrues when the injured person discovers the cause of his or her injury...
> Moreover, ... the claims were barred by the general statutes of limitation and by the limitations provisions in the [Georgia Tort Claims Act].
> ***
> ... [Francis'] cause of action ... would have accrued when she reached the age of majority. The time when [Francis] achieved her majority, however, had long passed when she filed this action, and was far beyond the two-year period of limitations for bringing personal injury actions....

1. Creation of Rights in a Corpse

[Francis'] claims based on [the Medical College's] possession and handling of her mother's body that arise from her personal, quasi-property right in her mother's body to ensure its proper handling and burial, however, are subject to the four-year period of limitations.[136]

In *Colavito v. New York Organ Donor Network, Inc.*,[137] a federal district court was asked in 2005, to decide whether the plaintiff, a kidney patient, had a claim against an organ donor network and physicians, on the grounds that a decedent's kidney was promised to the plaintiff by the decedent's wife, but was wrongfully transplanted into another patient by the defendants. The district court found that the plaintiff did not have a cause of action:

> Plaintiff ... argues that the defendants' actions constitute conversion because they intentionally and wrongfully acquired the second kidney when they misdirected it to another transplant recipient. To support a claim for conversion, a plaintiff must establish legal ownership of a specific identifiable piece of property and the defendant's exercise of dominion over or interference with the property in defiance of the plaintiff's rights.
>
> The issue of whether a specified donee of an anatomical gift may sustain a claim for conversion is an issue of first impression. The court has found no cases involving similar facts in either this or any other federal circuit or state court. However, courts have disallowed conversion claims in other cases involving the body of a deceased....
>
> ***
>
> ... [T]he courts in both New York and other states generally recognize a "quasi-property" right, belonging to the spouse or next of kin to possess the body for the purposes of ensuring proper burial. The quasi-property right in a corpse is not pecuniary in nature, nor should it be. The right encompasses only the power to ensure that the corpse is orderly handled and laid to rest, nothing more....
>
> ***
>
> ... [T]he court cannot allow plaintiff's conversion claim to go forward. Several courts, including a New York State appellate court, that have considered a claim for conversion in cases involving an unauthorized organ removal or other interference with the body of a deceased have concluded that it is not sustainable.... [I]t would be against public policy to engage in a valuation of [the] kidneys, which are not property. Based on the case law discussed above, the court also finds it inappropriate to expand the limited right that courts recognize in a deceased's body, which only belongs to the next of kin to ensure proper burial.[138]

Organ Transplants from Executed Prisoners

In 2002, a federal district court in Virginia was asked in the case of *Mazur v. Woodson*[139] whether the brother of a deceased woman could be sued by her husband and children because of the brother's handling of her body. The facts in the case show that Paul and Betty Mazur were married in Virginia in 1958. They lived in Virginia until 1965, when they moved to New Jersey. In 1994, Betty was suffering from the onset of Alzheimer's disease, so Paul brought her back to Virginia to stay with her aunt. However, shortly after Betty was left with her aunt, she was moved to the residence of her brother, Victor Woodson. Paul was not aware that Betty was moved to the home of her brother. When Paul and his children found out that Betty was living with Victor and that Victor was appointed guardian over Betty and her property, they filed a lawsuit seeking to remove Victor as a guardian of Betty. While the lawsuit was pending, Betty died in 2001. Victor arranged for Betty to be buried in Virginia without informing Paul and his children. Paul and his children sued Victor a second time in order to have Betty disinterred so that they could bury her in New Jersey. Victor agreed to have Betty reburied in New Jersey. However, after the agreement Paul and his children sued Victor again in federal court.[140] The third lawsuit sought monetary damages because of Victor's failure to inform Paul and his children about Betty's initial burial; and because Paul and his children were not able to give Betty a proper reburial as a result of the decomposition of her body. The federal court found that the lawsuit was improper for the following reasons:

> Plaintiffs argue that Virginia common law provides a hierarchy of relatives who have quasi-property rights over the corpse of a deceased family member. They claim that as Betty Mazur's spouse and children, their quasi-property rights to Betty Mazur's corpse are superior to those of her brother, defendant Woodson. Based on this reasoning, they contend that Woodson ... had a duty to inform them prior to burying Betty Mazur's corpse, and that failure to do so violated their quasi-property rights in her corpse. In short, plaintiffs claim that Woodson ... had a duty to determine their wishes prior to burying Betty Mazur's corpse.
>
> ***
>
> ... [T]he enactment of Virginia Code § 54.1–2807 indicates the legislature's intent to create a "broad and coequal" class of individuals who have rights to the deceased's body. Any member of this class would have a cause of action *against a third party* who interfered with that right....

1. Creation of Rights in a Corpse

Because each member of the deceased's "next of kin," as defined by the Virginia Code, has equal rights to "possess, preserve, and bury" a decedent's body, there can be no cause of action among members of that class for withholding a corpse from other members of the class. Woodson, Betty Mazur's brother, is a member of Betty Mazur's "next of kin," and has a quasi-property interest in Betty Mazur's body that is equal to that of the plaintiffs. Therefore, he is not subject to suit from other members of that class for withholding the body from them.[141]

The appellate courts in California and Ohio have recognized limits on the rights of next of kin to organs of a decedent that have been retained by a coroner for autopsy purposes. An appellate court in California held in *Benson v. Superior Court*[142] that "[a] county coroner conducting an inquiry into cause of death has no duty to obtain consent from next of kin before retaining a part of the decedent's body to determine cause of death, or for scientific investigation or coroner training."[143] The Ohio Supreme Court held in *Albrecht v. Treon*[144] that "[t]he next of kin of a decedent upon whom an autopsy has been performed do not have a protected right under Ohio law in the decedent's tissues, organs, blood, or other body parts that have been removed and retained by the coroner for forensic examination and testing."[145]

An appellate court in Tennessee addressed the issue of who has standing to file a lawsuit over the improper handling of a decedent's body. The issue was addressed in *Crawford v. J. Avery Bryan Funeral Home, Inc.*[146] In *Crawford* the parents and siblings of the decedent filed an action against a crematorium and funeral home as a result of their mishandling of the decedent's body. The trial court dismissed the case on the grounds that decedent's widow was the only person with standing to bring any of the claims.[147] The appellate court agreed with the trial court as follows:

> In *Hill v. Travelers' Ins. Co.*, 154 Tenn. 295, 294 S.W. 1097 (1927) ... [it was held that] it is the surviving spouse, if there is one, that has the right to possession and control of the body that the law protects.
>
> ***
>
> Other jurisdictions which have ... reached the same result ... include, but are not limited to: *Tomasits v. Cochise Memory Gardens, Inc.*, 150 Ariz. 39, 721 P.2d 1166 (1986); *Andrews v. McGowan*, 739 So.2d 132 (Fla.App.1999); *Walser v. Resthaven Memorial Gardens, Inc.*, 98 Md.App. 371, 633 A.2d 466, 475 (1993); *Whaley v. County of Saginaw*, 941 F.Supp.

1483 (E.D.Mich.1996); *Amaker v. King County,* 479 F.Supp.2d 1159 (W.D.Wash.2007).

When considering all of the above, we conclude that, in Tennessee, any tort claims for negligent, reckless or intentional interference with a dead body and the like can be brought only by the person or persons who have the right to control disposition of the body. Pursuant to *Hill,* it is the surviving spouse who has the superior right to control disposition of the body. Therefore, in the present case, the Trial Court correctly held that because Wife had the right to control disposition of the decedent's body, she alone had the right to bring the various tort claims against the Funeral Home and Tri-State. These claims were properly dismissed for lack of standing.[148]

The appellate court in *Akers v. Buckner-Rush Enterprises, Inc.*[149] set out the order of priority with regard to establishing standing to sue for mishandling of a decedent's body as follows: "(1) the spouse of the decedent; (2) adult children of the decedent; (3) parents of the decedent; (4) adult siblings of the decedent; (5) adult grandchildren of the decedent; and (6) grandparents of the decedent."[150]

An Ohio appellate court in *Walker v. Firelands Community Hosp.*[151] addressed the issue of quasi-property rights in a fetus. *Walker* involved a class action lawsuit against a hospital and morgue employee over the handling of fetuses that were terminated as a result of a miscarriage or were stillborn. The plaintiffs in the case alleged that they were told that the fetuses would be cremated. However, a morgue employee "for personal reasons based upon her religious beliefs, decided to keep intact fetal specimens in containers filled with formalin. She stored them on shelves used to retain tissue for teaching purposes. Approximately 88 specimens of fetal tissue were commingled in the same three containers for different time periods lasting up to ten years."[152] The trial court dismissed the plaintiffs' claim for mishandling a corpse. The appellate court affirmed as follows:

> Within the context of the present case, the trial court was required to decide whether a fetus of 20 weeks or less of gestation was a "person" within the meaning of [our statute]. In ascertaining this meaning, the court below could, therefore, consider the definition of "person" as developed in *Roe v. Wade,* 410 U.S. 113, 93 S.Ct. 705, 35 L.Ed.2d 147 (1973), and its progeny.
> ***

1. Creation of Rights in a Corpse

... [T]he trial court quoted ... references in *Roe* that would indicate that a fetus is not a "person" and found that it could not disregard the ruling in *Roe* by defining "fetus" (at or under 20 weeks of gestation) as a "person."
***
... [T]he trial judge acknowledged the existence of the tort of interference with a dead body or mishandling of a dead body, but declined to extend the meaning of "body" or "person" to include "fetal tissue." The judge then found that in order for the next of kin to bring a claim premised upon the tort of interference with a dead body, a fetus would have to survive birth.
***
... [W]e are not inclined to create a new cause of action for the negligent infliction of emotional distress that results from the interference with the burial or cremation of a fetus that is at or less than 20 weeks of gestation and does not survive birth.[153]

An exception to the ruling in *Walker* was found by a Connecticut court in *Janicki v. Hospital of St. Raphael*.[154] In *Janicki* the plaintiff gave birth to a stillborn, nonviable nineteen weeks old fetus. The plaintiff expressly instructed the hospital not to dissect the fetus. However, the hospital performed a dissection anyway. The plaintiff sued the hospital and physician. An issue that was addressed by the trial court was whether the plaintiff could recover damages for emotional distress caused by the dissection of the fetus. The court found that under the unique facts of the case, the plaintiff could recover damages for emotional distress:

> Most courts in this country now recognize that the next of kin have at least a "quasi-property" right in a decedent's body for purposes of burial or other lawful disposition. The reach of this "quasi-property" right is uncertain. What is important, for present purposes, is that American courts have recognized a rule that, where a nonofficial autopsy is performed without the consent of those who have the quasi-right of property in the corpse ... the one responsible for such act is liable in damages.
> ***
> ... [I]t can hardly be doubted that Janicki had at least a "quasi-property" right in the fetus in question. The hospital effectively acknowledged such a right at argument, conceding that it had a responsibility to return the fetus to Janicki for burial.... To some people, of course, the issue of dissection will be inconsequential, but to others it will be deeply consequential. As a policy matter, the law recognizes the diversity of views on this subject and (except for examinations done by the state medical examiner in cases of

suspected crime) allows decisions concerning dissection to be made by the next of kin rather than physicians.

Is the body of a stillborn fetus entitled to less consideration in this regard than the body of a once living human being? A stillborn fetus does not have survivors in the same legal sense that a once living human being has survivors (never having lived, it cannot have an estate) but, as we have just seen, the mother nevertheless retains at least a quasi-property right in the body. The real question that must be addressed is not one of property but one of symbolism. The body of a once living human being is entitled to respect because of its symbolic import, if for no other reason. It is hardly a stretch to conclude that the body of a stillborn fetus should be entitled to similar respect for the same reason....

***

For these reasons, the common law should recognize that the fetus in question here, while not a person, was not "property" or "tissue" either. Instead, it occupied an intermediate category in the law entitled to a special respect that would not be given ordinary tissue. The hospital concedes that it had an obligation to turn the fetus over to Janicki for burial. The well-established line of authority dealing with unauthorized autopsies on human corpses teaches us that this conceded duty is accompanied by another duty, namely that of preserving the body. The fact that the fetus here was entitled to a "special respect" not accorded ordinary tissue means, at a minimum, that the hospital and its physicians were not entitled to dissect it in the teeth of the mother's express instructions to the contrary.

***

For these reasons, Janicki has adequately pleaded a cause of action for the negligent infliction of emotional distress.[155]

2

THE MARKET FOR HUMAN BODY PARTS

Since time immemorial the human corpse has been a tool used in the efforts of medical science to preserve human life. Without doubt, scores of horror stories exist in this noble journey to find answers that would extend human life. There is truth in the well-worn adage that *nothing good comes without suffering*. And so it was with experiments conducted by medical science. Much suffering has been endured by countless surviving relatives who learned that medical science, without authorization, used the cadavers of their loved ones in medical experiments.

One monumental achievement made by medical science, in its endless use of human corpses, was that of unlocking the door that allows certain body parts of cadavers to be transplanted into living human beings. (Certain organs can also be transplanted from living donors.) This chapter presents a general overview of the *market* created by medical science when it unlocked the door that permitted certain cadaveric body parts to be transplanted into living human beings.

The following material has been divided into five major parts. The first part examines how medical science was able to successfully transplant specific cadaveric organs into living human beings. The second part looks at the actual donee market for transplantable cadaveric organs. Part three reviews the legal prohibition, in America, against selling transplantable organs. Part four reviews the method used for obtaining transplantable organs. The final part of the chapter briefly examines a few proposals for changing the way in which transplantable organs are obtained and distributed.

Organ Transplants from Executed Prisoners

Medical Science Breakthrough

Today approximately 25 human organs can be removed from cadavers and transplanted into living donees. Organs that are transplantable include: heart, nerves, skin, bone marrow, liver, kidneys, corneas, glands, blood vessels, and tendons.[1] Reaching this proud epic in medical history required centuries of torturous experimentations involving cadavers and live human beings. The great impediment to organ transplantation was the uniqueness that nature designed in all individuals. Each human body is configured so as to have a natural tendency to reject the organs of another human body (and the organs of any other life form). This natural tendency is called the rejection factor.[2]

In 1954 the first successful organ transplant took place in Boston, Massachusetts, at the Peter Bent Brigham Hospital. The organ transplanted was a kidney, and it came from a living donor. (The donor was the twin of the donee. The transplanted kidney reportedly functioned for nine years.)[3] In 1962 Peter Bent Brigham Hospital was also the site of the first successful transplantation of a kidney taken from a corpse.[4] In 1967 the first successful liver transplant took place.[5] In the same year, on December 3, 1967, the first recorded successful heart transplant was performed by Dr. Christian Barnard of South Africa.[6] One year later, in 1968, the first successful heart transplant in the United States took place in the state of California.[7]

The initial breakthrough in organ transplantation did not completely subdue the rejection factor. The immediate decades that followed the initial organ transplants saw only modest success in this new frontier. As a result of the rejection factor, it was preferable to obtain organs from living donors (ideally from a relative of the donee).

One commentary noted, "[T]he real breakthrough in organ transplantation occurred in the early 1980's, with the creation of a wonder drug called cyclosporine."[8] Cyclosporine is an immunosuppressive drug that allows for a greater success rate in cadaveric organ transplants.[9] At the start of the 1990s a new immunosuppressive drug, called FK-506, was introduced.[10] FK-506 has been reported to be 50 to 100 times more effective than cyclosporine in combating the rejection factor.[11]

As a result of the tremendous success of cyclosporine and FK-506,

2. The Market for Human Body Parts

"the human body part market shifted into high gear and hearts, lungs, livers, pancreas and kidneys became overnight stars."[12] For example, in 2012 physicians in the United States transplanted 2,378 hearts, 6,256 livers, 242 pancreases, 801 kidney/pancreases, 1,754 lungs, 29 heart/lungs, 106 intestines, and 16,485 kidneys.[13] Since 1988, approximately 580,302 organ transplants have occurred in the United States.[14] Table 2.0 lists the total number of organ transplants for the period 2000–2010.

Table 2.0 Organ Transplants, 2000–2010

Year	Number of Transplants
2000	23,266
2001	24,239
2002	24,910
2003	25,473
2004	27,040
2005	28,118
2006	28,940
2007	28,366
2008	27,964
2009	28,459
2010	28,661

SOURCE: Based on OPTN data (2013), United States Department of Health and Human Services.

Unfulfilled Demand for Body Parts

Although medical science has made tremendous advances in organ transplants, the utilization of these advances is limited by the availability of organ donors. For example, it has been estimated that the organ donee waiting list grew 64 percent over the past ten years, but the list of donors rose by only 39 percent during this time period. A grim result of this disparity is that in 2009 it was estimated that 6,453 organ candidates died while waiting for an organ donor. There are over 100,000 organ candidates listed on the national organ transplant registry.[15]

Of course, "[t]he organ shortage is an international crisis. Other countries have the same problem as the United States—the demand for organs exceeds the supply."[16] The global organ shortage has resulted in the development of an international organ trade, where organ candidates

Organ Transplants from Executed Prisoners

travel abroad to obtain organs through unlawful commercial transactions. This is commonly referred to as "transplant tourism."[17] Some of the countries involved in transplant tourism include Bolivia, Brazil, India, Iran, Iraq, Israel, Moldova, Nepal, Pakistan, Peru, Philippines, South Africa, and Turkey. It has been reported that Australia, Canada, Israel, Japan, Oman, Saudi Arabia and the United States are the major organ-importing countries.[18] China is the only country that relies heavily upon transplantable organs from executed prisoners. By the end of 2012, roughly 64 percent of transplanted organs in China came from executed prisoners.[19]

The grim result of the shortage in available human body parts is death.[20] Although each day an average of 79 people receive organ transplants,[21] an average of 18 people die each day waiting for transplant organs.[22] In October of 2013 the following specific human body-part waiting list existed in the United States: 1,193 pancreases; 16,562 livers; 3,633 hearts; 1,654 lungs, 263 intestines and 105,124 kidneys.[23] Table 2.1 lists the total number of people who died while waiting for an organ transplant during the period 1995–2013. Table 2.2 sets out the number of organ donors during the period 2000–2010.

Table 2.1 Total Deaths While Waiting on Organ Transplant, 1995–2013

Organ Needed	Deaths
Kidney	105,124
Liver	16,562
Pancreas	1,193
Kidney/Pancreas	2,122
Heart	3,633
Lung	1,654
Heart/Lung	49
Intestine	263

SOURCE: Based on OPTN data (2013), United States Department of Health and Human Services.

Table 2.2 Organ Donors Deceased and Living, 2000–2010

Year	Deceased	Living
2000	5,985	5,949
2001	6,080	6,622

2. The Market for Human Body Parts

2002	6,190	6,631
2003	6,457	6,828
2004	7,150	7,004
2005	7,593	6,904
2006	8,017	6,733
2007	8,085	6,315
2008	7,989	6,218
2009	8,022	6,609
2010	7,943	6,560

SOURCE: Based on OPTN data (2013), United States Department of Health and Human Services.

The real tragedy behind the death of donees waiting for organs is that the organs exist to fill the demand but are unavailable to the market in the United States.[24] The organ shortage is artificial because of the method currently being used in the United States for procuring organs. One commentator noted that nationally every year, 200,000 transplantable organs are buried for "maggots" to eventually convert to "swill."[25]

Sale of Body Parts Prohibited

As a result of the tremendous advances made in transplanting human body parts, "Congress felt the need to protect citizens from potential negative implications of the market."[26] It did this by enacting the National Organ Transplant Act of 1984 (NOTA).[27] Two aspects of NOTA are worthy of note here.

First, NOTA authorized the creation of the National Organ Procurement and Transplantation Network (Network). The purpose of Network is to set up procedures for matching human body-part donors with transplant patients.[28] Second, under NOTA it is a federal offense to sell human body parts in interstate commerce. The criminal component of NOTA is set out below:

> NOTA, 42 U.S.C.A. § 274e (2007):
> (a) It shall be unlawful for any person to knowingly acquire, receive, or otherwise transfer any human organ for valuable consideration for use in human transplantation if the transfer affects interstate commerce. The preceding sentence does not apply with respect to human organ paired donation.

Organ Transplants from Executed Prisoners

(b) Any person who violates subsection (a) of this section shall be fined not more than $50,000 or imprisoned not more than five years, or both.

(c) For purposes of subsection (a) of this section:

(1) The term "human organ" means the human (including fetal) kidney, liver, heart, lung, pancreas, bone marrow, cornea, eye, bone, and skin or any subpart thereof and any other human organ (or any subpart thereof, including that derived from a fetus) specified by the Secretary of Health and Human Services by regulation.

(2) The term "valuable consideration" does not include the reasonable payments associated with the removal, transportation, implantation, processing, preservation, quality control, and storage of a human organ or the expenses of travel, housing, and lost wages incurred by the donor of a human organ in connection with the donation of the organ.

(3) The term "interstate commerce" has the meaning prescribed for it by section 321(b) of Title 21.

(4) The term "human organ paired donation" means the donation and receipt of human organs under the following circumstances:

(A) An individual (referred to in this paragraph as the "first donor") desires to make a living donation of a human organ specifically to a particular patient (referred to in this paragraph as the "first patient"), but such donor is biologically incompatible as a donor for such patient.

(B) A second individual (referred to in this paragraph as the "second donor") desires to make a living donation of a human organ specifically to a second particular patient (referred to in this paragraph as the "second patient"), but such donor is biologically incompatible as a donor for such patient.

(C) Subject to subparagraph (D), the first donor is biologically compatible as a donor of a human organ for the second patient, and the second donor is biologically compatible as a donor of a human organ for the first patient.

(D) If there is any additional donor-patient pair as described in subparagraph (A) or (B), each donor in the group of donor-patient pairs is biologically compatible as a donor of a human organ for a patient in such group.

(E) All donors and patients in the group of donor-patient pairs (whether 2 pairs or more than 2 pairs) enter into a single agreement to donate and receive such human organs, respectively, according to such biological compatibility in the group.

(F) Other than as described in subparagraph (E), no valuable consideration is knowingly acquired, received, or otherwise transferred with respect to the human organs referred to in such subparagraph.

2. The Market for Human Body Parts

NOTA's blanket prohibition of the interstate sale of transplantable organs has been criticized.[29] Some have argued, "Removal of a monetary incentive to donate organs has drastically stunted the growth of the nation's organ bank and promoted a lucrative, but inefficient, black market trade in organs."[30] It has also been contended that by banning the sale of human organs, Congress incorrectly assumed that permitting organs to be sold would violate social norms.[31]

The constitutionality of NOTA was challenged in federal court in *Flynn v. Holder*.[32] The constitutional challenge in *Flynn* was very narrow. The plaintiffs in the case argued that the prohibition on the sale of "bone marrow" violated the Equal Protection Clause. A federal district court dismissed the case as having no merit. However, on appeal the Ninth Circuit found merit in one aspect of the plaintiffs' complaint. It was said in *Flynn* that NOTA did not prohibit compensation for bone marrow donations by the peripheral blood stem cell apheresis method. *Flynn* reasoned that extraction of bone marrow by apheresis was not prohibited by NOTA because this method of extraction did not exist when NOTA was enacted. On the other hand, the court in *Flynn* held that NOTA did prohibit the sale of bone marrow extracted by the aspiration method. *Flynn* found that this prohibition did not violate the constitution. *Flynn* addressed the issue as follows:

> The statute says that the term "human organ" includes "bone marrow." The soft, fatty stuff that the needle extracts is bone marrow. It is irrelevant that the legislative history indicates that Congress viewed certain types of regenerable tissue, such as blood, as falling outside the statutory definition of human organ....
>
> As for whether the distinction between the organs or other body substances for which compensation is permitted and those for which it is prohibited has a rational basis, there are two classes of rational basis here: policy concerns and philosophical concerns. The policy concerns are obvious. Some are mentioned in the legislative history, though they need not be. Congress may have been concerned that if donors could be paid, rich patients or the medical industry might induce poor people to sell their organs, even when the transplant would create excessive medical risk, pain, or disability for the donor. Or, looking from the other end, Congress might have been concerned that every last cent could be extracted from sick patients needful of transplants, by well-matched potential donors making "your money or your life" offers. The existing commerce in organs

extracted by force or fraud by organ thieves might be stimulated by paying for donations. Compensation to donors might also degrade the quality of the organ supply, by inducing potential donors to lie about their medical histories in order to make their organs marketable....

Congress may have had philosophical as well as policy reasons for prohibiting compensation. People tend to have an instinctive revulsion at denial of bodily integrity, particularly removal of flesh from a human being for use by another, and most particularly "commodification" of such conduct, that is, the sale of one's bodily tissue. While there is reportedly a large international market for the buying and selling of human organs, in the United States, such a market is criminal and the commerce is generally seen as revolting.[33]

It was reported in 2011, that a man called Levy Izhak Rosenbaum pleaded guilty in a New Jersey federal court to trafficking in illegal kidney transplants. Prosecutors in the case alleged that Mr. Rosenbaum was buying organs from people in Israel for as little as $10,000, and selling them to wealthy Americans for as much as $120,000.[34] In another unlawful organ sale, reported in 2005, an Israeli citizen named Nick Rosen flew to New York to donate one of his kidneys to a Long Island man. At the time of the operation the hospital carrying out the operation did not know that Mr. Rosen was paid $20,000 for "donating" his kidney.[35] Mr. Rosen subsequently "made an 11-minute documentary film he called 'Kidney Beans' to show how easy it was to sell an organ. A portion of the documentary shows him lying on a bed, covered in cash he says he was paid."[36]

In the criminal prosecution in *Commonwealth v. Garzone*[37] the opinion set out the sophisticated organ trafficking operation of Gerald Garzone, Louis Garzone[38] and Michael Mastromarino.[39] All three men were convicted of unlawfully selling human body-parts. The opinion in *Garzone* described the operation as follows:

> Louis and Gerald Garzone were licensed funeral home directors who operated separate funeral homes in Philadelphia. [The Garzones] were also co-owners of Liberty Crematorium in Philadelphia with co-defendant James McCafferty. In early 2004, [the Garzones] and Mr. McCafferty were approached by codefendant Michael Mastromarino, the founder and president of a business called Biomedical Tissue Services ("BTS") that sold human tissue harvested from cadavers to tissue banks. Mr. Mastromarino had initially partnered with funeral home directors in New York and New

2. The Market for Human Body Parts

Jersey. These funeral home directors provided Mr. Mastromarino with cadavers from which he and his team of "cutters" could harvest tissue without the consent of the deceased or their next of kin and then sell to tissue banks. However, this arrangement required Mr. Mastromarino and his cutters to reconstruct the cadavers with PVC pipe after harvesting to conceal their activity and prepare the bodies for viewing and burial. Therefore, Mr. Mastromarino approached [the Garzones] and Mr. McCafferty, who as owners of a crematorium, had access to cadavers destined for cremation and could provide these cadavers without concern for their post-harvesting condition.

[The Garzones] and McCafferty agreed to provide bodies that had been entrusted to their funeral homes and crematorium for cremation to Mr. Mastromarino, who would then harvest bones and tissue from the cadavers to sell to tissue banks. In exchange, Mr. Mastromarino agreed to pay [the Garzones] $1,000 for each cadaver. When Mr. Mastromarino and his cutters came to Philadelphia, [the Garzones] would direct them to the bodies in the embalming rooms of their funeral homes. There, Mr. Mastromarino and the cutters would remove the cadavers' arms, legs, bones, ligaments, tendons, and skin, often leaving only a head and a bloody torso behind in a bag for cremation.

Between visits from Mr. Mastromarino and his cutters, cadavers destined for harvesting would sit in an alley, unrefrigerated, for days. [The Garzones] never provided Mr. Mastromarino or his cutters with death certificates, identification, consent forms, or the names of the bodies' next of kin. Although Mr. Mastromarino told [the Garzones] that the tissue was destined for medical use and the cadavers had to be of individuals who were less than seventy-five years old and disease-free when they died, [the Garzones] provided cadavers of individuals who were more than eighty years old and sick with cancer, H.I.V., and hepatitis at the time of their passing. Over the course of their arrangement with Mr. Mastromarino, [the Garzones] provided more than 244 cadavers and received more than $245,000 in return.[40]

In *Specialty Nat. Ins. Co. v. English Bros. Funeral Home*[41] an insurance company filed a declaratory judgment case in a federal district court in New York, seeking to have the court declare that it had no duty to defend or indemnify its insured, English Brothers Funeral Home, in a series of lawsuits filed against the funeral home. The civil lawsuits against the funeral home involved the unlawful sale of body parts. The federal district court dismissed the insurer's complaint after concluding that the insurance policy might provide coverage. The opinion in the case set out the unlawful conduct by the funeral home and the lawsuits it faced:

Organ Transplants from Executed Prisoners

Beginning in the fall of 2005, English Brothers was named as a defendant in a series of lawsuits stemming from allegations that it, in conjunction with several other individuals and entities also named as defendants in those actions, illegally harvested body parts, organs, and tissue from corpses without the consent of the deceased or their families, and then caused those body parts, organs, and tissues to be implanted in individuals awaiting donations without their knowledge of where the implanted body parts, organs, or tissues had come from.

At least seventeen such suits were filed falling into two general categories. First, "donor cases" have been brought by living family members of decedents whose bodies were allegedly harvested without the consent of the decedents or their families; these donor cases seek relief for the resulting emotional, physical, and mental anguish suffered by surviving family members as a result.

Second, "implant cases" have been brought by persons who received tissue or other body parts from the harvested corpses; the implant cases seek relief for physical injuries suffered or likely to be incurred by the recipients as a result of defendants' conduct, as well as for the emotional and mental anguish suffered by the organ or tissue recipients and their families.[42]

Current Method of Obtaining Body Parts

The human body-part market in the United States is based on a system called the donation-based organ supply system (D-BOSS).[43] Under the D-BOSS system, human body parts are exchanged based on donor's compassion. Of course, procedures are needed to generate body parts from donors who will not be monetarily compensated. The D-BOSS system is regulated by the Uniform Anatomical Gift Act (UAGA).

UAGA was developed by the National Conference of Commissioners on Uniform State Laws. The original version of UAGA was provided in 1968 as a model for states to adopt in regulating the human body-part market.[44] The original version of UAGA did not ban the sale of human body parts. However, in response to NOTA's criminal prohibition against the interstate sale of human organs, UAGA was amended in 1987.[45] The 1987 version of UAGA prohibited the intrastate sale of human body parts. All 50 states and the District of Columbia have adopted and codified UAGA in its original or amended form.[46]

The principal areas addressed by the 1987 version of UAGA are as follows:

2. The Market for Human Body Parts

1. Persons who may execute an anatomical gift
2. Persons who may become donees
3. Purposes for which anatomical gifts may be made
4. Recovery of corneas
5. Manner of executing anatomical gifts
6. Request for consent to an anatomical gift
7. Delivery of document of gift
8. Amendment or revocation of the gift
9. Rights and duties at death
10. Prohibition of sales and purchases of human organs

The current organ donation system in the United States is an opt in system. This system requires donors provide explicit consent to donate an organ. Under the opt in system there is a presumption that a decedent did not wish to donate his or her organs. The ways in which a person can opt in, i.e., consent to donating his or her organs include (1) registering with a state donor registry, (2) designating donor status on a driver's license, (3) carrying a donor card, and (4) informing family members of the desire to be an organ donor upon death.[47]

Proposals for Commercializing the Body-Part Market

The D-BOSS system does not work.[48] Too many patients needing transplantable organs die while waiting for nonexistent organs. Relying on people to donate transplantable organs on death (a few organs can be transplanted from a living person), based purely on their moral belief and commitment to human life, runs counter to the essence of the nation's existence. That essence is grounded in the profit motive.

A thriving black-market system has emerged in the nation as a result of the inefficiency of the D-BOSS system. Cadavers are routinely being pillaged for transplantable organs. Pillaged transplantable organs are being sold on the black market for enormous profits. Only the pillagers share in the monetary benefits. The heirs of cadavers receive nothing, because they are not aware that the corpses of their loved ones are hollow shells.

Organ Transplants from Executed Prisoners

Proposals have been made to replace the inefficient D-BOSS system with a futures-market organ supply system (F-MOSS). Currently, four noteworthy models of an F-MOSS system are on the table: (1) the Schwindt-Vining model; (2) the Hansmann model; (3) the Cohen model; and (4) the Crespi model.[49] It should be noted that for any F-MOSS system to operate, the criminal sanctions for selling human body parts would have to be repealed.

THE SCHWINDT-VINING F-MOSS MODEL

Under the Schwindt-Vining model[50] the government (state) would act as the exclusive buyer of transplantable organs. The transplantable organ bearer would act as the seller. The buyer and the seller would enter into a binding contract that provides immediate monetary consideration to the seller in exchange for the seller's agreement to give the buyer the right to *harvest* the seller's transplantable organs upon the death of the seller. The contract between the buyer and the seller could not be rescinded unless both parties mutually agreed to this.

Under this model, the buyer would pay the seller an amount that would be based on the inventory needs of the buyer. However, the buyer would be able to provide such organs to transplant patients at a cost that was not based on the purchase price of the buyer.

The Schwindt-Vining model has special provisions for contracting with minors. The parent or legal guardian of a minor would execute the contract on behalf of the minor. The monetary consideration would be placed into a trust fund and held until the minor reached majority age. On reaching majority age, the minor would have the option of nullifying the contract and retaining a small portion of the contract proceeds. Should the minor, on reaching majority, decide to honor the contract, he or she would then be entitled to all of the proceeds immediately.

THE HANSMANN F-MOSS MODEL

In the Hansmann model[51] the buyer of transplantable organs would be large health-insurance corporations. The seller of organs would be the individual bearer. Under this model, the buyer and the seller would

2. The Market for Human Body Parts

execute a contract requiring the buyer to immediately pay the seller a certain sum in exchange for the seller's transplantable organs at death. This model would allow the buyer to sell its contract.

The price paid by a buyer to a seller under this model would be based on prices set by the competitive market. However, the model proposes that transplant patients be charged based on an administratively set price or market demand prices.

The model would prohibit heirs of a decedent from selling the decedent's transplantable organs if the decedent had failed to enter into a contract with a buyer, unless the decedent specifically provided for such sale by heirs in a will.

A buyer under this model would have to provide a central registry with information on each contract executed. Hospitals would be required to consult the central registry whenever a patient died, to learn if the patient had previously executed a contract disposing of his or her transplantable organs. If a patient has entered into such a contract, the hospital would have an obligation to notify the buyer and preserve the organs in a harvestable condition until they are retrieved by the buyer.

THE COHEN F-MOSS MODEL

The buyer in the Cohen model[52] could be a government (state) or private entrepreneur. The seller would be the bearer of transplantable organs. The contract executed between the buyer and the seller in this model provides for contingent compensation that is not paid directly to the seller. In this model, the buyer would agree to pay a certain sum to the seller's estate on death, on the condition that transplantable organs are actually harvested from the seller's cadaver.

The price determination between the buyer and the seller would be based on administrative figures or market demand. This model projects payment to a decedent's estate to be as much as $30,000.

The Cohen model would allow contracts to be entered into with minors, if the parents of the minors also executed contracts involving their own transplantable organs.

To ensure that hospitals notify buyers of the death of a seller and preserve transplantable organs in a harvested state, the Cohen model

The Crespi F-MOSS Model

The Crespi model[53] does not indicate explicitly whether the buyer is a government or private entity or both. The seller is identified as the bearer of transplantable organs. This model calls for the buyer and the seller to execute an agreement wherein the buyer agrees to pay a sum to the estate of the seller at death, on the condition that the buyer actually harvests transplantable organs from the seller's cadaver. Market demand would determine the price paid for the organs harvested. Contracts under this model may be unilaterally terminated by the seller before death, without liability exposure. The heirs of the seller would not be allowed to terminate a contract.

This model provides that proceeds from a contract could not be attached by creditors of the seller. The proceeds would also be subject to the same tax treatment that is provided for life insurance proceeds that are payable to a decedent's estate.

The buyer is permitted to assign away the rights of a contract. However, the seller would not be able to assign away the proceeds from the contract. A seller is also prohibited from selling and having removed any transplantable organ while alive.

Parents or guardians of minors would be able to enter into contracts on behalf of minors. A minor would be able to terminate such a contract on reaching majority age.

This model would permit relatives of a decedent to sell the decedent's transplantable organs even if the decedent had not previously entered into a contract while living. However, any proceeds from such a sale would have to be given to a nonprofit organization or church.

The federal government, under the Crespi model, would be obligated to establish a national registry for transplantable organ contracts. Hospitals would be required to consult the national registry whenever a patient died, to determine whether the patient had executed a transplantable organ contract. The hospital would have a duty to notify the buyer and preserve transplantable organs in a harvested state.

2. The Market for Human Body Parts

Finally, buyers would be able to provide transplantable organs to transplant patients at a cost determined by market demand.

Presumed Consent

There is another internationally recognized option for increasing organ supply that is called presumed consent.[54] This system creates a presumption that people want to donate their organs upon death.[55] In 2013, the government of Wales joined a growing list of countries that have presumed consent laws.[56] The other nations include Austria, Belgium, Bulgaria, Croatia, Cyprus, Czech Republic, Estonia, Finland, France, Greece, Hungary, Italy, Latvia, Luxemburg, Norway, Poland, Portugal, Slovak Republic, Slovenia, Spain, Sweden, and Turkey.[57]

In theory the presumed consent system allows people to opt out of donating their organs, by registering their decision in online data bases, carrying an opt out card, or telling their relatives.[58] It has been said that presumed consent systems can be tough, as in Austria, where the views of family members are not seriously considered, or friendly, as in Spain and France, where the opinion of family members is earnestly considered.[59]

A study was conducted to determine whether organ donation rates across Europe differed. It was found that four countries that do not have presumed consent laws, Denmark, Netherlands, United Kingdom, and Germany, have low donation rates: Denmark 4.25 percent, Germany 12 percent, United Kingdom 17.17 percent, and Netherlands 27.5 percent. Whereas seven countries with presumed consent laws, Austria, Belgium, France, Hungary, Poland, Portugal, and Sweden, all have higher rates of donation, ranging from a low of 85.9 percent to a high of more than 99 percent.[60]

Although presumed consent organ donation laws do not exist in the United States, many states do have mild variations of presumed consent for cornea transplantation. "These laws generally provide that a coroner or medical examiner may remove the corneas from a cadaver in the course of a legally-required autopsy, provided that a need for the tissues is demonstrated and that no objection from either the decedent or the next-of-kin is known."[61] The mild form of presumed consent laws in the United States have been challenged in various courts.

For example, in *Tillman v. Detroit Receiving Hosp.*[62] the mother of a decedent challenged the constitutionality of a Michigan law that allowed a medical examiner to remove and retain corneas. The mother in *Tillman* alleged that her daughter's corneas and eyes were removed without her consent and in violation of state law. The trial court dismissed the case as having no merit. A court appeals affirmed as follows:

> Plaintiff claims that as next of kin she has an inherent, fundamental right to bury her decedent's body without mutilation. While there is no property right in the next of kin to a dead body, Michigan jurisprudence recognizes a common law cause of action on behalf of the person or persons entitled to the possession, control, or burial of a dead body for the tort of interference with the right of burial of a deceased person without mutilation.
>
> We do not find this common law right to be of constitutional dimension. The privacy right encompasses the right to make decisions concerning the integrity of one's body. This right is, however, a personal one. It ends with the death of the person to whom it is of value. It may not be claimed by his estate or his next of kin. Accordingly, we reject plaintiff's constitutional challenge predicated on the right to privacy.
>
> ***
>
> Even assuming that plaintiff's allegations are true and that the eyes of her decedent were removed, a medical examiner may retain body portions for further criminal investigation.[63]

In another example, the parents of two decedents in *State v. Powell*[64] filed a lawsuit to invalidate a Florida statute that allowed a medical examiner to retain corneas of their deceased sons. A trial court found that the statute authorizing a medical examiner to remove corneal tissue from the decedents was unconstitutional. The Florida Supreme Court disagreed as follows:

> The unrebutted evidence in this record establishes that the State of Florida spends approximately $138 million each year to provide its blind with the basic necessities of life. At present, approximately ten percent of Florida's blind citizens are candidates for cornea transplantation....
>
> The record reflects that the key to successful corneal transplantation is the availability of high-quality corneal tissue and that corneal tissue removed more than ten hours after death is generally unsuitable for transplantation. The implementation of [the statute] has, indisputably,

2. The Market for Human Body Parts

increased both the supply and quality of tissue available for transplantation. Statistics show that, in 1976, only 500 corneas were obtained in Florida for transplantation while, in 1985, more than 3,000 persons in Florida had their sight restored through corneal transplantation surgery.

***

Our review of [the statute] reveals certain safeguards which are apparently designed to limit cornea removal to instances in which the public's interest is greatest and the impact on the next of kin the least: corneas may be removed only if the decedent is under the jurisdiction of the medical examiner; an autopsy is mandated by Florida law; and the removal will not interfere with the autopsy or an investigation of the death. Further, medical examiners may not automatically remove tissue from all decedents subject to autopsy; rather, a request must be made by an eye bank based on a present need for the tissue.

We conclude that this record clearly establishes that this statute reasonably achieves the permissible legislative objective of providing sight to many of Florida's blind citizens.[65]

The Israeli Organ-for-Organ Law

In 2010, a law took effect in Israel which made it the first nation in the world to attempt to increase organ donations by giving priority to organ donors. Under this approach if a person signs an organ donor card, he or she will have priority for an organ if the need arises.[66] Under the groundbreaking law "priority would also be 'granted to transplant candidates with a first-degree relative who was a deceased organ donor and to any live donor of a kidney, liver lobe, or lung lobe who subsequently needs an organ.'"[67]

The Israeli system is also heralded as being the first to incorporate "nonmedical" requirements into the allocation priority system.[68] The Israeli law establishes three levels of priorities in organ allocation. Top priority is given to candidates who have a first-degree relative who donated organs after death or to candidates who have donated kidneys, lung-lobes or liver-lobes. The second priority is given to donors who have registered as organ donors at least 3 years prior of being listed. The third priority is to candidates who have not actually signed a donor card, but they have first-degree relatives who registered as organ donors at least 3 years prior of their listing.[69]

It has been reported that under the new Israeli system in 2012, 52 people received priority for organ donations. It was also reported that "by the end of 2012, a total of 717,826 [people] had signed organ donor cards, an increase of 13 percent over the previous year."[70]

Mandated Choice

Mandated choice is a proactive method of increasing the organ supply. Under the mandated choice system individuals are required to register their decision regarding organ donation through various registration mechanisms. This system is designed to allow individuals to affirmatively make a decision about donating their organs upon death. The mandated choice system assures that only the individual, and not his or her relatives, will dictate the fate of his or her organs. Under mandated choice, an individual registers his or her decision to donate or decline to donate while, for example, renewing a driver's license or filing a tax return. This process requires the individual respond to questions regarding organ donation. Whatever choice the individual makes, it is binding upon his or her death and cannot be reversed by relatives.[71]

In 2006, the state of Illinois enacted a mandated choice statute it called the First Person Consent Act ("Act"). Under the Act citizens over the age of eighteen are required to inform the state, when obtaining their driver's licenses, whether they consent to being an organ donor upon their death.[72] The relevant text of the Act is set out below.

> 625 Illinois Comp. Stat. 5/6–117(g):
> The Secretary of State may establish a First Person Consent organ and tissue donor registry in compliance with subsection (b–1) of Section 5–20 of the Illinois Anatomical Gift Act, as follows:
> (1) The Secretary shall offer, to each applicant for issuance or renewal of a driver's license or identification card who is 18 years of age or older, the opportunity to have his or her name included in the First Person Consent organ and tissue donor registry. The Secretary must advise the applicant or licensee that he or she is under no compulsion to have his or her name included in the registry. An individual who agrees to having his or her name included in the First Person Consent organ and tissue donor registry has given full legal consent to the donation of any of his or her organs or

2. The Market for Human Body Parts

tissue upon his or her death. A brochure explaining this method of executing an anatomical gift must be given to each applicant for issuance or renewal of a driver's license or identification card. The brochure must advise the applicant or licensee (i) that he or she is under no compulsion to have his or her name included in this registry and (ii) that he or she may wish to consult with family, friends, or clergy before doing so.

3

REMOVING TRANSPLANTABLE ORGANS OF CAPITAL FELONS

Currently, a majority of states allow the imposition of the death penalty for the crime of capital murder.[1] Capital punishment jurisdictions allow for the burial of an executed prisoner by relatives, friends or the government if the body is unclaimed. However, such disposition was not always the case. The state of Massachusetts once had a statute which provided that, "Upon conviction of murder in the first degree, the court may order the body of the convict after his execution to be dissected."[2] Moreover, it was reported that "[i]n 1789 there was a law passed by the state of New York to the effect that where persons were convicted of murder and sentenced to death therefor, the court might, at its discretion, add to the judgment that the body of such offender be delivered to a surgeon for dissection[.]"[3] Additionally, the federal system had a dissection-enhanced punishment statute that was repealed in the 1980s. The now repealed federal statute read as follows:

> 18 U.S.C.A. § 3567:
> The court before which any person is convicted of murder in the first degree, or rape, may, in its discretion, add to the judgment of death, that the body of the offender be delivered to a surgeon for dissection; and the marshal who executes such judgment shall deliver the body, after execution, to such surgeon as the court may direct; and such surgeon, or some person appointed by him, shall receive and take away the body at the time of execution.[4]

These dissection-enhanced punishment statutes were for the purpose of medical experimentation only and were not intended for removing organs for donation to transplant patients.

3. Removing Transplantable Organs of Capital Felons

A natural extension of the dissection-enhanced punishment is to have all capital-punishment jurisdictions harvest the transplantable organs of capital felons as part of the death sentence. The intent of this chapter is to provide an examination of the nonconstitutional issues involved in a court order to remove transplantable organs of capital felons as part of the death sentence.

The material in this chapter is presented in three major parts. The first part sets forth the ways in which capital punishment jurisdictions currently dispose of the cadavers of executed felons. The second part discusses the two primary reasons for the slowness of the law to incorporate, as punishment, the removal of transplantable organs of executed capital murderers. The third part gives four dominant justifications for permitting courts the authority to order, as punishment, the removal of transplantable organs of capital felons as part of the death sentence.

Table 3.0 Capital Punishment Jurisdictions, 2013

Alabama	Idaho	Nebraska	South Carolina
Arizona	Indiana	Nevada	South Dakota
Arkansas	Kansas	New Hampshire	Tennessee
California	Kentucky	North Carolina	Texas
Colorado	Louisiana	Ohio	Utah
Delaware	Mississippi	Oklahoma	Virginia
Florida	Missouri	Oregon	Washington
Georgia	Montana	Pennsylvania	Wyoming
			Federal system

Source: Louis J. Palmer, Jr., *The Death Penalty in the United States: A Complete Guide to Federal and State Laws* (2013) 91, Box 11.0 (2013).

Statutory Disposal of Corpses

The death-penalty statutes in a minority of U.S. capital-punishment jurisdictions set out the method of disposition of an executed capital felon's corpse. The five statutorily recognized dispositions for the cadavers of executed capital felons reflect an acknowledgment of the quasi-property rights in corpses. Descriptions of the dispositions follow.[5]

Permit Relatives to Take the Corpse. Twelve capital punishment jurisdictions require the corpse of an executed felon be turned over to a requesting relative.[6] Five of those jurisdictions pay the cost of shipping the corpse to a requesting relative.[7]

Permit a Friend to Take the Corpse. Eight capital punishment jurisdictions allow the corpse of an executed felon to be turned over to a requesting friend.[8] In this situation the corpse would be given to a friend of the capital felon only if no relative made a request for the corpse.

Permit a Person Designated by the Felon to Take the Corpse. The statute in one capital punishment jurisdiction provides that the corpse of an executed felon may be turned over to a person designated by the capital felon before the execution.[9]

Permit the Unclaimed Corpse to be Donated to a Medical Center or Physician. The statutes in two capital punishment jurisdictions provide that the corpse of a capital felon may be turned over to a medical center for research.[10] Another jurisdiction allows a requesting physician to take the corpse.[11] Disposition in this category is triggered only if neither relatives nor friends of the capital felon request the corpse.

Permit the Unclaimed Corpse to Be Buried by the Jurisdiction. If no claim is made for the corpse of an executed felon, the statutes in eleven capital punishment jurisdictions provide for burial by the jurisdiction.[12]

Removing Organs as Part of the Death Sentence

Presently no American court has been given the authority to order the removal of transplantable organs from a convicted capital murderer as part of the imposition of a death sentence. Two fundamental reasons explain the slowness of legislatures to empower the legal system to punitively recycle transplantable organs of capital murderers: (1) the impact of Furman, and (2) an uninformed public.

IMPACT OF FURMAN

In 1972 the U.S. Supreme Court caused the *Richter scale* to register 9.9 when it abolished the death penalty through its decision in *Furman*

3. Removing Transplantable Organs of Capital Felons

v. Georgia.[13] The decision in *Furman* concluded that the death penalty was imposed in an arbitrary and capricious manner and, therefore, violated the Eighth Amendment's prohibition of cruel and unusual punishment.

The decision in *Furman* was narrowly reached by a 5–4 vote of the justices. Each of the justices voting to bar the death penalty wrote separate concurring opinions. The concurring opinion that ultimately had the greatest impact on future capital-punishment law was that of Justice William Douglas. Set out below is an excerpt from Justice Douglas:

> It has been assumed in our decisions that punishment by death is not cruel, unless the manner of execution can be said to be inhuman and barbarous....
>
> It would seem to be incontestable that the death penalty inflicted on one defendant is "unusual" if it discriminates against him by reason of his race, religion, wealth, social position, or class, or if it is imposed under a procedure that gives room for the play of such prejudices.
>
> There is evidence that the provision of the English Bill of Rights of 1689, from which the language of the Eighth Amendment was taken, was concerned primarily with selective or irregular application of harsh penalties and that its aim was to forbid arbitrary and discriminatory penalties of a severe nature....
>
> The words "cruel and unusual" certainly include penalties that are barbaric. But the words, at least when read in light of the English proscription against selective and irregular use of penalties, suggest that it is "cruel and unusual" to apply the death penalty—or any other penalty—selectively to minorities whose numbers are few, who are outcasts of society, and who are unpopular, but whom society is willing to see suffer though it would not countenance general application of the same penalty across the board....
>
> ... Juris (or judges, as the case may be) have practically untrammeled discretion to let an accused live or insist that he die....
>
> Former Attorney General Ramsey Clark has said, "It is the poor, the sick, the ignorant, the powerless and the hated who are executed." One searches our chronicles in vain for the execution of any member of the affluent strata of this society. The Leopolds and Loebs are given prison terms, not sentenced to death....
>
> ... [W]e deal with a system of law and of justice that leaves to the uncontrolled discretion of judges or juries the determination whether defendants ... should die or be imprisoned. Under [current] laws no standards govern the selection of the penalty. People live or die, dependent on the whim of one man or of 12....

Organ Transplants from Executed Prisoners

Those who wrote the Eighth Amendment knew what price their forebears had paid for a system based, not on equal justice, but on discrimination. In those days the target was not the blacks or the poor, but the dissenters, those who opposed absolutism in government, who struggled for a parliamentary regime, and who opposed governments' recurring efforts to foist a particular religion on the people. But the tool of capital punishment was used with vengeance against the opposition and those unpopular with the regime. One cannot read this history without realizing that the desire for equality was reflected in the ban against "cruel and unusual punishments" contained in the Eighth Amendment.

In a Nation committed to equal protection of the laws there is no permissible "cast" aspect of law enforcement. Yet we know that the discretion of judges and juries in imposing the death penalty enables the penalty to be selectively applied, feeding prejudices against the accused if he is poor and despised, and lacking political clout, or if he is a member of a suspect or unpopular minority, and saving those who by social position may be in a more protected position. In ancient Hindu Law a Brahman was exempt from capital punishment, and under that law, "[g]enerally, in the law books, punishment increased in severity as social status diminished." We have, I fear, taken in practice the same position, partially as a result of making the death penalty discretionary and partially as a result of the ability of the rich to purchase the services of the most respected and most resourceful legal talent in the Nation.

The high service rendered by the "cruel and unusual" punishment clause of the Eighth Amendment is to require legislatures to write penal laws that are evenhanded, nonselective, and nonarbitrary, and to require judges to see to it that general laws are not applied sparsely, selectively, and spottily to unpopular groups....

Thus, these discretionary statutes are unconstitutional in their operation. They are pregnant with discrimination and discrimination is an ingredient not compatible with the idea of equal protection of the laws that is implicit in the ban on "cruel and unusual" punishments.[14]

Furman did not hold that the death penalty or the punishment of death was unconstitutional per se. The decision was narrow in merely holding that the method used to determine who was sentenced to die violated the constitution. *Furman* invalidated the capital-punishment selection process, not capital punishment.

Furman left the door open for the death penalty to be reinstated if a method could be designed to impose death in a fair and nondiscriminatory manner. The state of Georgia was one of the first jurisdictions to overcome the aftershock of *Furman*. In doing so, Georgia designed

3. Removing Transplantable Organs of Capital Felons

new procedures for determining when the death penalty could be imposed. Georgia's new death-penalty procedures were challenged and brought to the U.S. Supreme Court in 1976, in the case of *Gregg v. Georgia*.[15]

Gregg resurrected the death penalty in the nation. The *Gregg* opinion approved of the new death-penalty procedures enacted by the state of Georgia. Under those procedures, a capital prosecution was divided into two distinct phases: guilt phase and penalty phase. Justice Potter Stewart, writing the opinion in *Gregg*, reviewed the new procedures:

> [I]t is necessary to understand the Georgia statutory scheme for the imposition of the death penalty. The Georgia statute [was] amended after our decision in *Furman v. Georgia*.... The capital defendant's guilt or innocence is determined in the traditional manner, either by a trial judge or a jury, in the first stage of a bifurcated trial.
>
> > If trial is by jury, the trial judge is required to charge lesser included offenses when they are supported by any view of the evidence. After a verdict, finding, or plea of guilty to a capital crime, a presentence hearing is conducted before whoever made the determination of guilt. The sentencing procedures are essentially the same in both bench and jury trials. At the hearing:
>
> "[T]he judge [or jury] shall hear additional evidence in extenuation, mitigation, and aggravation of punishment, including the record of any prior criminal convictions and pleas of guilty or pleas of nolo contendere of the defendant, or the absence of any prior conviction and pleas: Provided, however, that only such evidence in aggravation as the State has made known to the defendant prior to his trial shall be admissible. The judge [or jury] shall also hear argument by the defendant or his counsel and the prosecuting attorney ... regarding the punishment to be imposed."
>
> The defendant is accorded substantial latitude as to the types of evidence that he may introduce. Evidence considered during the guilt stage may be considered during the sentencing stage without being resubmitted.
>
> In the assessment of the appropriate sentence to be imposed the judge is also required to consider or to include in his instructions to the jury "any mitigating circumstances or aggravating circumstances otherwise authorized by law and any of [10] statutory aggravating circumstances which may be supported by the evidence...." The scope of the nonstatutory aggravating or mitigating circumstances is not delineated in the statute. Before a convicted defendant may be sentenced to death, however, ... the jury, or the trial judge in cases tried without a jury, must find beyond a reasonable doubt one of the 10 aggravating circumstances specified in the statute. The sentence of death may be imposed only if the jury (or judge) finds one of

the statutory aggravating circumstances and then elects to impose that sentence. If the verdict is death, the jury or judge must specify the aggravating circumstance(s) found. In jury cases, the trial judge is bound by the jury's recommended sentence.

In addition to the conventional appellate process available in all criminal cases, provision is made for special expedited direct review by the Supreme Court of Georgia of the appropriateness of imposing the sentence of death in the particular case. The court is directed to consider "the punishment as well as any errors enumerated by way of appeal," and to determine:

"(1) Whether the sentence of death was imposed under the influence of passion, prejudice, or anything arbitrary factor, and

"(2) Whether ... the evidence supports the jury's or judge's finding of a statutory aggravating circumstance as enumerated in [the statute], and

"(3) Whether the sentence of death is excessive or disproportionate to the penalty imposed in similar cases, considering both the crime and the defendant."

If the court affirms a death sentence, it is required to include in its decision reference to similar cases that it has taken into consideration.

A transcript and complete record of the trial, as well as a separate report by the trial judge, are transmitted to the court for its use in reviewing the sentence. The report is in the form of a ... questionnaire, designed to elicit information about the defendant, the crime, and the circumstances of the trial. It requires the trial judge to characterize the trial in several ways designed to test for arbitrariness and disproportionality of sentence. Included in the report are responses to detailed questions concerning the quality of the defendant's representation, whether race played a role in the trial, and, whether, in the trial court's judgment, there was any doubt about the defendant's guilt or the appropriateness of the sentence. A copy of the report is served upon defense counsel. Under its special review authority, the court may either affirm the death sentence or remand the case for resentencing. In cases in which the death sentence is affirmed there remains the possibility of executive clemency....

The basic concern of *Furman* centered on those defendants who were being condemned to death capriciously and arbitrarily. Under the procedures before the Court in that case, sentencing authorities were not directed to give attention to the nature or circumstances of the crime committed or to the character or record of the defendant. Left unguided, juries imposed the death sentence in a way that could only be called freakish. The new Georgia sentencing procedures, by contrast, focus the jury's attention on the particularized nature of the crime and the particularized characteristics of the individual defendant. While the jury is permitted to consider any aggravating or mitigating circumstances, it must find and

3. Removing Transplantable Organs of Capital Felons

identify at least one statutory aggravating factor before it may impose a penalty of death. In this way the jury's discretion is channeled. No longer can a jury wantonly and freakishly impose the death sentence; it is always circumscribed by the legislative guidelines. In addition, the review function of the Supreme Court of Georgia affords additional assurance that the concerns that prompted our decision in *Furman* are not present to any significant degree in the Georgia procedure applied here.

For the reasons expressed in this opinion, we hold that the statutory system under which [the defendant] was sentenced to death does not violate the Constitution. Accordingly, the judgment of the Georgia Supreme Court is affirmed.[16]

In the wake of *Gregg*, a majority of the nation's jurisdictions eventually created new death-penalty procedures patterned, with variations, along the lines of Georgia's procedures.[17]

In the final analysis, *Furman* traumatized all legislators. The decision created a legislative climate of ultra-extreme caution in all matters pertaining to capital punishment. As a result of this climate, post–*Gregg* capital-punishment legislation has moved in a slow, snail-like fashion. No capital-punishment jurisdiction wants its internal integrity challenged and emasculated as was done through the *Furman* decision.

The *Furman*-induced caution is one of the central reasons legislators have been slow in creating statutes that permit the removal of transplantable organs from capital murderers as part of the sentence of death. At this juncture, however, the temperament of the nation's highest court permits legislators to throw capital-punishment caution to the wind. As documented in the next chapter, there is no constitutional impediment to ultimately saving lives by the nonconsensual removal of transplantable organs from executed capital murderers. The nation's highest court will not find death-penalty statutes unconstitutional merely because they require the removal of a capital murderer's transplantable organs as part of the sentence of death.[18]

Uninformed Public

A great disservice has been done to the American public by the failure of public officials to educate the public about the tremendous beneficial achievements made in the transplantable organ frontier.[19] This matter was recognized by the American Bar Association in 1992, when it passed a resolution supporting "efforts to educate the public about the critical need for organ ... donations[.]"[20] At present there is no national consciousness of, or sensitivity to, medical science's ability to prolong life through organ transplantation. Primordial taboos and innocent ignorance continue to cast an evil eye on this new life-giving frontier.

One of the major negative consequences flowing from the general public's lack of awareness and understanding of the full import of organ transplantation, is public silence on the disposition of the transplantable organs of executed capital murderers. In the post–*Furman* era, the general public in a majority of states demanded that the death penalty be reinstated for capital murder. Legislators in those states (and the federal government) heard and reacted positively to the public's demand for the death penalty.

The general public's demand for reinstatement of the death penalty is no great mystery. The death penalty means the end of life for a criminal who has taken the life of another in a profoundly cruel way. The public understands the formula of *a life for a life*. This formula has ancient, Biblical roots. It is a formula that, in one sense, is instinctive to human nature. On the other hand, the general public has heretofore made no demand on legislators to enact statutes requiring the removal of transplantable organs of capital felons as an incident to the sentence of death.

This silence is no great mystery either. The thought of removing the organs of executed capital murderers, for donation to transplant patients, is not instinctive to human nature. Organ transplantation is a new phenomenon on the world stage, not something that existed when human life began. Thus, no basis exists for human nature to *instinctively* connect this medical breakthrough with the punishment of a capital murderer. The public must be sufficiently sensitized to the general moral benefits of organ transplantation. If this necessary educational process had already occurred, it would today be common practice to remove transplantable organs from capital murderers. That is, once the general public understands the formula that permits a capital murderer to involuntarily give life back, the halls of every legislature will tremble with the public's demand for the imposition of this formula. Legislators will heed

3. Removing Transplantable Organs of Capital Felons

this moral demand and enact statutes requiring the removal of the organs of capital felons as part of the sentence of death.

Justification for Removing Organs

The physical life of every human being is not and never will be eternal. Each person must die. The inevitability of death, however, does not command that each individual go out and end his or her life. Longevity has its place and purpose. This simple truth is expressed in the very existence of life.

When a capital felon brutally cuts short the life of a citizen, such conduct is not the inevitability of death being played out on the world stage. Capital murder is the unjustifiable denial of the inherent right to life. Society recognizes that capital murder deprives the victim of the inherent right to life; consequently, the majority of jurisdictions require that the capital murderer forfeit his or her life.

Legal scholars and courts justify the imposition of criminal punishment on four grounds: moral, deterrent, retributive and restitution.[21] The following discussion applies these justification principles to the issue of requiring capital murderers to forfeit their transplantable organs as part of the sentence of death. Additionally, factual case illustrations follow the discussion of each justification principle.

MORAL JUSTIFICATION

In the abstract, the law does not concern itself with the moral tenor or position of its pronouncements. However, the humanity of lawmakers requires them to wrestle with the moral correctness of their legislative actions before those actions are undertaken. And too, the humanity of the will of the people demands that all citizens weigh the moral uprightness of the legislation they impose on legislators. Thus, morality is embedded in the creative spirit of each law, though it will not be found in the text of any law.

The question of the morality of the death penalty has been intellectually explored by legislators and the public. The majority of both have concluded that it is morally correct to impose the death penalty on capital murderers. The will of the majority, right or wrong, must always be the law of the land.

The death penalty is morally justified. The truth of this proposition is not a logical deduction from the mere fact that a majority of our society approve of the death penalty for capital murder. Its truth is rationally deduced from life's essence: *survival*. All life form is endowed with a constitution that demands taking all measures necessary to survive. Without such an inherent prime directive, life would not long exist. Life must exist for life to exist.

To permit a capital murderer to snuff out life without a societal response in proportion to the murderer's act is immoral. It would be immoral not to punish a capital murderer with death, because to do otherwise is a direct assault on the integrity of life and its prime directive—survival. A capital murderer, in the final summation, establishes an example that says: *"Human life is nothing more than dung for the soil."* Such an example is immoral and must never be allowed to stand as a model for emulation. Therefore, society must assert the moral legitimacy and worthiness of life by taking the life of a capital murderer.

No one will question the fact that it is immoral to permit a person, innocent of any wrongdoing, to die when the means for saving that person's life are readily at hand. When a capital murderer is buried with his or her transplantable organs intact, an immoral act has been committed. In burying the healthy transplantable organs of a capital murderer, society is intentionally and knowingly allowing innocent transplant patients to die. This is wrong and immoral. Therefore, it must logically follow that requiring capital murderers to forfeit their transplantable organs as part of the sentence of death is morally justified.[22]

Case Illustration # 1. The moral justification for the nonconsensual removal of the transplantable organs of a capital murderer is illustrated by the facts reported in the case *Commonwealth v. Edmiston*[23]:

> Following a non-jury trial in the Court of Common Pleas of Cambria County, the appellant, Stephen Rex Edmiston, was convicted of murder of the first degree, rape, statutory rape, and involuntary deviate sexual intercourse with a two-year-old female child. A sentencing jury concluded that a sentence of death was appropriate....

3. Removing Transplantable Organs of Capital Felons

> The record reflects that appellant committed the heinous acts designed to produce death and intended to commit those acts. Here, a two-year-old girl, weighing thirty-four pounds and standing thirty-six inches tall, suffered the following serious injuries: scalping, blunt force to her torso, obliteration of her genital area, burning of her body and skull fracture. She was scalped by being cut with a sharp knife-like instrument from the ear up across the front hair line of her forehead and down to the other ear. Her scalp was then peeled back to the nape of her head exposing the entire skull. Blunt force trauma to her chest and stomach was so forceful that it caused the tearing of her liver and lungs. This force was also one of two possible causes of two feet of the infant's intestines to protrude from her genital area. (The other possible cause was pulling the intestines out of the genital area.) The genital area of the two-year-old child was completely obliterated and ripped to such an extent that there was only one large and bloody cavity where there originally were the anal and vaginal orifices. There were also areas of burning of the infant's body, many other lacerations and abrasions and a skull fracture.
>
> All of the these separate and gruesome injuries occurred while the child was living.... The separate inflictions of these injuries demonstrate a methodical step-by-step process of killing, i.e., a willful, premeditated, deliberate, and intentional killing by a fully developed adult man of a helpless two-year-old infant girl.[24]

Case Illustration # 2. The brief facts from the case of *Maynard v. Cartwright*[25] provide a second example of the moral justification for nonconsensually removing the transplantable organs of capital felons:

> On May 4, 1982, after eating their evening meal in their Muskogee County, Oklahoma, home, Hugh and Charma Riddle watched television in their living room. At some point, Mrs. Riddle left the living room and was proceeding towards the bathroom when she encountered respondent Cartwright standing in the hall holding a shotgun. She struggled for the gun and was shot twice in the legs. The man, whom she recognized as a disgruntled ex-employee, then proceeded to the living room where he shot and killed Hugh Riddle. Mrs. Riddle dragged herself down the hall to a bedroom where she tried to use a telephone. Respondent, however, entered the bedroom, slit Mrs. Riddle's throat, stabbed her twice with a hunting knife the Riddles had given him for Christmas, and then left the house. Mrs. Riddle survived and called the police. Respondent was arrested two days later and charged with first-degree murder.[26]

The capital murderers in *Edmiston* and *Maynard* looked on human life as nothing more than dung for the soil. Their crimes cannot stand as a model for what society thinks of itself. Life is more precious and sacred than the model erected in *Edmiston* and *Maynard*. A moral duty arises from the crimes committed in *Edmiston* and *Maynard,* a moral duty that demands society revoke those murderers' membership in the human family. Revocation of their rights to exist in the human family is not only morally correct, but a moral obligation.

However, morality would be half served by merely revoking the life membership cards of such capital murderers. In the wake of medical advancements, moral duty—moral obligation—takes on a broader agenda. The moral agenda now includes saving lives by methodically removing healthy transplantable organs from those who would treat life as did the capital murderers in *Edmiston* and *Maynard*. The moral agenda cannot bring back the victims in *Edmiston* and *Maynard*, but it can increase the life span of thousands of citizens.

Voices of dissent may cry out that morality is not being served by taking healthy transplantable organs from executed capital murderers. Patience must never have a boundary. Let the chorus of dissenters sing their song. Once the dissenters are through, turn up the volume and let the praise and advocacy from those who received new life from healthy transplantable organs of executed capital murderers be heard around the world. The beneficiaries of healthy transplantable organs taken from executed capital murderers will articulate the moral legitimacy of the organs they received.

Deterrent Justification

Legal theorists have long embraced deterrence as a justification for criminal punishment in general. A massive volume of literature explains the necessity for attaching the appropriate punishment to every penal law, with a view toward effectively deterring individuals from violating those laws. Effective deterrence has never embraced the expectation that appropriate penal consequences would forever prevent laws from being violated. A fundamental premise embedded in the deterrence principle is minimizing violations of criminal laws, not completely abating violations. Human nature has made it quite clear that, like the Biblical prophecy that the poor will always exist, so too will violations of criminal

3. Removing Transplantable Organs of Capital Felons

laws always exist. Deterrence, then, in a rational compromise with reality, has sought only to keep criminal conduct at a level tolerable to society.

Attaching a fine to a law prohibiting speeding will not completely deter speeding. The prospect of the fine will, however, reduce the incidence of such prohibited conduct. Enacting a law that requires incarcerating anyone who dumps toxic waste into rivers and streams will not forever deter such conduct. The threat of incarceration will, however, reduce the level of such prohibited activity. Creating a law that imposes the punishment of death for taking a human life in a profoundly cruel way will not deter capital murder from ever occurring. However, the ominous specter of the death penalty will reduce the potential incidence level of capital murder.

Deterrence and reduction are like the two opposite sides of a coin: both exist because of the other, and neither can exist without the other. This unadorned proposition must not be lost sight of, in the examination of deterrence as a justification for enacting laws that require the removal of transplantable organs from those who are convicted of capital murder.

Although it may be a tragic confession and reflection in the mirror, capital murder occurs at a tolerable level. Toleration has been reached because of the deterrent effect of the death penalty. However, as a result of magnificent achievements by medical science, a new level of toleration is at society's fingertips. Appending to the sentence of death the removal of a capital murderer's transplantable organs will further reduce the incidence of capital murder. An immediate grasp of the truth of this statement is evident in the brutal intimidation the statement impresses on the mind.[27]

Case Illustration # 1. An understanding of the deterrent justification for removing the transplantable organs of a capital murderer, as part of the sentence of death, may be gleamed from the facts reported in the case *Blystone v. Pennsylvania*[28]:

> A Pennsylvania jury sentenced petitioner Scott Wayne Blystone to death after finding him guilty of robbing and murdering a hitchhiker who was unlucky enough to have accepted a ride in his car....
> On a September night in 1983, Dalton Charles Smithburger, Jr., an indi-

vidual characterized at trial as possessing a learning disability, was attempting to hitch a ride along a Pennsylvania road. Petitioner, who was driving an auto carrying his girlfriend and another couple, observed Smithburger and announced: "I am going to pick this guy up and rob him, Okay...?" His friends acquiesced in the idea. Once petitioner had Smithburger in the car, he asked him if he had any money for gas. Smithburger responded that he only had a few dollars and began searching a pocket for money. Dissatisfied, petitioner pulled out a revolver, held it to Smithburger's head and demanded that Smithburger close his eyes and put his hands on the dash. Petitioner then pulled off the road and ordered Smithburger out of the car and into a nearby field. After searching his victim at gunpoint and recovering $13, petitioner told Smithburger to lie face down in the field....

Petitioner then ordered his victim not to move, and crept back to the car to tell his companions he was going to kill Smithburger. Petitioner returned to the field where, paralyzed by fright, Smithburger remained with his face to the ground. Petitioner asked his victim what kind of car he had been in. Smithburger responded with the wrong answer—he accurately described the car as green with a wrecked back end. Petitioner then said "good-bye" and discharged six bullets into the back of Smithburger's head. During a subsequent conversation with a friend, petitioner was recorded on a concealed device "bragging in vivid and grisly detail of the killing of that unlucky lad." In response to a query during the conversation as to whether petitioner dreamed about, or felt anything from, the murder, petitioner stated: "We laugh about it .... [I]t gives you a realization that you can do it.... You can walk up and blow somebody's brains out and you know that you can get away with it. It gives you a feeling of power, self-confidence...."[29]

Case Illustration # 2. The deterrent justification for the nonconsensual removal of transplantable organs from capital murders is highlighted again in the case *Walton v. Arizona*[30]:

Petitioner Walton and his two codefendants, Robert Hoover and Sharold Ramsey, went to a bar in Tucson, Arizona, on the night of March 2, 1986, intending to find and rob someone at random, steal his car, tie him up, and leave him in the desert while they fled the State in the car. In the bar's parking lot, the trio encountered Thomas Powell, a young, off-duty Marine. The three robbed Powell at gunpoint and forced him into his car which they then drove out into the desert. While driving out of Tucson, the three asked Powell questions about where he lived and whether he had any more money. When the car stopped, Ramsey told a frightened Powell that he would not be hurt. Walton and Hoover then forced Powell out of

3. Removing Transplantable Organs of Capital Felons

the car and had him lie face down on the ground near the car while they debated what to do with him. Eventually, Walton instructed Hoover and Ramsey to sit in the car and turn the radio up loud. Walton then took a .22 caliber derringer and marched Powell off into the desert. After walking a short distance, Walton forced Powell to lie down on the ground, placed his foot on Powell's neck, and shot Powell once in the head. Walton later told Hoover and Ramsey that he had shot Powell and that he had "never seen a man pee in his pants before." Powell's body was found approximately a week later, after Walton was arrested and led police to the murder site. A medical examiner determined that Powell had been blinded and rendered unconscious by the shot but was not immediately killed. Instead, Powell regained consciousness, apparently floundered about in the desert, and ultimately died from dehydration, starvation, and pneumonia approximately a day before his body was found.[31]

Society has an obligation to do all that is in its power to deter the senseless and vicious types of murders that were carried out in *Blystone* and *Walton*. Detractors may very well argue that removing healthy transplantable organs from murderers like those in *Blystone* and *Walton* will not deter this category of murderers. However, the issue cannot be resolved in academic debate, books, articles, or television or on the Internet. The obligation imposed on society is to use all means at its disposal in the war against murderers of the *Blystone* and *Walton* type. Creating laws that require the removal of healthy transplantable organs from executed murderers is justified, even if only one potential murder victim is spared death because of the deterrent effect of such laws.

RETRIBUTIVE JUSTIFICATION

When the life of an innocent person is hideously taken by a capital murderer, the victim's family and friends endure justifiable anger toward the murderer. The law has been eternally sympathetic to the aggressive anger harbored by the loved ones of a victim of capital murder. This sympathy is embodied in the law's recognition that the penalty of death for capital murder is justified as retribution for the victim's loved ones.

Retribution, in the abstract, is ignoble. However, retribution is an instinctive attribute of human nature and, as such, must be understood and controlled. Retribution is the buzzword on the lips of every victim of a robbery, carjacking, or other similar crime. The stability of society makes it imperative that individual retribution be channeled toward the acceptance of potential grave legal consequences to criminals, as a replacement for individual "get-even" conduct. Failure to control the retribution of victims on a large scale would doom any society.

Capital punishment has served as a tool to control the retributive impulse of loved ones of capital murder victims. Imagine what it must be like to be informed that one's spouse, child, parent, or aged grandparent had his or her limbs and head brutally cut off by an assailant. Once grief recedes to a bearable level, anger toward the assailant most likely consumes the victim's loved ones. Capital punishment serves to channel this natural retributive rage. Knowing that the life of the assailant will be forfeited calms a person's instinct to seek individual retribution.

Requiring that the transplantable organs of a capital murderer be extracted is justified as retribution for the victim's loved ones. Such punishment is the ultimate balm for tempering the anger that the victim's loved ones must live with for the rest of their lives.[32]

Case Illustration # 1. The retributive justification for allowing courts to order the removal of transplantable organs of convicted capital murderers is illustrated by the case *State v. Simpson*[33]:

> Defendant confessed that ... he and his pregnant, sixteen-year old girlfriend, Stephanie Eury, went for a walk to look for some money. Stephanie went to the front door of the Reverend [Jean] Darter's house and rang the doorbell. She told the Reverend Darter she was hungry, so he brought her a diet soft drink and gave the defendant a glass of milk. Stephanie asked if they could come inside, so the three went into the front living room. Stephanie told the Reverend that she and defendant were traveling to Florida and had gotten stuck in Reidsville. The Reverend suggested they contact the Salvation Army or the police. Stephanie asked [the Reverend] Darter if he could give them some money, and the Reverend Darter gave her four dollars, explaining that was all the money he had in cash....
> Defendant told the police that before he and Stephanie left the house, the Reverend gave them some sponge cake and peaches to take with them....
> The next day ... defendant said that he and Stephanie "both talked about going back to preacher Darter's house to get some money. Stephanie and I decided we would go back to Darter's house and we would not come back empty-handed no matter what[.]" Once it was dark enough, the two walked to the Reverend Darter's house, looking around to make sure no one saw them. They rang the doorbell, and when the Reverend Darter answered the door, they forced their way inside. The Reverend Darter ran

3. Removing Transplantable Organs of Capital Felons

to the telephone, but defendant "pulled the preacher's hands off the telephone." Defendant told Stephanie to cut the telephone cords, and in the meantime, he was "struggling with Preacher Darter holding onto the preacher's arms to control him and force him back in his bedroom so he would tell me where some money was." Defendant held the Reverend down on the bed, with his hands around his neck, telling him he wanted money "or else," but the Reverend told defendant he did not have any money.

... Defendant reached across the bed and got a belt and "looped it around his neck and tightened the belt.... Then I called Stephanie to bring me something in the bedroom to kill this preacher with."

When defendant did not receive any weapon to his liking, he called for Stephanie to come and hold the belt while he "went in the kitchen and looked for some device to beat the old preacher and finish him off." He picked up a full pop bottle and then decided to put it back and get an empty bottle. He returned to the bedroom, pulled tight on the belt, and "hit the old preacher hard three times with this bottle and on the third blow the soft drink bottle broke." Defendant then decided to tie the end of the belt to the bedpost, and he went into the bathroom and got a double-edged razor blade. "I held this double-edged razor blade between my right index finger and right thumb and then I sliced the preacher's arms from the biceps all of the way down the under side of the forearms to the wrist. I cut both of the preacher's arms." Stephanie gathered a bag of food, a porcelain lamp, a radio, and boxes of Kleenex and packed them in a plastic laundry bag. "The last thing we did before leaving the preacher's house was to turn off all the lights except the bathroom light[.]"

Pathologist Michael James Shkrum performed an autopsy on the Reverend Darter and testified the Reverend sustained blunt-trauma injuries to his face causing swelling and bruising. The bone between the eye socket and the brain was fractured, the cheek and the jaw bone were broken, and the Reverend's tongue was torn.[34]

Case Illustration # 2. The retributive justification for nonconsensually removing a capital felon's transplantable organs is again illustrated in the case *Payne v. Tennessee*[35]:

Petitioner, Pervis Tyrone Payne, was convicted by a jury on two counts of first degree murder and one count of assault with intent to commit murder in the first degree. He was sentenced to death for each of the murders and to 30 years in prison for the assault.

The victims of Payne's offenses were 28-year-old Charisse Christopher, her 2-year-old daughter Lacie, and her 3-year-old son Nicholas. The three lived together in an apartment ... across the hall from Payne's girlfriend, Bobbie Thomas....

Organ Transplants from Executed Prisoners

Payne passed the morning and early afternoon [of Saturday, June 27, 1987] injecting cocaine and drinking beer. Later, he drove around the town [of Millington, Tennessee] with a friend ... each of them taking turns reading a pornographic magazine. Sometime around 3 p.m. Payne returned to the apartment complex [his girlfriend was not at home], entered the Christophers' apartment, and began making sexual advances towards Charisse. Charisse resisted and Payne became violent. A neighbor who resided in the apartment directly beneath the Christophers heard Charisse screaming, "Get out, get out," as if she were telling the children to leave. The noise briefly subsided and then began, "horribly loud." The neighbor called the police after she heard a "blood curdling scream" from the Christophers' apartment.

When the first police officer arrived at the scene, he immediately encountered Payne, who was leaving the apartment building, so covered with blood that he appeared to be "sweating blood." The officer confronted Payne, who responded, "I'm the complainant." When the officer asked, "What's going on up there?" Payne struck the officer ... and fled.

Inside the apartment, the police encountered a horrifying scene. Blood covered the walls and floor throughout the unit. Charisse and her children were lying on the floor in the kitchen. Nicholas, despite several wounds inflicted by a butcher knife that completely penetrated through his body from front to back, was still breathing. Miraculously, he survived.... Charisse and Lacie were dead.

Charisse's body was found on the kitchen floor on her back, her legs fully extended. She had sustained 42 direct knife wounds and 42 defensive wounds on her arms and hands....

Lacie's body was on the kitchen floor near her mother. She had suffered stab wounds to the chest, abdomen, back, and head. The murder weapon, a butcher knife, was found at her feet....

Payne was apprehended later that day hiding in the attic of the home of a former girlfriend.... He had blood on his body and clothes and several scratches across his chest. It was later determined that the blood stains matched the victims' blood types[.][36]

Retribution is a word that legal scholars use to sanitize discussions involving a primitive human instinct—revenge. The families of the victims in *Simpson* and *Payne* deserve revenge against those who savagely cut short the lives of their loved ones. Mere infliction of traditional methods of capital punishment will not placate the justifiable rage of those families. Removing the healthy transplantable organs of the *Simpson* and *Payne* type of murderers will go a long way in filling the cup of vengeance. No doubt, voices of reason will cry out that revenge is too

3. Removing Transplantable Organs of Capital Felons

pedestrian to be a justification for removing the transplantable organs of capital murderers. Reason has its place. However, when surviving family members confront the sadistic behavior that inflicts the *Simpson* and *Payne* type of murder, reason must be swept aside. The ignoble pedigree of revenge does not prevent it from having a royal voice in demanding that the healthy transplantable organs of this type of murderer be removed on execution.

RESTITUTION JUSTIFICATION

Restitution is a central component of the criminal law. The aim of restitution is to require criminals to pay back any monetary loss they have caused their victims. Like incarceration or a fine, monetary restitution is a component of a criminal's sentence.

In the context of capital murder, restitution, to be meaningful, must necessarily take on a different form of compensation. Moreover, the tragic fact that the victim of capital murder is not alive means that the recipient of restitution will not be the victim.

Although a capital murderer cannot be ordered by a court to give back the life of the victim, a court can order the murderer to restore the life of those dying for want of particular transplantable organs. Restitution, therefore, in the context of capital murder must take on the form of restoration of the life of transplant patients. No greater justification exists than that of restitution for requiring capital murderers to forfeit their healthy transplantable organs as part of the sentence of death.[37]

Case Illustration # 1. The restitution justification for allowing courts to order transplantable organs of capital murderers to be removed is underscored by the case *Tison v. Arizona*.[38]

> Gary Tison was sentenced to life imprisonment as the result of a prison escape during the course of which he had killed a guard. After he had been in prison a number of years, Gary Tison's ... three sons Donald, Ricky, and Raymond ... made plans to help Gary Tison escape again.... Plans for escape were discussed with Gary Tison, who insisted that his cellmate, Randy Greenawalt, also a convicted murderer, be included in the prison break....
>
> On July 30, 1978, the three Tison brothers entered the Arizona State Prison at Florence carrying a large ice chest filled with guns. The Tisons

Organ Transplants from Executed Prisoners

armed Greenawalt and their father, and the group, brandishing their weapons, locked the prison guards and visitors present in a storage closet....

After leaving the prison, the men ... proceeded on to an isolated house in a white Lincoln automobile that the brothers had parked at a hospital near the prison. At the house, the Lincoln automobile had a flat tire; the only spare tire was pressed into service. After two nights at the house, the group drove toward Flagstaff. As the group traveled on back roads and secondary highways through the desert, another tire blew out. The group decided to flag down a passing motorist and steal a car. Raymond stood out in front of the Lincoln; the other four armed themselves and lay in wait by the side of the road. One car passed by without stopping, but a second car, a Mazda occupied by John Lyons, his wife Donnelda, his 2-year-old son Christopher, and his 15-year-old niece, Theresa ... pulled over to render aid.

As Raymond showed John Lyons the flat tire on the Lincoln, the other Tisons and Greenawalt emerged. The Lyons family was forced into the backseat of the Lincoln. Raymond and Donald drove the Lincoln down a dirt road ... into the desert; Gary Tison, Rick Tison, and Randy Greenawalt followed in the Lyons' Mazda. The two cars were parked trunk to trunk and the Lyons family was ordered to stand in front of the Lincoln's headlights. The Tisons transferred their belongings from the Lincoln into the Mazda....

Gary Tison then told Raymond to drive the Lincoln still farther into the desert. Raymond did so.... The Lyons and Theresa ... were then escorted to the Lincoln and again ordered to stand in its headlights.... John Lyons asked the Tisons and Greenawalt to "give us some water ... just leave us out here, and you all go home." Gary Tison then told his sons to go back to the Mazda and get some water....

[Ricky and Raymond] went back towards the Mazda, along with Donald, while Randy Greenawalt and Gary Tison stayed at the Lincoln guarding the victims. [When the brothers returned they] gave the water jug to Gary Tison who then, with Randy Greenawalt, went behind the Lincoln, where they spoke briefly, then raised the shotguns and started firing. [Rick and Raymond said] they saw Greenawalt and their father brutally murder their four captives with repeated blasts from their shotguns. Neither made an effort to help the victims, though both later stated they were surprised by the shooting. The Tisons got into the Mazda [with Greenawalt] and drove away.... Physical evidence suggested that Theresa ... managed to crawl away from the bloodbath, severely injured. She died in the desert....

Several days later the Tisons and Greenawalt were apprehended after a shootout at a police roadblock. Donald Tison was killed. Gary Tison escaped into the desert where he subsequently died of exposure. Raymond and Ricky Tison and Randy Greenawalt were captured....

3. Removing Transplantable Organs of Capital Felons

The State then individually tried each of the [defendants] for capital murder of the four victims. The capital murder charges were based on Arizona felony-murder law.... Each of the [defendants were] convicted of the four murders....

[Ultimately] the judge sentenced [the defendants] to death.[39]

Case Illustration # 2. The restitution justification for the nonconsensual removal of transplantable organs from capital murderers is again shown in the case *Ford v. State*[40]:

Melbert Ray Ford, Jr., was found guilty by a Newton County jury of murdering his former female companion, Martha Chapman Matich, and her 11-year-old niece, Lisa Chapman, and of committing the offenses of armed robbery, burglary, and possession of a firearm during the commission of a felony. He was sentenced to death on each of the murder convictions.

After his relationship with Martha Matich broke up, Ford began harassing her by telephone. Two weeks prior to her death, Ford told a friend of his that he "was going to blow her ... brains out." The day before her death, Ford unsuccessfully tried to convince a friend to drive him to the convenience store where Matich worked. Ford told the friend that he planned to rob the store and work revenge upon Matich by killing her.

On March 6, 1986, Ford talked to several people about robbing the store. He told one that he intended to kidnap Ms. Matich, take her into the woods, make her beg, and then shoot her in the forehead. Ford tried to talk another into helping him with his robbery (Ford had no car). When this effort failed, Ford responded that "there wasn't anybody crazy around here anymore."

Finally, Ford met 19-year-old Roger Turner, who was out of a job and nearly out of money. By plying him with alcohol, and promising him that they could easily acquire eight thousand dollars, Ford persuaded Turner to help him.

They drove in Turner's car to Chapman's Grocery, arriving just after closing time. Ford shot away the lower half of the locked and barred glass door and entered the store. Turner, waiting in the car, heard screams and gunshots. Then Ford ran from the store to the car, carrying a bag of money.

At 10:20 p.m. the store's burglar alarm sounded. A Newton County sheriff's deputy arrived at 10:27 p.m. Ms. Matich was lying dead behind the counter, shot three times. Lisa Chapman was discovered in the bathroom, shot in the head but still alive, sitting on a bucket, bleeding from the head, and having convulsions. She could answer no questions. She died later.[41]

Organ Transplants from Executed Prisoners

The innocence of murder victims like those in *Tison* and *Ford* demand the restoration of life from the lives of their murderers. Restitution has a bold, prominent, and unassailable place in justifying the removal of transplantable organs from murderers like those in *Tison* and *Ford*. In the final analysis, the idea behind restitution—restoring lives—makes it the single most potent justification for creating and maintaining laws that require the removal of transplantable organs from executed murderers.

4

ORGAN REMOVAL STATUTES AND THE UNITED STATES CONSTITUTION

The U.S. Constitution is the great protector of civil liberties and human rights. It advances the interests of the wealthy and poor alike. It is the beacon that lights the destiny of America.

The power and responsibility vested in the Constitution necessarily make it a complex document to grasp. No document that is designed to give expression to the freedom all human beings must strive to achieve is capable of immediate understanding by all or even by a few. Such a document is *otherworldly*, even though it is in and of this world.

The complexity of the Constitution is not in its literal textual pronouncements. Its complexity is in its ability to make pronouncements about matters embedded in the future of each succeeding generation. The mercurial adaptability of the Constitution is the essence of its complexity. The generation that follows the present generation will see and learn matters about the Constitution that the present generation is unable to conceive. And so it was, is, and will be for all generations that will come under its protection.

The question the Constitution must now answer is one that no past generation asked or could reasonably discern: *Will the Constitution permit the removal of transplantable organs of capital murderers as part of the sentence of death?* For several decades into the 21st century, this question will be litigated by capital murderers who will have this type of sentence imposed on them. The litigation will necessarily be protracted because each constitutional attack will be concluded with a holding that

Organ Transplants from Executed Prisoners

will say, in effect: *Yes, the Constitution permits governments to impose, as punishment for capital murder, a death sentence that includes and mandates the removal of transplantable organs of executed murderers.*

This chapter will examine the principal constitutional clauses that capital murderers will invoke in vain attempts to prevent the removal of their transplantable organs. As will be seen, the present generation has cast the die on this issue. The Constitution will not stand in the way of saving lives through the use of healthy organs of executed murderers.

Free Exercise Clause

The First Amendment to the Constitution provides, "Congress shall make no law respecting an establishment of religion, or prohibiting the free exercise thereof[.]" Two distinct religion clauses have developed from this amendment: the Free Exercise Clause and the Establishment Clause. The religion clauses are intended to facilitate religious freedom by curtailing the nature and scope of governmental support or interference with religion.

The Free Exercise Clause is intended to prevent coercive governmental action that would interfere with religious belief and practice.[1] It has been said, "[R]eligious beliefs need not be acceptable, logical, consistent, or comprehensible to others in order to merit First Amendment protection."[2] As a result, convicted capital murderers will contend that their *particular* religion requires that all of their organs be buried with them or be disposed of in some manner other than transplantation to another human being (e.g., cremation). Therefore, death sentence laws that deny the religiously required disposition of their organs will be labeled governmental interference with religious practice and thus violative of the Free Exercise Clause.

Yet the mere fact that a religious practice may be interfered with by laws that require the removal of transplantable organs of capital murderers does not, in and of itself, violate the Free Exercise Clause. A successful invocation of the Free Exercise Clause requires filtering through a three-pronged constitutional test. Three basic inquiries are made when examining allegations of a violation of the Free Exercise Clause: (1) neu-

4. Organ-Removal Statutes and the Constitution

trality of the law, (2) general applicability of the law, and (3) compelling governmental interest in promulgating the law.

Neutrality and general applicability are intertwined, so that the failure to satisfy one requirement is a likely indication that the other will not be satisfied. When a government cannot satisfy the neutrality or general applicability requirements, it must demonstrate that the law is justified by a compelling governmental interest and is narrowly tailored to advance that interest. A separate examination of the three requirements follow.

NEUTRALITY REQUIREMENT

The protections of the Free Exercise Clause are invoked if a law impairs some or all religious practices or regulates or prohibits conduct undertaken for religious reasons.[3] A law is not neutral if it is intended to infringe on or restrict practices because of the religious basis of those practices.

The initial focus of the neutrality requirement is the actual text of a law. Under the neutrality requirement, the text or face of a law cannot blatantly discriminate on religious grounds. A law lacks facial neutrality if it refers to a religious practice without an overriding secular meaning discernible from its language or context.

There is absolutely no need to draft death sentence organ removal statutes with language that is not neutral (see the Appendix). In fact, most jurisdictions will undoubtedly simply amend their death penalty statutes, as opposed to overhauling them, so as to add a few words instructing courts to impose death sentences that require the removal of transplantable organs of convicted capital felons. This conservative approach will unequivocally pass constitutional muster because the Supreme Court has never invalidated a traditional death penalty statute on neutrality grounds. To the extent that some jurisdictions overhaul their death penalty statutes and use words associated with religion, this will not be fatal. The neutrality requirement will still be satisfied so long as secular connotations are reasonably discernible from such loose wording.

Neutrality analysis does not end with an examination of the text of a law. The Supreme Court has stated that the Free Exercise Clause "forbids subtle departures from neutrality."[4] A law that targets a religious practice for distinctive treatment will not be shielded by mere compliance with the requirement of facial neutrality. An examination of the impact of the law, in general, is part of the neutrality analysis. What this means is that the text of a law may be neutral, but its practical effect may be that of affecting exclusively or predominately a religious practice. The Free Exercise Clause prohibits such an adverse impact.

There is no doubt that death sentence organ removal statutes will affect religious belief of some capital murderers. But, this coincidental impact does not rise to a constitutional level. Most penal laws affect to some minute degree, the religious beliefs of many criminals. Such impact is constitutionally meaningless because the laws were not created with the intent of adversely influencing the religious beliefs of any criminal.

Death sentence organ removal statutes are not created with the intent of adversely restricting the religious belief of any capital murderer. The impact of those statutes will be felt just as strongly on capital murderers who are atheist, who are nonreligious, and whose religions are indifferent to the disposal of their organs. More important, such statutes are not intended to restrict, nor will they restrict, the religious practices of those who do not commit capital murder.

Death sentence organ removal statutes satisfy both prongs of the neutrality analysis. All neutrality arguments advanced by capital murderers will fail.

General Applicability Requirement

The second requirement of the Free Exercise Clause is that laws burdening religious practice must be of general applicability. The Free Exercise Clause protects religious adherents against unequal treatment by governments. What this means is that a general governmental interest cannot be advanced through a law that targets only conduct that has a religious motivation. General governmental interest must be advanced with laws that have general applicability.

A key point of analysis in the general applicability requirement is

4. Organ-Removal Statutes and the Constitution

a determination of whether a law is *underinclusive* in advancing a governmental interest. To determine whether a law is underinclusive, a legitimate governmental interest behind the law must be made known. In the context of this discussion, a legitimate governmental interest advanced by death sentence organ removal statutes includes (but is not limited to) deterring capital murder.

A government's legitimate interest in curtailing the occurrence of capital murder shuts the door on any underinclusiveness argument. That is, death sentence organ removal statutes seek to deter everyone from committing capital murder, not just those who may commit capital murder and have religious convictions about the disposal of their organs. Death sentence organ removal statutes extend to those who commit capital murder for nonreligious reasons as well as to those who may be motivated by religious beliefs to commit capital murder.

Capital felons' arguments advanced under the general applicability requirement will fail. Death sentence organ removal statutes seek to deter capital murder everywhere and by everyone in society.

COMPELLING GOVERNMENTAL INTEREST REQUIREMENT

The compelling governmental interest requirement is triggered only if there has been a judicial finding that a challenged law is not neutral or not of general applicability. That is, if a government establishes that a law is neutral and of general applicability, courts will not subject the law to the compelling governmental interest test (also called *strict scrutiny*). The reason for this is that it is almost impossible for any statute to successfully pass this test. The Supreme Court has remarked, "A law that targets religious conduct for distinctive treatment or advances legitimate governmental interests only against conduct with a religious motivation will survive strict scrutiny only in rare cases."[5] In other words, if the compelling governmental interest test is reached, the chances immensely favor a finding that the law violates the Free Exercise Clause.

The compelling governmental interest test will never be reached as a result of Free Exercise Clause challenges to death sentence organ removal statutes. However, for purposes here, an analysis of the compelling governmental interest test will be given. To start, the compelling governmental interest test has two components, both of which must be satisfied by a government: (1) articulating a compelling interest behind the law, and (2) establishing that the law is narrowly tailored to address that interest.

There are several compelling governmental interests behind the creation of death sentence organ removal statutes. Only one such interest will be mentioned here. All jurisdictions in the nation, not merely capital punishment jurisdictions, have a compelling interest in making transplantable organs available to transplant patients. Lives are saved to the extent that transplantable organs are available. It is well documented that the nation has a drastic shortage in available transplantable organs. Therefore, a compelling governmental interest in creating death sentence organ removal statutes is that of making more transplantable organs available for transplant patients.

Death sentence organ removal statutes are narrowly tailored to serve the compelling governmental interest in adding to the nation's supply of available transplantable organs. The statutes do not permit the nonconsensual removal of transplantable organs from convicted offenders who have not been sentenced to death. Nor do the statutes authorize the nonconsensual removal of transplantable organs from members of society who have not been convicted of any crime. The statutes authorize removal of transplantable organs only from executed capital felons. All nontransplantable parts of a capital felon's corpse are made available for burial. The statutes do not single out, and disproportionately affect, capital felons whose religious practices require burial or other disposition of their organs. Finally, the statutes apply across the board to anyone sentenced to death, without regard to religion.

Although it is rare that a law survives the compelling governmental interest test, if for some illogical reason the test *is* applied to a death sentence organ removal statute, through a Free Exercise Clause challenge, the statute will prevail. Death sentence organ removal statutes serve a compelling governmental interest and are narrowly tailored to meet that interest.

4. Organ-Removal Statutes and the Constitution

Establishment Clause

The Establishment Clause is intended to prohibit support for religion, as well as the usurpation of governmental authority by religious communities. Extremely spurious and untenable legal arguments can (and no doubt will) be made by capital felons, who will allege that death sentence organ removal statutes violate the Establishment Clause. In spite of the absolute implausibility of such arguments, an examination of whether death sentence organ removal statutes violate the Establishment Clause will be provided.[6]

In the 1971 decision of *Lemon v. Kurtzman*[7] the Supreme Court set out the following three-pronged test for analyzing a statute purporting to violate the Establishment Clause: "First, the statute must have a secular legislative purpose; second, its principal or primary effect must be one that neither advances nor inhibits religion; finally, the statute must not foster an excessive government entanglement with religion."[8] Recent decisions by the Supreme Court strongly suggest that the *Lemon* test is too constraining and ill-suited for the factual situations brought under the Establishment Clause by litigants.[9] But in spite of the recognized limitations of the test, it has yet to be abandoned and replaced. Therefore, the analysis here will embrace *Lemon's* three-pronged test.

SECULAR PURPOSE OF STATUTE

The first prong of the test used to discern whether a law violates the Establishment Clause requires a determination of the legislative purpose of the statute. The Establishment Clause has been interpreted to prohibit, generally, enactment of laws that have no secular purpose.

A desperate legal contention that capital murderers will make is that although death sentence organ removal statutes have a slight secular goal, the overriding purpose behind the statutes is religious. This argument lacks merit. It is nothing more than legal sophistry turned on its head. Death sentence organ removal statutes are purely secular in purpose. Religion does not enter the purpose equation whatsoever.

One of the secular purposes guiding death sentence organ removal statutes is that of saving the lives of innocent people in need of transplantable organs. Of course, it may be legitimately postured that legislative concern with transplant patients dying while waiting for unavailable organs is a moral concern. However, this moral concern must be contained within its proper context. The moral concern of legislators is deeply rooted in secular soil. Morality may be inextricably intertwined with religion in general, but religion has no exclusive grip on morality. Fundamental human instincts, like that of a lioness concerned with the safety of her cubs, decry the unnecessary death of innocent people. Such instincts predate religion and exist independent of religion. Therefore, conceptualizing one of the legislative purposes behind death sentence organ removal statutes as a moral purpose does not transform that purpose into a religious objective.

No rational argument exists to connect death sentence organ removal statutes with a religious purpose. Therefore the first prong of the *Lemon* test will not be proven by capital felons.

Neither Advance nor Inhibit Religion

The second requirement of *Lemon* is that the primary effect of a law must not advance or inhibit religion.

Effect Must Not Advance Religion. In failing to show that a religious legislative purpose was behind death sentence organ removal statutes, capital murderers will contend that the effect of such statutes advances religion. In spite of the facially spurious reflection of this contention, it will rear its head. The effect of death sentence organ removal statutes does not advance any religion.

To understand the hollowness of the position taken by capital felons on this matter, we must examine the word "advance." No great mystery surrounds this word. In the context of *Lemon's* second prong, "advance" simply refers to promoting or benefiting a particular religion.

Nonconsensual removal of the transplantable organs of capital felons will not produce an effect that promotes or advances a particular religion. True, a few people who anonymously receive organs of capital felons may feel a deeper sense of appreciation toward God for the extension of their life due to the timely receipt of the organs. However, such an effect is incidental and inconsequential and does not advance the

4. Organ-Removal Statutes and the Constitution

donees' religion in any meaningful way. In such situations, the individual donees may have "advanced" spiritually closer to God, but the donees' religion will not thereby advance one iota.

No legitimate argument exists to bring death sentence organ removal statutes under *Lemon's* prohibition against legislation that has the effect of advancing religion. Such statutes will not promote a particular religion or religion in general.

Effect Must Not Inhibit Religion. There is a legitimate place for religion in society. Religion should always be in a growth or upsizing posture. *Lemon's* second prong seeks to ensure that the effect of secular legislation is not that of downsizing or inhibiting the growth of religion. As an alternative contention for capital murderers, the argument will be made that the effect of death sentence organ removal statutes is that of inhibiting the growth of religion. Of course, this averment has no altar to stand on, but it will be raised.

From a narrow corner of irrationality, it can be argued that a few individuals will be disillusioned by the will of the majority to allow the nonconsensual removal of organs of capital murderers and that, as a consequence of this disillusionment, those few individuals will abandon their faith in God and religion. But religion as an institution will not thereafter be inhibited from continuing its inherent course of growth. The inhuman horrors and atrocities of wars have not inhibited the valiant march of religion—even though wars have caused millions to cast aside their faith in God and religion. Death sentence organ removal statutes will not do what wars have failed to do—inhibit the growth of religion.

NO EXCESSIVE ENTANGLEMENT WITH RELIGION

The last prong of *Lemon's* test bars excessive government entanglement with religion. This prong must be approached with caution. The Supreme Court has stated: "Interaction between church and state is inevitable, and we have always tolerated some level of involvement between the two. Entanglement must be 'excessive' before it runs afoul of the Establishment Clause."[10] For example, in *Roemer v. Board of Public Works of Md.*[11] it was held that there is no excessive entanglement when a state conducts annual audits to ensure that categorical state grants to religious colleges are not used to teach religion.

The Supreme Court has bowed to reality and recognized that governments and religion do not exist on separate planets. Interaction between the two is inevitable. The concern expressed in *Lemon's* third prong is that such interaction or entanglement must not be excessive.

The concern with excessive entanglement between governments and religion (which could advance or inhibit religion) is not evident in death sentence organ removal statutes. Such statutes will not require the participation of religion. True, death-penalty statutes in general have always allowed religious representatives to be with death-row inmates in their final hour of life. However, the presence of a religious representative at an execution is a privilege granted to capital felons, not a requirement of law.

No valid argument can be advanced to establish that death sentence organ removal statutes produce an excessive entanglement between governments and religion. Any involvement with religion and the execution of the death sentence is a matter requested by the capital felon, not a requirement of death sentence organ removal statutes.

Involuntary Servitude Clause

The Thirteenth Amendment declares, "Neither slavery nor involuntary servitude, except as a punishment for crime whereof the party shall have been duly convicted, shall exist within the United States[.]" The primary purpose of this amendment was to abolish the system of slavery as it had existed in the United States at the time of the Civil War. However, the amendment was not limited to that purpose. The phrase "involuntary servitude" was intended to extend "to cover those forms of compulsory labor akin to … slavery which in practical operation would tend to produce like undesirable results."[12] Thus two separate but related clauses unfold from the amendment: the Involuntary Servitude Clause and the Slavery Clause.

Capital murderers will argue that death sentence organ removal statutes violate the Involuntary Servitude Clause. Their position will be buttressed by the contention that the use of their organs after their death, by transplant patients, constitutes an imposition of involuntary servitude on their living organs. This argument is without substance for two reasons.

First, the Supreme Court noted in *United States v. Kozminski*,[13] "While the general spirit of the phrase 'involuntary servitude' is easily comprehended, the exact range of conditions it prohibits is harder to define."[14] In spite of the difficulty in pinpointing the scope of the Involuntary Servitude Clause, the clause clearly permits "involuntary servitude [to be] imposed as a punishment for crime[.]"[15] In *Kozminski* the Court said, "The fact that the drafters [of the amendment] felt it necessary to exclude this situation indicates that they thought involuntary servitude includes ... situations in which the [defendant] is compelled to work by law."[16] Therefore, assuming for a moment that the organs of capital felons' are subject to involuntary servitude, this would not amount to a constitutional violation. The Thirteenth Amendment expressly permits governments to impose involuntary servitude as a punishment for the commission of crime.[17]

Second, assuming that capital felons were able to skirt the penal exception for nonconsensual servitude, they would still be unable to mount a successful attack based on a violation of the Involuntary Servitude Clause. A prerequisite for asserting a violation of the Involuntary Servitude Clause is that the victim must be a person. Death sentence organ removal statutes subject extracted transplantable organs of a capital murderer to "involuntary work," not the capital murderer. A transplantable organ of a capital felon is not a person, within the meaning of the Constitution. Therefore, the Involuntary Servitude Clause is not violated by death sentence organ removal statutes.

Slavery Clause

The Supreme Court has said that the Slavery Clause "is not a mere prohibition of State laws establishing or upholding slavery, but an absolute declaration that slavery ... shall not exist in any part of the United States."[18] Capital murderers will contend that death sentence organ removal statutes violate the Slavery Clause because the effect of the statutes is to enslave their transplantable organs.

The latter argument is no different from that discussed in the previous section on the Involuntary Servitude Clause. Of course, there is no exception in the Thirteenth Amendment that permits the imposition of slavery as a penal sanction. However, the exclusive purpose of the Slavery Clause is to protect people from enslavement. It was not intended to protect the extracted transplantable organs of capital murderers.

Capital felons will not prevail under the Slavery Clause, regardless of the "free labor" performed by their transplantable organs. The "enslavement" of an organ is simply not the equivalent of the enslavement of a person. The Constitution stands as a fortress preventing the occurrence of the latter, but the gates of that fortress have a welcome sign for the former. Death sentence organ removal statutes do not violate the Slavery Clause.

Takings Clause

The Takings Clause is succinctly set out in the Fifth Amendment: "[N]or shall private property be taken for public use, without just compensation." The Supreme Court indicated in *Armstrong v. United States*[19] that the purpose of the Takings Clause is "to bar Government from forcing some people alone to bear public burdens which, in all fairness and justice, should be borne by the public as a whole."[20] The "burden" expressed by *Armstrong* concerns the government usurpation of "pure" property, that is, realty or personality.

The Takings Clause may be used to attack a statute that burdens pure property without providing for fair compensation to its owner. Capital murderers will offer the argument that death sentence organ removal statutes violate the Takings Clause because the statutes deprive them of their transplantable organs without compensation (to their estates). This argument, at first blush, would appear to have merit. However, closer scrutiny reveals that it is a hollow "jest by [capital felons] seeking controversy upon grounds where the wind [has never] blow[n]."[21]

The Takings Clause was intended to protect inviolate pure property.

4. Organ-Removal Statutes and the Constitution

The transplantable organs of capital felons are not pure property in the sense contemplated by the Takings Clause. Transplantable organs, like the corpse from which they derive, have a status as mere quasi-property. A commentator has pointed out that Anglo-American jurisprudence found it "necessary to label a corpse [and its parts] *quasi-property* in order to establish that not all legal principles attendant to *pure property* were applicable to a corpse [or its parts]."[22]

The status of transplantable organs as quasi-property denies them the full "bundle of rights that are commonly characterized as property."[23] Only pure property is able to rise to the heights of the Constitution and obtain its protection. The Takings Clause cannot be invoked to require compensation to the estate of capital murderers for the nonconsensual removal of their transplantable organs. Nor can the Takings Clause be called on to strike down death sentence organ removal statutes because governments do not provide compensation to the estate of capital felons.

Assuming for a moment that capital felons were able to show that as a result of the commercial value of transplantable organs in general, such organs should be accorded a property status greater than that recognized in the cadavers from which they derive. This assumption, appealing as it may be intellectually, would still not invalidate death sentence organ removal statutes or require governments to compensate the estates of capital murderers.

The Supreme Court has long recognized the common law right of a government to require convicted criminals to forfeit property as an incident of punishment. When this occurs "[t]he government may not be required to compensate an owner for property which it has already lawfully acquired under the exercise of governmental authority[.]"[24]

The sentence of death by a court of law effectively gives a government the right to "take" the life of a capital felon. From this fact it becomes axiomatic that a capital felon has no personal rights to life. A government does not have to compensate the estate of a capital felon for taking his life because the capital felon had no property interest in his life once the sentence of death was pronounced—his life thereafter was lawfully forfeited to the government.

An expressed purpose of death sentence organ removal statutes is that of giving governments all interests in the transplantable organs of capital felons as an incident of punishment for capital murder. This lawful forfeiture of transplantable organs exempts governments from having to compensate capital felons for "property" that the governments have already lawfully "acquired."

In sum, death sentence organ removal statutes do not violate the Takings Clause compensation requirement because transplantable organs of capital felons are mere quasi-property and do not come within the meaning of property contemplated by the clause. To the extent that transplantable organs may be brought closer to property in the commercial sense, death sentence organ removal statutes require forfeiture of those organs and, therefore, such statutes do not violate the Takings Clause compensation requirement.

Seizure Clause

The Fourth Amendment of the Constitution provides that the "right of the people to be secure in their persons ... and effects, against unreasonable ... seizures, shall not be violated[.]" The Seizure Clause requires "consent or a warrant permitting seizure [or] such seizures can be justified only if they meet the probable-cause standard."[25] In the case of *United States v. Jacobsen*[26] the Supreme Court held that a seizure of property occurs when "there is some meaningful interference with an individual's possessory interests in that property."[27] The Supreme Court noted in *Soldal v. Cook County*,[28] "In holding that the Fourth Amendment's reach extends to property as such, we are mindful that the Amendment does not protect possessory interests in all kinds of property."[29] For example, in *Hudson v. Palmer*[30] the Court said that because of the status of a prison inmate as an incarcerated felon, the Seizure Clause did not prevent unreasonable seizure of his personal effects by prison officials.

The argument that capital felons will offer under the Seizure Clause is that death sentence organ removal statutes permit an unreasonable seizure of their transplantable organs. The novelty of the argument will not legitimize it. In the final analysis, death sentence organ removal statutes do not violate the Seizure Clause for several reasons.

4. Organ-Removal Statutes and the Constitution

To begin, long before a capital felon's sentence of death, the prosecuting government will have legal custody (seizure) of the capital felon pursuant to an arrest warrant. Once a sentence of death and transplantable organ removal has been imposed, neither the life of the capital felon nor his organs belong to him. The sentence imposed automatically transfers possession of his life and organs to the prosecuting government. Therefore, the Seizure Clause would not require a government to issue a warrant to seize that which was already forfeited to it and is in its possession. Nothing pertaining to such a seizure is unreasonable within the meaning of the Seizure Clause because it was obtained after a valid warrant was issued giving the government the authority to take custody of the capital felon for the purpose of prosecuting him. The imposition and execution of punishment is part of the prosecution.

Equal Protection Clause

The Equal Protection Clause is explicitly set out in the Fourteenth Amendment (it is implicit in the Fifth Amendment).[31] The pertinent language in the Fourteenth Amendment provides, "No State shall ... deny to any person within its jurisdiction the equal protection of the laws." In *Jones v. Helms*[32] the Supreme Court held, "The Equal Protection Clause provides a basis for challenging legislative classifications that treat one group of persons as inferior or superior to others, and for contending that general rules are being applied in an arbitrary or discriminating way."[33]

Convicted and sentenced capital murderers will make two basic arguments under the Equal Protection Clause. First, they will allege that death sentence organ removal statutes deny equal protection of the laws because the transplantable organs of similarly situated murderers are not removed. Second, they will contend that death sentence organ removal statutes are arbitrarily applied.

SIMILARLY SITUATED MURDERERS

The argument by capital murderers that similarly situated murderers are not compelled to give up their transplantable organs involves the legal distinction between murder and capital murder. The maximum punishment for murder is life imprisonment. The maximum punishment for capital murder is death. To understand why the similarly situated argument will fail, some discussion is necessary regarding the types of offenses that may be categorized as capital offenses.

The Nature of Capital Offenses. Under the common law, all felony offenses could be punished with a sentence of death.[34] The laws of the American colonies incorporated the common law's position that all felonies were subject to punishment by death. The first codified capital punishment laws in the American colonies were drawn up in 1636 by the Massachusetts Bay colony. The *Capital Laws of New England*, as they were called, provided the death penalty for the following crimes: rebellion, perjury, manstealing, rape, statutory rape, adultery, buggery, sodomy, murder, blasphemy, idolatry, witchcraft, and assault in sudden anger.[35]

All jurisdictions in the nation, at some point in time, provided the death penalty for crimes that did not involve the death of a human being. For example, between 1930 and 1968, a total of 3,859 defendants were executed for criminal offenses. The executions were for the following crimes: 3,334 executions were for murder; 455 executions were for rape; and 70 executions were for crimes other than murder or rape.[36]

The constitutional issue of whether or not the death penalty could be inflicted for nonhomicide offenses was not addressed by the Supreme Court until it heard the 1977 case of *Coker v. Georgia*.[37] The narrow issue presented to the Supreme Court in *Coker*, was whether or not the Constitution prohibited the imposition of the death penalty for the crime of the rape of an adult woman. In addressing this issue the Court observed, "Georgia is the sole jurisdiction in the United States at the present time that authorizes a sentence of death when the rape victim is an adult woman, and only two other jurisdictions provide capital punishment when the victim is a child."[38] The Supreme Court concluded:

> Rape is without doubt deserving of serious punishment; but in terms of moral depravity and of the injury to the person and to the public, it does not compare with murder, which does involve the unjustified taking of human life. Although it may be accompanied by another crime, rape by definition does not include the death of or even the serious injury to

4. Organ-Removal Statutes and the Constitution

another person. The murderer kills; the rapist, if no more than that, does not. Life is over for the victim of the murderer; for the rape victim, life may not be nearly so happy as it was, but it is not over and normally is not beyond repair. We have the abiding conviction that the death penalty, which "is unique in its severity and irrevocability," is an excessive penalty for the rapist who, as such, does not take human life.[39]

Coker stands for the proposition that it is unconstitutional to impose capital punishment for the offense of rape of an adult, without more. The issue of whether capital punishment may constitutionally be imposed for rape of a child was not directly addressed in *Coker*. This issue was confronted in 2008, in *Kennedy v. Louisiana*.[40]

The narrow issue presented to the Supreme Court in *Kennedy* was whether the Constitution prohibited imposition of the death penalty for the crime of rape of a child, without more. The defendant in *Kennedy* was charged by the state of Louisiana with the aggravated rape of his 8-year-old stepdaughter. After a jury trial the defendant was convicted and sentenced to death under a state statute authorizing capital punishment for the rape of a child less than 12 years of age. The Supreme Court was called upon to decide whether the Constitution permitted such punishment. The Court held that the Constitution prohibited such punishment when the victim was not killed.

At this juncture in Anglo-American jurisprudence, it may be reasonably asserted that, with *Coker* and *Kennedy* as the barometer, *capital punishment for any offense that does not involve the death of a victim would be found unconstitutional by the Supreme Court*.[41] There may be a limitation to the application of *Coker* and *Kennedy*. While both cases counseled against the general imposition of capital punishment for non-homicide crimes, *Kennedy* cautioned that "[w]e do not address, for example, crimes defining and punishing treason, espionage, terrorism, and drug kingpin activity, which are offenses against the State."[42] In other words, the jury is still out on whether the Constitution will allow capital punishment to be imposed for crimes against the government that does not involve the loss of life.

Table 4.0 Murder Time Clock, 1999–2010

Year	Frequency of Murder
1999	every 34 minutes

2000	every 33 minutes
2001	every 32 minutes
2002	every 32 minutes
2003	every 31 minutes
2004	every 32 minutes
2005	every 31 minutes
2006	every 30 minutes
2007	every 31 minutes
2008	every 32 minutes
2009	every 34 minutes
2010	every 35 minutes

SOURCE: Louis J. Palmer, Jr., *The Death Penalty in the United States: A Complete Guide to Federal and State Laws* 92, Table 11.0 (2013).

As a result of the Supreme Court's interpretation of the Constitution, capital punishment today does not resemble its common law counterpart. The Supreme Court has indicated that the Constitution requires "narrowing the categories of murders for which a death sentence may ... be imposed[.]"[43] In an effort to pull out a subclass of death-eligible murders from among all murders, legislators have singled out specific factors or conduct that may appear in some murders. These specific factors or types of conduct are called *aggravating circumstances* and form the basis of a sentence of death. In other words, capital punishment jurisdictions have taken the offense of murder and surrounded it with a variety of *aggravating circumstances*, that permit the imposition of the death penalty.[44]

The Failure of the Similarly Situated Argument. The fact that not all intentional homicides are punished with death does not deny capital murderers equal protection of the laws. The Supreme Court, pursuant to its interpretation of the Constitution, requires that all capital punishment jurisdictions narrow the class of murderers who are subject to capital punishment. No jurisdiction may impose capital punishment on all intentional homicides. The Supreme Court has expressly prohibited this.[45] In *Jurek v. Texas*[46] the Supreme Court quoted, approvingly, the following language by the Texas Supreme Court:

> [The Constitution] limits the circumstances under which the State may seek the death penalty to a small group of narrowly defined and particularly brutal offenses. This insures that the death penalty will only be imposed for the most serious crimes [and] ... that [it] will only be imposed for the

4. Organ-Removal Statutes and the Constitution

same type of offenses which occur under the same types of circumstances.[47]

The argument raised by capital murderers—that similarly situated murderers are not subject to a sentence of death—is true. However, it is an unavailing truth. The reason for this is simple yet complex, obvious yet subtle. The Supreme Court, in its wisdom, has deemed it constitutionally necessary to take the crime of murder and split it into murder and capital murder. This division is made according to *aggravating circumstances*. If a murder is accompanied by aggravating circumstances, it becomes capital murder and is subject to capital punishment. In permitting this distinction, the Supreme Court has stated that the Equal Protection Clause is not offended. Merely adding to the sentence of death the additional punishment of removal of transplantable organs does not thereby inject an Equal Protection Clause violation. To do so is inconsistent with the constitutionally permissible distinction between murder and capital murder.

ARBITRARY APPLICATION

In a majority of capital punishment jurisdictions, the sentence of death is determined arbitrarily. (This issue is elaborated on in Chapter 6.) The Supreme Court has repeatedly indicated that the current factors that permit the arbitrary application of the death penalty do not violate the Equal Protection Clause. The factors have been labeled "discretionary" by the Supreme Court.

Capital murderers will contend that death sentence organ removal statutes are applied arbitrarily and, therefore, violate the Equal Protection Clause. If the recommendations proffered in Chapter 6 are not incorporated by capital punishment jurisdictions, then the arbitrariness claim will have validity. However, its validity will not rise to constitutional proportions. Death sentence organ removal statutes that do not incorporate the recommendations of Chapter 6 will merely continue the current constitutionally acceptable standard of arbitrariness.

The gist of the arbitrariness argument resides in the fact that the death penalty statutes currently on the books in a majority of jurisdictions permit the rejection of the death penalty by a judge or jury, even though all of the prerequisites for imposing the sentence have been met. The Supreme Court has consistently approved of this. Therefore, in spite of this legitimate argument, capital felons will not succeed in invalidating death sentence organ removal statutes that are applied arbitrarily.

Due Process Clause

The Fourteenth Amendment prohibits governments from depriving citizens of life, liberty, or property without due process of law.[48] The Due Process Clause of the Fourteenth Amendment is composed of two distinct analytical tools: substantive due process and procedural due process. Capital felons will utilize the substantive due process component in their attempts to invalidate death sentence organ removal statutes. No discussion, therefore, will be provided regarding procedural due process.

A substantive due process claim may be brought to attack any statute that purportedly infringes on life, liberty, or property. Capital felons will raise the argument that death sentence organ removal statutes infringe on their rights to liberty and property. The substantive due process property allegation will fail for the reasons discussed under the Seizure and Takings Clauses. Therefore, the discussion here will not revisit the property argument. The sole issue examined here will be the claim that death sentence organ removal statutes violate the liberty interest guaranteed under the Due Process Clause.

LIBERTY INTEREST

In a succession of cases the Supreme Court has recognized a number of liberty interest rights protected by the Due Process Clause: to marry,[49] to have children,[50] to control the upbringing of one's children,[51] to keep marital privacy,[52] to use contraception,[53] to maintain bodily integrity,[54] and to have an abortion.[55] To facilitate an understanding of the substantive due process liberty interest concept, we will review the Supreme Court's decision in the 1997 case *Washington v. Glucksberg*[56]

4. Organ-Removal Statutes and the Constitution

before discussing the liberty interest argument that will be made by capital felons.

Washington v. Glucksberg. The decision in *Glucksberg* involved the question of whether the state of Washington's penal law banning assisted suicide violated the liberty interest protected by the Due Process Clause. The plaintiffs in the case were three terminally ill patients, several physicians, and a nonprofit organization. The defendants were the state of Washington and its attorney general.

The plaintiffs in *Glucksberg* contended that the decision of a mentally competent, terminally ill adult to commit physician-assisted suicide was a personal choice, and that this personal choice was a liberty interest protected by the Due Process Clause. The plaintiffs were able to convince a federal district court and the Court of Appeals for the Ninth Circuit (en banc) that their argument was valid. Both courts found that personal choice to commit physician-assisted suicide was a liberty interest protected by the Due Process Clause. Therefore, both courts went on to find Washington's penal law banning assisted suicide unconstitutional. The case then proceeded to the Supreme Court.

The Supreme Court's opinion in *Glucksberg* started out methodically slow. It began by retracing the history of suicide and assisted-suicide laws. It noted, "The earliest American statute explicitly to outlaw assisting suicide was enacted in New York in 1828[.]"[57] It further pointed out, "By the time the Fourteenth Amendment was ratified, it was a crime in most States to assist a suicide."[58] The opinion then shifted to a discussion of the impact of medical advances on extending life:

> Because of advances in medicine and technology, Americans today are increasingly likely to die in institutions, from chronic illnesses. Public concern and democratic action are therefore sharply focused on how best to protect dignity and independence at the end of life, with the result that there have been many significant changes in state laws and in the attitudes these laws reflect. Many States, for example, now permit "living wills," surrogate health-care decisionmaking, and the withdrawal or refusal of life-sustaining medical treatment.[59]

With the historical and medical discourses concluded, the opinion confronted the question presented by the appeal: "whether the protections of the Due Process Clause include a right to commit suicide with another's assistance."⁶⁰ The opinion foreshadowed its conclusion by noting, "The mere novelty of such a claim is reason enough to doubt that substantive due process sustains it."⁶¹ It added "That many of the rights and liberties protected by the Due Process Clause sound in personal autonomy does not warrant the sweeping conclusion that any and all important, intimate, and personal decisions are so protected[.]"⁶² The Supreme Court ultimately concluded, "[T]he asserted 'right' to assistance in committing suicide is not a fundamental liberty interest protected by the Due Process Clause."⁶³

Personal Choice to Dispose of Transplantable Organs. Capital felons will invoke the Due Process Clause by asserting that they have a constitutionally protected personal choice in deciding what happens to their transplantable organs after they are executed. This personal choice, it will be argued, is a liberty interest that is violated by death sentence organ removal statutes. The Supreme Court's decision in *Glucksberg* has foretold the shattered outcome of this argument.

Capital felons will lose their substantive due process claim because they will not be able to demonstrate that they have a fundamental right of personal choice in disposing of their transplantable organs. (Of course, capital felons will attempt to couch their personal choice argument in such a way as to implicate the right of personal choice of all citizens to determine the disposition of their organs. However, this legal maneuver will fail, and the focus will remain on the narrower issue involving the transplantable organs of capital murderers.) Legal history is against the capital murderers' claim that they have a fundamental right of personal choice in disposing of their transplantable organs. It was noted in Chapter 1 that the common law permitted courts, as part of the sentence of death, to order the corpses of executed capital murderers be turned over to anatomy schools for dissection. Additionally, Chapter 3 pointed out that two former capital punishment jurisdictions and the federal government had statutes that permitted courts, at the sentencing phase of a capital prosecution, to order that the corpses of executed capital felons be turned over for dissection and experimentation. There is no fundamental right of personal choice by capital felons to direct the disposition of their transplantable organs.

Assume, for a moment, that capital felons were able to show that

4. Organ-Removal Statutes and the Constitution

they have a constitutionally protected liberty interest in their transplantable organs. This assumption will not unseat death sentence organ removal statutes. The Supreme Court has indicated that a law that infringes on a liberty interest may still be valid if it is shown that a government has a legitimate interest in promulgating the law and that the interest is rationally related to that law.

Governments will be able to proffer a legitimate interest in enacting death sentence organ removal statutes. That interest is to help save lives by supplying transplantable organs to transplant patients. Death sentence organ removal statutes are rationally related to this interest because they provide governments with a source for transplantable organs: the cadavers of executed capital murderers.

Cruel and Unusual Punishment Clause

The Eighth Amendment provides, "Excessive bail shall not be required, nor excessive fines imposed, nor cruel and unusual punishments inflicted." The primary tool used by the Supreme Court to address issues raised under traditional death penalty statutes is the Cruel and Unusual Punishment Clause. In his concurring opinion in *Furman v. Georgia*,[64] Justice William Brennan reviewed prior Supreme Court cases that involved the Cruel and Unusual Punishment Clause. This examination was done to ascertain the general principles that the Supreme Court relied on to decide whether or not a particular punishment was cruel and unusual. Justice Brennan determined that four basic principles were relied upon:

(1) The punishment must not be so severe as to be degrading to the dignity of human beings.

(2) A government cannot arbitrarily inflict a severe punishment.

(3) A severe punishment must not be unacceptable to contemporary society.

(4) A severe punishment must not be excessive.

Based on the above principles, Justice Brennan concluded:

> The test, then, will ordinarily be a cumulative one: If a punishment is unusually severe, if there is a strong probability that it is inflicted arbitrar-

ily, if it is substantially rejected by contemporary society, and if there is no reason to believe that it serves any penal purpose more effectively than some less severe punishment, then the continued infliction of that punishment violates the command of the Clause that the State may not inflict inhuman and uncivilized punishments upon those convicted of crimes.[65]

The following material will examine arguments that will be made by capital murderers under Justice Brennan's first, third, and fourth principles. The second principle found by Justice Brennan was touched on in the discussion on the Equal Protection Clause (and is elaborated on in Chapter 6); therefore, it will not be revisited here. Additionally, due to the enormous legal significance of the Eighth Amendment in death penalty law, a few words about its origin will precede the discussion of Justice Brennan's principles.

THE LEGAL ROOTS OF THE EIGHTH AMENDMENT

The Eighth Amendment became a part of the Constitution in 1791.[66] The history of this amendment, however, does not begin with its insertion into the Constitution. The birth of the Eighth Amendment reaches back to the shores of England and the English Bill of Rights of 1689.

The tenth clause of the English Bill of Rights provided, "[E]xcessive bail ought not to be required, nor excessive fines imposed, nor cruel and unusual punishments inflicted."[67] Justice Thurgood Marshall, in his concurring opinion in *Furman*, said that scholars were in debate over "[w]hether, the English Bill of Rights prohibition against cruel and unusual punishments is properly read as a response to excessive or illegal punishments, as a reaction to barbaric and objectionable modes of punishment, or both[.]"[68] Justice William Douglas concluded, in his concurring opinion in *Furman*, "There is evidence that the provision of the English Bill of Rights ... was concerned primarily with selective or irregular application of harsh penalties and that its aim was to forbid arbitrary and discriminatory penalties of a severe nature."[69] Although there is no unanimous agreement as to why the English Rill of Rights included a clause prohibiting cruel and unusual punishments, there is no dissent over the fact that the Eighth Amendment owes its existence to the English Bill of Rights.

4. Organ-Removal Statutes and the Constitution

The Eighth Amendment did not leap directly from the English Bill of Rights into the U.S. Constitution. "The precise language used in the [Eighth Amendment] first appeared in America on June 12, 1776, in Virginia's Declaration of Rights[.]"[70] A delegate named George Mason was responsible for taking the tenth clause of the English Bill of Rights and placing it into Virginia's Declaration of Rights. Delegate Mason was also a strong advocate, at the Constitutional Convention, for placing the tenth clause into the Constitution as the Eighth Amendment.[71] Delegate Mason's foresight eventually paid off, and in 1791 the tenth clause of the English Bill of Rights, with slight modifications, became the Eighth Amendment of the Constitution.

PUNISHMENT MUST NOT DEGRADE

Decisions of the Supreme Court have made it clear that the Cruel and Unusual Punishment Clause prohibits punishments that are so severe as to degrade human dignity. Below, an excerpt will be provided from the concurring opinion of Justice Brennan, in *Furman*, on the meaning of punishments that degrade human dignity. Next, the capital felons' argument—that death sentence organ removal statutes degrade their dignity—will follow.

Justice Brennan on Degradation.

In *Trop v. Dulles*,[72] it was said that "[t]he question is whether [a] penalty subjects the individual to a fate forbidden by the principle of civilized treatment guaranteed by the [Cruel and Unusual Punishment Clause]." It was also said that a challenged punishment must be examined "in light of the basic prohibition against inhuman treatment" embodied in the Clause. It was said, finally, that:

> The basic concept underlying the [Clause] is nothing less than the dignity of man. While the State has the power to punish, the [Clause] stands to assure that this power be exercised within the limits of civilized standards.

At bottom, then, the Cruel and Unusual Punishments Clause prohibits the infliction of uncivilized and inhuman punishments. The State, even as it punishes, must treat its members with respect for their intrinsic worth as human beings. A punishment is "cruel and unusual," therefore, if it does not comport with human dignity....

[A] primary principle, [then], is that a punishment must not be so severe as to be degrading to the dignity of human beings. Pain, certainly, may be a factor in the judgment. The infliction of an extremely severe punishment will often entail physical suffering. Yet ... there could be exercises of cruelty by laws other than those which inflicted bodily pain.... Even though "[t]here may be involved no physical mistreatment, no primitive torture," severe mental pain may be inherent in the infliction of a particular punishment....

More than the presence of pain, however, is comprehended in the judgment that the extreme severity of a punishment makes it degrading to the dignity of human beings. The barbaric punishments condemned by history, "punishments which inflict torture, such as the rack, the thumbscrew, the iron boot, the stretching of limbs, and the like," are, of course, "attended with acute pain and suffering." When we consider why they have been condemned, however, we realize that the pain involved is not the only reason. The true significance of these punishments is that they treat members of the human race as nonhumans, as objects to be toyed with and discarded. They are thus inconsistent with the fundamental premise of the Clause that even the vilest criminal remains a human being possessed of common human dignity.

The infliction of an extremely severe punishment, then, ... may reflect the attitude that the person punished is not entitled to recognition as a fellow human being. That attitude may be apparent apart from the severity of the punishment itself.... Indeed, a punishment may be degrading to human dignity solely because it is a punishment. A State may not punish a person for being "mentally ill, or a leper, or ... afflicted with a venereal disease," or for being addicted to narcotics.... Finally, of course, a punishment may be degrading simply by reason of its enormity.[73]

Capital Felons' Argument. Capital murderers will vigorously argue that death sentence organ removal statutes violate the Cruel and Unusual Punishment Clause because such statutes degrade their dignity as human beings. This contention has inviting emotional appeal. It does not, however, comport with reality.

Justice Brennan isolated the two primary factors that would render a punishment degrading to human dignity: severe physical pain and severe mental pain. But capital murderers will not be able to establish that death sentence organ removal statutes inflict either severe physical pain or severe mental pain.

Regarding severe physical pain, the methods of inflicting capital punishment under traditional death penalty statutes have been documented as causing great physical pain and suffering.[74] (See Chapter 5.) In spite of such pain and suffering, the Supreme Court has found that

4. Organ-Removal Statutes and the Constitution

all current methods of execution comply with constitutional standards. The method of execution that occurs under death sentence organ removal statutes does not cause any pain whatsoever. (See Chapter 5 and the Appendix.) To ensure that no healthy transplantable organ of a capital murderer is destroyed or damaged, execution under death sentence organ removal statutes must be humane and painless.

As for the contention that death sentence organ removal statutes inflict severe mental pain, it is true that before actual execution, many capital murderers will endure severe mental pain over the thought of their transplantable organs being removed. So be it. Severe mental pain is endured by most capital murderers, before actual execution, under traditional death penalty statutes (death row is not meant to be a picnic). The constitutional prohibition on severe mental pain does not attach to the pre-execution stage; it focuses on the period in which the execution is actually being carried out. And under the method of execution authorized by death sentence organ removal statutes, capital felons will not endure any mental pain during the execution. Contrast this with the documented fact that execution by electrocution, for example, can last several minutes—with accompanying mental and physical pain throughout the procedure.[75]

Death sentence organ removal statutes do not degrade the dignity of capital murderers as human beings. Execution under such statutes is the equivalent of dying in one's sleep.

PUNISHMENT MUST BE ACCEPTABLE TO SOCIETY

The Supreme Court has held that the Cruel and Unusual Punishment Clause prohibits punishments that are unacceptable to society. Below, an excerpt will be provided from the concurring opinion of Justice Brennan, in *Furman*, on how the determination is made as to whether a punishment is accepted by society. Next, capitol felons' argument—that death sentence organ removal statutes are unacceptable to society—follows.

Justice Brennan on the Acceptability of a Punishment.

A[nother] principle inherent in the Clause is that a severe punishment must not be unacceptable to contemporary society. Rejection by society, of course, is a strong indication that a severe punishment does not comport with human dignity. In applying this principle, however, we must make certain that the judicial determination is as objective as possible. Thus, for example, ... one factor that may be considered is the existence of the punishment in jurisdictions other than those before the Court. [A]nother factor to be considered is the historic usage of the punishment....

The question under this principle, then, is whether there are objective indicators from which a court can conclude that contemporary society considers a severe punishment unacceptable. Accordingly, the judicial task is to review the history of a challenged punishment and to examine society's present practices with respect to its use. Legislative authorization, of course, does not establish acceptance. The acceptability of a severe punishment is measured, not by its availability, for it might become so offensive to society as never to be inflicted, but by its use.[76]

Capital Felons' Argument. Capital murderers will argue that society does not accept death sentence organ removal statutes. Based on this assertion, they will contend that death sentence organ removal statutes violate the Cruel and Unusual Punishment Clause. The proponents do not actually believe in this argument—but feel the need to throw in the kitchen sink.

When this argument is made, all current capital punishment jurisdictions will likely have adopted death sentence organ removal statutes. Moreover, because of the life-saving benefits of such statutes, many states that do not now permit the punishment of death will probably have enacted capital punishment legislation allowing the removal of transplantable organs of capital murderers.

The support for the latter assertion is found in society's current position on the issue of transplantable organs in general. In a 2005 poll of American citizens it was determined that 95 percent of the American public supported organ transplantation.[77] This overwhelming public support of organ transplantation in general suggests that society may be willing to accept utilizing the transplantable organs of executed murderers to save the lives of innocent citizens.

PUNISHMENT MUST NOT BE EXCESSIVE

The Cruel and Unusual Punishment Clause prohibits punishments that are excessive. Below, an excerpt will be provided from the concur-

4. Organ-Removal Statutes and the Constitution

ring opinion of Justice Brennan, in *Furman*, on the meaning of excessive punishment. Next, the capital felons' argument—that death sentence organ removal statutes are excessive—will follow.

Justice Brennan on Excessiveness.

> The final principle inherent in the Clause is that a severe punishment must not be excessive. A punishment is excessive under this principle if it is unnecessary[.] The infliction of a severe punishment by the State cannot comport with human dignity when it is nothing more than the pointless infliction of suffering. If there is a significantly less severe punishment adequate to achieve the purposes for which the punishment is inflicted, the punishment inflicted is unnecessary and therefore excessive.
> ... Although the determination that a severe punishment is excessive may be grounded in a judgment that it is disproportionate to the crime, the more significant basis is that the punishment serves no penal purpose more effectively than a less severe punishment.[78]

Capital Felons' Argument. Capital murderers will argue that death sentence organ removal statutes violate the Cruel and Unusual Punishment Clause because they allow excessive punishment. The "unpersuasive hollow-point platitudes"[79] of this argument may be properly exposed in the context of death per se as punishment.

The Supreme Court's decision in *Furman* found capital punishment unconstitutional because it was inflicted in an arbitrary way. *Furman* did not hold that death per se was excessive or unconstitutional as punishment. Subsequent to *Furman*, the Supreme Court ruled in *Gregg v. Georgia*[80] that the death penalty was not, per se, unconstitutional. In making this ruling, the Court said:

> [C]apital punishment is an expression of society's moral outrage at particularly offensive conduct. This function may be unappealing to many, but it is essential in an ordered society that asks its citizens to rely on legal process rather than self-help to vindicate their wrongs....
> ... [T]he moral consensus concerning the death penalty and its social utility as a sanction, require us to conclude ... that the infliction of death as a punishment for murder is not without justification and thus is not unconstitutionally [excessive]....
> Finally, ... when a life has been taken deliberately by the offender, we cannot say that the punishment [of death] is invariably disproportionate to the crime. It is an extreme sanction, suitable to the most extreme crimes.[81]

Organ Transplants from Executed Prisoners

With the pronouncements of *Gregg* in full view, it is inconceivable that the punishment of removing transplantable organs from executed capital murderers is excessive when the actual infliction of death as punishment is not deemed excessive. Both must fall as excessive punishment, or neither may fall as excessive punishment. Both must fall as being disproportionate punishment for capital murder, or neither may fall as being disproportionate punishment for capital murder.

5

THE NEED FOR A NEW METHOD OF EXECUTION

The intent of this chapter is threefold. First, to provide a summary of the methods of execution used to inflict death under traditional death penalty statutes. Second, to illustrate why current methods of execution are inefficient. Finally, to introduce a new and efficient method of execution for use under death sentence organ removal statutes

Current Methods of Execution

Traditional death penalty statutes provide for five methods of execution: firing squad, hanging, lethal injection, electrocution, and lethal gas. A discussion of each method of execution is provided in this section. Additionally, this section discusses those jurisdictions that permit more than one method of execution.

Table 5.0 Methods of Execution, 1977–2010

Method of Execution	Number of Executions
Firing squad	3
Hanging	3
Lethal gas	11
Electrocution	147
Lethal injection	1,060

SOURCE: U.S. Department of Justice, Bureau of Justice Statistics, Corrections, Capital Punishment, TABLE 10 (2011).

Organ Transplants from Executed Prisoners

EXECUTION OPTION JURISDICTIONS

The phrase "execution option jurisdictions" refers to capital punishment jurisdictions that have statutes which provide for alternative methods of execution. The jurisdictions providing for more than one method of execution do so for a variety of reasons, including: (1) give inmate an option[1]; (2) use alternative if primary method found unconstitutional or if necessary for any reason[2]; (3) option for inmate sentenced before a certain date[3]; (4) option for inmate committing crime before a certain date.[4]

Table 5.1 Execution Methods Used by Jurisdictions

Jurisdiction	Lethal Injection	Electrocution	Hanging	Lethal Gas	Firing Squad
Alabama	X	X[1]			
Arizona	X			X[7]	
Arkansas	X	X[2]			
California	X			X[1]	
Colorado	X				
Delaware	X		X[2]		
Florida	X	X[1]			
Georgia	X				
Idaho	X				
Indiana	X				
Kansas	X				
Kentucky	X	X[4]			
Louisiana	X				
Mississippi	X				
Missouri	X			X[1]	
Montana	X				
Nebraska	X				
Nevada	X				
New Hampshire	X		X[3]		
North Carolina	X				
Ohio	X				
Oklahoma	X	X[2]			X[2]
Oregon	X				
Pennsylvania	X				
South Carolina	X	X[1]			
South Dakota	X				
Tennessee	X	X[5]			
Texas	X				
Utah	X				X[6]
Virginia	X	X[1]			

5. The Need for a New Method of Execution

Washington	X	X[1]	
Wyoming	X		X[2]
Federal System	X		

[1]Inmate's option. [2] Used if alternative method found unconstitutional. [3] If necessary for any reason. [4] Option for inmate sentenced before March 31, 1998. [5] Option for inmate committing crime before January 1, 1999. [6] Option for inmate sentenced before May 3, 2004; and used if alternative method found unconstitutional. [7] Option for inmate sentenced before November 23, 1992.

Case Illustration. Capital murderers have argued against having to choose the method of their execution. In the following case, *Campbell v. Wood*,[5] the defendant contended that it was unconstitutional for the state of Washington to allow him to select between hanging and lethal injection as the method of his execution.

In 1974, Charles Campbell assaulted and sodomized Renae Wicklund in her residence in Clearview, Washington. Campbell held a knife to the throat of Wicklund's one-year-old daughter Shannah, threatening to harm her if Renae did not submit. After the attack, Wicklund ran to the house of her neighbor, Barbara Hendrickson, for help. Campbell was tried and convicted on the assault and sodomy charges in 1976. Both Renae Wicklund and Barbara Hendrickson testified at the trial. Campbell was sentenced to a prison term. In March 1982, Campbell was transferred to a work-release facility in Everett, Washington.

On April 14, 1982, Renae Wicklund, Shannah Wicklund (then eight years old), and Barbara Hendrickson were found brutally slain in the Wicklund residence. Wicklund had been sick and remained at home that day. Hendrickson had gone to Wicklund's residence to assist her.

The evidence at trial showed that Wicklund had been the first victim. She was found naked on her bedroom floor. She had been beaten with a blunt instrument on her head, back, and upper chest. Her jaw and nose were broken, and she had been strangled. She had a seven-inch cut across her neck, from which she had bled to death. After her death, she had been vaginally assaulted with a blunt instrument which left a one-inch cut in her vaginal wall.

Wicklund's daughter had also been strangled, and she had a seven-and-one-half-inch cut across her upper neck. She had lost so much blood that a sample was difficult to obtain.

Hendrickson's throat also had been cut, leaving a seven-inch wound. She died of a massive hemorrhage.

Campbell was charged and tried on three counts of aggravated first degree murder....

Items seized from Campbell on the day of the murders included a pair of earrings that a witness identified as belonging to Renae Wicklund. An earring found in Campbell's car was identified by a business associate of Renae's as a birthday present he had given to Shannah. A glass found in the Wicklunds' kitchen bore a fingerprint matching Campbell's. Finally, another work-release resident directed police to a place on the Snohomish River where he and Campbell had been on the evening of April 14. Investigators and divers found a bracelet, three earrings, two necklaces, a piece of pottery, and a brass object, all of which were linked to the Wicklund residence and the victims.

The jury convicted Campbell on November 26, 1982.... In a separate proceeding ... Campbell was sentenced to death.

Campbell claims that his First and Eighth Amendment rights are violated by the statutory provision that allows him to elect death by lethal injection rather than by hanging....

Campbell's First Amendment challenge is premised on the Free Exercise Clause. He contends that his religious beliefs preclude him from participating at any level in his own execution, and that these beliefs are infringed upon by [the statute] which allows him to elect lethal injection and avoid death by judicial hanging.

We see no infringement upon Campbell's free exercise of his religious beliefs....

First, Campbell is not required to make any choice or to participate in the selection of the method to be employed in his execution. He may remain absolutely silent and refuse to participate in any election. The statute provides for imposition of the death penalty by hanging, and does not require him to choose the method of his execution.... The statute does not compel Campbell to compromise one constitutional right to avoid the infringement of another.

Campbell also argues that the statutory provision of an option for death by lethal injection constitutes cruel and unusual punishment.... Campbell faces a heavy burden in attempting to show that the existence of an option related to his execution is cruel and unusual. We cannot say the State descends to inhuman depths by allowing the condemned to exercise such an election. We believe that benefits to prisoners who may choose to exercise the option and who may feel relieved that they can elect lethal injection outweigh the emotional costs for those who find the mere existence of an option objectionable.

EXECUTION BY FIRING SQUAD

Death by firing squad is traced to military tradition. Mutiny and desertion were among the offenses that the military punished with death by firing squad. The common law did not accept or reject execution by

5. The Need for a New Method of Execution

firing squad. Common law judges simply never resorted to this method of execution.[6]

The exact date that execution by firing squad was adopted by civilian law in the United States is uncertain. Records reflect, however, that by the 1850s, death by firing squad was a part of civilian law in the nation.[7]

Firing Squad Jurisdictions. Only two capital punishment jurisdictions, Utah and Oklahoma, allow execution by firing squad. In Utah the firing squad is an option for inmates sentenced before a specific date; the firing squad is also designated for use in the event the State's primary method of execution is found unconstitutional. Oklahoma provides for the use of a firing squad in the event that its other two designated methods of execution are found unconstitutional.

The most publicized firing squad execution in the last half of the twentieth century was the January 17, 1977, execution of Gary Gilmore by the state of Utah. Two issues made Gilmore's execution noteworthy. First, Gilmore refused to appeal his conviction. However, his attorneys filed a state court appeal without his permission. Gilmore demanded the appeal be withdrawn. The appeal eventually reached the Supreme Court as *Gilmore v. Utah*.[8] Chief Justice Warren Burger summed up the matter:

> This case may be unique in the annals of the Court. Not only does Gary Mark Gilmore request no relief himself, but on the contrary he has expressly and repeatedly stated since his conviction in the Utah courts that he had received a fair trial and had been well treated by the Utah authorities. Nor does he claim to be innocent of the crime for which he was convicted. Indeed, his only complaint against Utah or its judicial process ... has been with respect to the delay on the part of the State in carrying out the sentence.[9]

The second legal dilemma posed by Gilmore was the constitutionality of Utah's death penalty statute. As was pointed out in previous chapters, in 1972 *Furman v. Georgia*[10] led to the invalidity of all capital punishment statutes. It was not until the 1976 decision in *Gregg v. Georgia*[11] that capital punishment was resumed in the nation. Gilmore's execution was the first since the *Furman* decision.

In response to *Furman*, the state of Utah revised its death penalty in 1973. However, the constitutionality of those procedures had not been determined at the time of Gilmore's trial in 1976. Chief Justice Burger explained the problem:

Organ Transplants from Executed Prisoners

[Gilmore's attorneys] informed the trial court that they had advised Gilmore ... that the constitutionality of the Utah death penalty statute had not yet been reviewed by either the Utah Supreme Court or the United States Supreme Court, and that in their view there was a chance that the statute would eventually be held unconstitutional. The trial court itself advised Gilmore ... that the constitutional issue had not yet been resolved, and that both counsel for the State and Gilmore's own counsel would attempt to expedite an appeal to avoid unnecessary delay. Gilmore stated that he did not "care to languish in prison for another day," that the decision was his own.[12]

After additional amendments in 1977 and 1982, Utah's death penalty statute was found constitutional by a federal court of appeals in the 1986 case *Andrew v. Shulsen*.[13]

Case Illustration. The Supreme Court addressed the constitutionality of death by firing squad over 100 years ago, in *Wilkerson v. Utah*.[14]

> Congress organized the Territory of Utah on the 9th of September, 1850, and provided that the legislative power and authority of the Territory shall be vested in the governor and legislative assembly.
>
> [T]he prisoner named in the record was legally charged with the wilful, malicious, and premeditated murder of William Boxter, with malice aforethought, by indictment of the grand jury in due form of law, as fully set forth in the transcript; and that he, upon his arraignment, pleaded that he was not guilty of the alleged offense. Pursuant to the order of the court, a jury for the trial of the prisoner was duly impanelled and sworn; and it appears that the jury, after a full and fair trial, found, by their verdict, the prisoner was guilty of murder in the first degree.
>
> Regular proceedings followed, and the record also shows that the presiding justice in open court sentenced the prisoner as follows: That "you be taken from hence to some place in this Territory, where you shall be safely kept until Friday, the fourteenth day of December next; that between the hours of ten o'clock in the forenoon and three o'clock in the afternoon of the last-named day you be taken from your place of confinement to some place within this district, and that you there be publicly shot until you are dead."
>
> Proceedings in the court of original jurisdiction being ended, the prisoner sued out a writ of error and removed the cause into the Supreme Court of the Territory, where the judgment of the subordinate court was affirmed....
>
> ... [T]he assignment of error [here] being that the court below erred in ... sentencing the prisoner to be shot to death....
>
> Duly convicted of murder in the first degree as the prisoner was by the

5. The Need for a New Method of Execution

verdict of the jury, it is conceded that the existing law of the Territory provides that he "shall suffer death"; nor is it denied that the antecedent law of the Territory which was in force from March 6, 1852, to March 4, 1876, provided that "when any person shall be convicted of any crime the punishment of which is death ... he shall suffer death by being shot, hung, or beheaded, as the court may direct[.]"

When the Revised Penal Code went into operation, it ... repealed that provision....

... [T]he existing law of the Territory provides that every person guilty of murder in the first degree shall suffer death, without any other statutory regulation as to the mode of executing the sentence than ... [that it is] a duty upon the court authorized to pass sentence to determine and impose the punishment prescribed....

... Territories are invested with legislative power which extends to all rightful subjects of legislation not inconsistent with the Constitution and laws of the United States. By virtue of that power the legislative branch of the Territory may define offenses and prescribe the punishment of the offenders, subject to the prohibition of the Constitution that cruel and unusual punishments shall not be inflicted....

Offenses of various kinds are defined in the rules and articles of war where the offender, if duly convicted, may be sentenced to the death penalty. In some of those cases the provision is that the accused, if convicted, shall suffer death, and in others the punishment to be awarded depends upon the finding of the court-martial; but in none of those cases is the mode of putting to death prescribed in the articles of war or the military regulations....

Repeated instances occur where the death penalty is prescribed in those articles; but the invariable enactment is that the person guilty of the offence shall suffer death, without any specification as to the mode in which the sentence shall be executed, and the regulations of the army are as silent in that respect as the rules and articles of war.... [T]he custom of war, says a learned writer upon the subject, has, in the absence of statutory law, determined that capital punishment be inflicted by shooting....

Military laws, says another learned author, do not say how a criminal offending against such laws shall be put to death, but leave it entirely to the custom of war; and his statement is that shooting ... is the method determined by such custom....

Cruel and unusual punishments are forbidden by the Constitution, but the ... punishment of shooting as a mode of executing the death penalty for the crime of murder in the first degree is not included in that category, within the meaning of the eighth amendment. Soldiers convicted of desertion or other capital military offenses are in the great majority of cases sentenced to be shot....

Organ Transplants from Executed Prisoners

Where the conviction is in the civil tribunals, the rule of the common law was that the sentence or judgment must be pronounced or rendered by the court in which the prisoner was tried or finally condemned, and the rule was universal that it must be such as is annexed to the crime by law. Of these, says Blackstone, some are capital, which extend to the life of the offender, and consist generally in being hanged by the neck till dead.

Such is the general statement of that commentator, but he admits that in very atrocious crimes other circumstances of terror, pain, or disgrace were sometimes superadded. Cases mentioned by the author are, where the prisoner was drawn or dragged to the place of execution, in treason; or where he was embowelled alive, beheaded, and quartered, in high treason. Mention is also made of public dissection in murder, and burning alive in treason committed by a female....

Difficulty would attend the effort to define with exactness the extent of the constitutional provision which provides that cruel and unusual punishments shall not be inflicted; but it is safe to affirm that punishments of torture, such as those mentioned by the commentator referred to, and all others in the same line of unnecessary cruelty, are forbidden by that amendment to the Constitution.

Concede all that, and still it by no means follows that the sentence of the court in this case falls within that category.

EXECUTION BY HANGING

The common law accepted death by hanging as a legitimate method of execution.[15] Hanging has also been a traditional part of Anglo-American jurisprudence as a result of its common law lineage. Although not reproduced here, the opinion in *Wilkerson v. Utah* discussed hanging in conjunction with its discussion of the firing squad. In nonbinding dicta, *Wilkerson* approved of hanging as a constitutional method of execution.

Hanging Jurisdictions. In the early history of the nation, hanging was a method of execution used by all capital punishment jurisdictions. However, industrial and medical technological advances have reduced the reliance on hanging as a method of execution.

Only three capital punishment jurisdictions employ hanging as a method of execution. One jurisdiction, Washington, provides hanging as an option for all capital felons. Another jurisdiction, Delaware, designated hanging as the method of execution in the event its primary

5. The Need for a New Method of Execution

method is found unconstitutional. The third jurisdiction, New Hampshire, utilizes hanging in the event its primary method of execution cannot be used for any reason.

Case Illustration. In the following case, *Rupe v. Wood*,[16] the defendant weighed over 400 pounds. Before a federal district court, he argued that it would be almost impossible to hang him without causing decapitation. Therefore, he contended that his execution by hanging could not be carried out, under the Eighth Amendment.

The executing jurisdiction in *Rupe* was the state of Washington, which provides capital murderers with a choice in the method of execution. The problem the state faced in this case was that the defendant refused to select one of the two methods available under the state's laws. The default method of execution was hanging. Therefore, if the state was to execute the defendant, execution by hanging had to be the method used.

> This matter comes before the Court in connection with Mitchell Edward Rupe's petition for habeas corpus alleging that Petitioner's hanging would constitute cruel and unusual punishment because of his peculiar circumstances. Petitioner contends that because of his excessive weight, he is likely to be decapitated if judicially executed in accordance with the State's protocol for hanging....
>
> Petitioner Mitchell Rupe has been sentenced to death under Washington State law.
>
> Pursuant to [the state's laws] the punishment of death in Washington shall be inflicted by hanging by the neck or, at the election of the defendant, by intravenous injection of a substance or substances in a lethal quantity sufficient to cause death.
>
> As of September 2, 1993, Mitchell Rupe weighed 409 1/4 pounds and measured 6'1/4" in height.... Petitioner's obesity presents an unusual and exceptional circumstance which is likely to dramatically affect the execution process.
>
> In Washington, execution by judicial hanging is carried out at the Washington State Penitentiary in Walla Walla, and is generally conducted pursuant to the Washington Field Instruction. The Washington Field Instruction requires use of manila hemp rope of a diameter between ∫3/4 inch and 1 1/4 inches. The rope is soaked and then stretched. The knot is treated with wax, soap, and clear oils to ensure a smooth sliding action.
>
> The Washington Field Instruction uses a "long drop" method of hanging, in which the condemned person is dropped a particular distance based on his or her weight. The Washington Field Instruction contains altering drop lengths for persons ranging from 120 pounds to 220 pounds.

Organ Transplants from Executed Prisoners

Under the Washington Field Instruction, persons weighing more than 220 pounds will be dropped a distance of five (5) feet....

Tana Wood is the Superintendent of the Washington State Penitentiary and the person who is now responsible for the preparation and carrying out of executions in the State of Washington. On December 7, 1993, Superintendent Wood testified during her deposition that Mitchell Rupe would be dropped a distance of five feet, as is set forth in the Washington Field Instruction, if judicially hanged at the weight of approximately 409 pounds. Superintendent Wood also testified, however, that she might consult with experts and the drop distance might be changed based on such consultation.

At a telephone conference with counsel on May 9, 1994, the Court ordered the Respondent to determine by June 10, 1994, the drop length to be used for Mr. Rupe's hanging. On June 9, 1994, Superintendent Wood determined that Mr. Rupe would be dropped a distance of 3 feet 6 inches if judicially hanged at the weight of approximately 409 pounds, using a rope with a 7/8 inch diameter. Wood testified at the hearing that this decision was based upon advice given to her by Dr. Bahram Ravani, an engineering expert consultant hired by the State of Washington, as well as her observations of the hanging executions of Westley Allen Dodd and Charles Rodman Campbell which have recently been carried out at the Washington State Penitentiary. Wood received no input from medical experts in connection with this decision.

Wood testified that she made the decision to reduce the drop length to 3 feet 6 inches and to fix the rope size at 7/8 inch diameter in order to reduce or eliminate the possibility of decapitation....

Petitioner contends that there is an 80 percent–90 percent risk of decapitation if Petitioner is hanged using a 3 foot 6 inch drop length and a 7/8 inch diameter rope. Petitioner relies upon the testimony of Alan Tencer, Ph.D. Tencer holds formal degrees in mechanical engineering and is the director of the Biomechanics Laboratory at Harborview Hospital in Seattle.... Petitioner also relies upon the testimony of Donald P. Becker, M.D., Chief of Neurological Surgery at the University of California at Los Angeles Medical Center.

Dr. Tencer testified that ... the Rupe hanging would involve an energy level of 1435 foot-pounds (410 pounds multiplied by a drop length of 3.5 feet).... Because of the ... energy that will be applied in the proposed Rupe hanging, Tencer concluded that decapitation is very likely to occur.

Dr. Becker also testified for the Petitioner. Becker testified that assuming a drop distance sufficient to disrupt Mr. Rupe's cervical column, it is his opinion that Rupe would be decapitated....

... Petitioner's counsel have also produced graphic pictures showing the decapitation of Black Jack Ketchum in New Mexico in 1901. The Court

5. The Need for a New Method of Execution

finds that decapitation is a recurrent phenomenon in the history of judicial hanging. While it is difficult to quantify the frequency of decapitation and the precise cause of any particular decapitation which is described in the historical literature, it appears that there is some correlation between the size of the condemned person and the risk of decapitation. The historical literature supports a conclusion that decapitation is more likely to occur during a long-drop hanging when the condemned person has excessive body weight....

Based on the ... limited tests conducted by the experts who testified at the hearing, the Court finds that Petitioner has established by credible evidence that there is a significant risk of decapitation if Petitioner is judicially hanged using a drop length of 3.5 feet under the Washington protocol outlined in the Washington Field Instruction. In the event decapitation occurred, it would result in immediate or near immediate unconsciousness and death, and in mutilation to Rupe's body.

The Washington judicial hanging protocol, as modified by Superintendent Wood's decision to use a 3 foot 6 inch drop length for Petitioner, was not based on adequate investigation or reliable testing and does not eliminate the significant risk of decapitation if Petitioner is hanged....

The Eighth Amendment prohibits cruel and unusual punishment. Judicial hangings, as conducted pursuant to the Washington Field Instruction, generally do not violate the Eighth Amendment. The issue presented here is whether the Washington Field Instruction, as modified by Superintendent Wood to accommodate Rupe's peculiar physical characteristics, violates the Eighth Amendment as it relates to Petitioner. Because the Court has found that there is significant risk that Rupe's hanging will result in decapitation, the question is whether such decapitation violates the Eighth Amendment.

The Eighth Amendment does not require a State's execution procedure to remove every single possibility of error. The risk of accident cannot and need not be eliminated from the execution process in order to survive constitutional review. However ... there is significant risk of decapitation if Petitioner is hanged. Thus, the risk of decapitation cannot be dismissed as a possible error or accident....

The Eighth Amendment must draw its meaning from the evolving standards of decency that mark the progress of a maturing society. Public attitudes toward hangings that might carry a light risk of decapitation cannot be equated with public attitudes toward hangings that carry a significant risk of decapitation. Objective indicia of this attitude are found in the history of court decisions that list beheading as one of the traditional methods of execution barred by the Eighth Amendment. No state has ever provided for execution by axe or guillotine. A hanging that is likely to result in decapitation is contrary to public perceptions of standards of decency.

Organ Transplants from Executed Prisoners

Because the Court concludes that there is a significant risk that Rupe's hanging would result in decapitation, such a hanging would also violate basic human dignity....

The Court concludes that the hanging of petitioner under the procedures selected by the State of Washington would result in a significant risk of decapitation and therefore violates the Eighth Amendment to the United States Constitution....

Petitioner is entitled to have his writ of habeas corpus granted.

EXECUTION BY LETHAL INJECTION

Lethal injection as a method of execution was not known to the common law. In the 1978 decision of *Ex parte Granviel*[17] the court of Criminal Appeals of Texas noted, "The intravenous injection of a lethal substance as a means of execution has not been heretofore utilized in this nation[.]"[18]

Injection of a barbiturate and a paralytic agent into the bloodstream of a capital felon represents a new method of execution. Lethal injection, as this new method is called, appeared in the 1970s. Oklahoma was the first jurisdiction to provide by statute for execution by lethal injection. It did so on May 10, 1977. The first state to actually execute a prisoner by lethal injection was Texas. It did so on December 7, 1982, when Charlie Brooks became the first inmate to die by lethal injection.

Lethal Injection Jurisdictions. Lethal injection is provided as a method of execution in every capital punishment jurisdiction. The statutes in seven of those jurisdictions, Alabama, California, Florida, Missouri, South Carolina, Virginia, and Washington, provide for lethal injection as an option for all capital felons. Nine jurisdictions, Arizona, Arkansas, Delaware, Kentucky, New Hampshire, Oklahoma, Tennessee, Utah, and Wyoming, set out alternative methods of execution that are triggered upon the occurrence of a specific event. The remaining lethal injection jurisdictions utilize this method exclusively.

Case Illustration. Lethal injection has been challenged on two fronts. First, it has been attacked on the grounds that the Food and Drug Administration has not approved of using drugs for lethal injection purposes. Second, it has been challenged as unconstitutional on the grounds that various factors can make it a physically and mentally painful death. The following case, *Woolls v. McCotter*,[19] illustrates both issues.

5. The Need for a New Method of Execution

On October 8, 1979, the appellant, Randy Lynn Woolls, was convicted of capital murder. He is scheduled to be executed before sunrise on August 20, 1986....

The appellant first asserts that the Food and Drug Administration's (FDA) refusal to evaluate certain drugs used for lethal injection to determine whether those drugs quickly and effectively cause a painless death is judicially reviewable.... Congress' failure to provide for judicial review of FDA's discretionary decision not to investigate the lethal use of sodium thiopental does not constitute a denial of appellant's right to due process of law. The action or inaction of the administrative agency is not a punishment and so cannot be characterized as cruel or unusual.

Although not clearly raised in his petition as a separate ground for relief, we will nevertheless review the appellant's apparent assertion that use by the Texas Department of Corrections of sodium thiopental violates his eighth amendment right to be free from cruel and unusual punishment because, when administered by untrained personnel or in improper dosages, this drug may cause conscious death by suffocation. Appellant's argument is premised on supposition unsupported by fact. The appellant proffers the affidavit of Dr. Ward Casscells, which recites an American Medical Association recommendation that a physician should not be a participant in a legally authorized execution. The appellant then offers the affidavit of Dr. Leroy David Vandam, which asserts that, even if administered by an expert, the injection of sodium thiopental may cause physical and mental pain due to possible technical difficulties in administering the drug. Finally, the appellant submits the affidavit of Dr. Richard S. Hodes, who concludes that, even if administered by a professional, individual responses to this drug can be quite varied. Thus, if an individual is not rendered unconscious before the injection of the paralytic drug, the individual would be aware of the onset of loss of consciousness and the paralytic drug would produce a sense of shortness of breath and suffocation over a two to three minute period. Depending on the specific paralytic drug administered, the individual may also experience a sensation of multiple electric shocks over the entire body with erratic muscle twitching followed by acute paralysis and suffocation.

First, the appellant has not even alleged, much less produced any evidence, that the Texas Department of Corrections allows anyone other than trained medical personnel to administer lethal injection. Second, the appellant has neither alleged nor produced evidence that would indicate that improper dosages of sodium thiopental have been or will be administered so as to result in physical or mental pain. Finally, even if the physical and mental manifestations noted by Dr. Hodes were experienced by an individual, this showing of discomfort or unnecessary pain falls far short of ... a substantial showing of the denial of his right to be free from cruel and unusual punishment under the eighth amendment....

... Because the appellant has failed to make a substantial showing of the denial of a federal right ... this appeal is dismissed.

EXECUTION BY ELECTROCUTION

The use of electricity to carry out the death penalty dates back to the late 19th century. The constitutionality of this method of execution was challenged in 1890, in the case *In re Kemmler*.[20] The Supreme Court was asked in *Kemmler* to decide whether electrocution was a cruel and unusual method of execution.

The relevant facts of the opinion in *Kemmler* reveal that on January 6, 1885, the governor of New York gave the annual *"State of the State Address"* to the legislature. In that address, the governor made the following observation and suggestion:

> The present mode of executing criminals by hanging has come down to us from the dark ages, and it may well be questioned whether the science of the present day cannot provide a means for taking the life of such as are condemned to die in a less barbarous manner. I commend this suggestion to the consideration of the legislature.[21]

As a result of prompting by the governor, the legislature assembled a commission to determine "the most humane and practical method known to modern science of carrying into effect the sentence of death in capital cases."[22] The commission eventually reported that execution by electricity was the most humane method of imposing the death penalty. The New York Legislature heeded the advice and, in 1888, signed into law what is reported to be the first electrocution death penalty statute. The statute, by its terms, went into effect on January 1, 1889.

On March 29, 1889, the defendant in *Kemmler* murdered Matilda Zeigler-Hort in Erie County, New York. He was prosecuted for the crime and sentenced to death on May 14, 1889. The method of execution was death by electrocution. The defendant, after unsuccessful arguments in front of state appellate courts, asked the Supreme Court to rule that electrocution was a cruel and unusual method of execution.

The initial observation made by the Supreme Court was that pun-

5. The Need for a New Method of Execution

ishments generally regarded as manifestly cruel and unusual were burning at the stake, crucifixion, and breaking on the wheel. The Court then noted, "The courts of New York held that the mode adopted in this instance (electrocution) might be said to be unusual because it was new, but that it could not be assumed to be cruel in the light of that common knowledge which has stamped certain punishments as such[.]"[23]

The Supreme Court agreed with the New York courts that electrocution was not a cruel and unusual method of execution. In doing so, the Court nailed the coffin shut, so to speak, with the following oft-quoted passage: Punishments are cruel when they involve torture or a lingering death; but the punishment of death is not cruel, within the meaning of that word as used in the Constitution. It implies there be something inhuman and barbarous, something more than the mere extinguishment of life.[24]

Notwithstanding the 19th century determination by *Kemmler* that execution by electrocution was not a constitutionally cruel and unusual form of punishment, the constitutionality of this method has been litigated into the 21st century.

Electrocution Jurisdictions. A total of eight capital punishment jurisdictions permit electrocution to be used as a method of execution. Four of those jurisdictions, Alabama, Florida, South Carolina, and Virginia, provide electrocution as an option for all capital felons. Two jurisdictions, Arkansas and Oklahoma, utilize electrocution if their primary method of execution is ever found unconstitutional. Kentucky utilizes electrocution as an option for inmates sentenced prior to a specific date. Tennessee permits electrocution for inmates who committed their crime before a specific date.

Case Illustration # 1. In the case *Francis v. Resweber*,[25] the defendant was electrocuted but did not die. The state of Louisiana then sought to electrocute him a second time. The defendant presented three constitutional arguments as to why Louisiana should be prohibited from again attempting an execution:

> This writ of certiorari brings before this Court a unique situation. The petitioner, Willie Francis, is a ... citizen of Louisiana. He was duly convicted of murder and in September, 1945, sentenced to be electrocuted for the crime. Upon a proper death warrant, Francis was prepared for execu-

tion and on May 3, 1946, pursuant to the warrant, was placed in the official electric chair of the state of Louisiana in the presence of the authorized witnesses. The executioner threw the switch but, presumably because of some mechanical difficulty, death did not result. He was thereupon removed from the chair and returned to prison where he now is. A new death warrant was issued by the Governor of Louisiana, fixing the execution for May 9, 1946....

To determine whether or not the execution of the petitioner may fairly take place after the experience through which he passed, we shall examine the circumstances....

First. Our minds rebel against permitting the same sovereignty to punish an accused twice for the same offense. But where the accused successfully seeks review of a conviction, there is no double jeopardy upon a new trial.... When an accident, with no suggestion of malevolence, prevents the consummation of a sentence, the state's subsequent course in the administration of its criminal law is not affected on that account by any requirement of due process under the Fourteenth Amendment. We find no double jeopardy here which can be said to amount to a denial of federal due process in the proposed execution.

Second. We find nothing in what took place here which amounts to cruel and unusual punishment in the constitutional sense.... The traditional humanity of modern Anglo-American law forbids the infliction of unnecessary pain in the execution of the death sentence....

Petitioner's suggestion is that because he once underwent the psychological strain of preparation for electrocution, now to require him to undergo this preparation again subjects him to a lingering or cruel and unusual punishment. Even the fact that petitioner has already been subjected to a current of electricity does not make his subsequent execution any more cruel in the constitutional sense than any other execution. The cruelty against which the Constitution protects a convicted man is cruelty inherent in the method of punishment, not the necessary suffering involved in any method employed to extinguish life humanely. The fact that an unforeseeable accident prevented the prompt consummation of the sentence cannot, it seems to us, add an element of cruelty to a subsequent execution. There is no purpose to inflict unnecessary pain nor any unnecessary pain involved in the proposed execution.... We cannot agree that the hardship imposed upon the petitioner rises to that level of hardship denounced as denial of due process because of cruelty.

Third. The Supreme Court of Louisiana also rejected petitioner's contention that death inflicted after his prior sufferings would deny him the equal protection of the laws, guaranteed by the Fourteenth Amendment. This suggestion ... is based on the idea that execution, after an attempt at execution has failed, would be a more severe punishment than is imposed

5. The Need for a New Method of Execution

upon others guilty for a like offense. That is, since others do not go through the strain of preparation for execution a second time or have not experienced a non-lethal current in a prior attempt at execution, as petitioner did, to compel petitioner to submit to execution after these prior experiences denies to him equal protection. Equal protection does not protect a prisoner ... against accidents during his detention for execution. Laws cannot prevent accidents nor can a law equally protect all against them. So long as the law applies to all alike, the requirements of equal protection are met. We have no right to assume that Louisiana singled out Francis for a treatment other than that which has been or would generally be applied.

... On this record, we see nothing upon which we would conclude that the constitutional rights of petitioner were infringed.

Case Illustration # 2. In the case *Thomas v. Jones*,[26] the defendant argued that because the state of Alabama had a defective electric chair, incompetent electrocutionists, and a history of bungling executions, it would be cruel and unusual punishment to allow the state to electrocute him.

Thomas was convicted on November 3, 1977, for the capital offense of robbery where the victim is intentionally killed. He was sentenced to death on March 13, 1978. On March 31, 1981, the Alabama Court of Criminal Appeals reversed Thomas' conviction ... and remanded the case for a new trial.

In May 1982, Thomas was tried for the second time, was found guilty, and was sentenced to death....

Thomas argued that "the State of Alabama's use of an antiquated electric chair, improperly trained correctional staff with no expertise in electrical execution and execution equipment which results in excessive mutilation of the body and torturous death constitutes cruel and unusual punishment in violation of the Eighth Amendment warranting a stay of execution." Thomas contended that the history of executions in Alabama in the post–*Furman* era show excessive mutilation and burning of the body, that Alabama corrections officers are not competent to manage executions, and that these conditions combine to cause unconstitutionality. Thomas requested that his execution be stayed until Alabama's new electric chair is installed....

The following is a summary of the relevant evidence presented through documents, exhibits, affidavits, depositions, and testimony at the hearing [held on this matter].

Alabama's wooden electric chair is in a separate "execution chamber" with its back to the wall on which the receptacles for the electrical connectors are located. There are four receptacles, arranged two by two. To properly connect the chair to the power source the cables should run from the two bottom receptacles to the back of the chair. The top receptacles lead to a bank of test resistors from which no power can flow.

If the cables are connected from the top receptacles to the electric chair, no electrical power reaches the chair.

During the execution of Horace Dunkins, Jr., on July 14, 1989, two cycles of the electric chair were necessary to complete the execution. Near midnight, Dunkins was taken to the chamber, placed in the chair, and prepared for execution. The switch was thrown, and the electrical power source proceeded through its cycle. After the cycle was completed, attending physicians found that Dunkins was not dead. The switch was thrown again, and after the second cycle the attending physicians found that Dunkins was dead.

Lt. Robert Skipper and Lt. David Craft were the prison officials responsible for connecting the electric chair to the wall for the execution of Horace Dunkins on July 14, 1989. Each man states that they mistakenly connected the cables from the chair to the wrong two receptacles on the wall....

After the Dunkins execution, Warden Jones of Holman Prison, directed that the cables be attached to the wall receptacles in such a way that the cables cannot be removed from the bottom receptacles. James Brooks, Jr., Holman's electrician supervisor, made the directed adjustments, and the jacks which are fastened to the wall panel cannot now be removed from their receptacles.

Fred A. Leuchter (engineer engaged in the design and manufacture of "execution hardware") states that Alabama's execution equipment is like that most electrocution states use to carry out their electrocutions. Leuchter opines that, properly operated, Alabama's electric chair can be used to carry out a humane execution. Leuchter also states that the old electric chair is being replaced because of the difficulty in getting spare parts, and because the newer electric chair will be easier to use....

Although the Eighth Amendment prohibits cruel and unusual punishment, execution by electrocution is not inherently unconstitutional. Although it is clear that death by torture is unacceptable under the Eighth Amendment, in the instant action, the Court is unable to find any credible evidence that Alabama prison inmates who have been executed have suffered pain. Neither does the Court find any credible evidence that prison inmates, including Thomas, who are to be executed in this electric chair in the foreseeable future will suffer any pain. In fact, the Court has heard no credible evidence that prisoners executed in Alabama feel any pain at all. Quite the contrary, the Court had heard ample testimony that death by electrocution in Alabama's electric chair is painless....

5. The Need for a New Method of Execution

John Louis Evans was the first inmate executed in Alabama after *Furman*. During that execution, Evans was given three separate jolts of electricity because attending doctors found heartbeats after the first two jolts. Because the electrode connectors were not secure, arching and burning occurred during the process, and Evans sustained third and fourth degree burns. Evans' co-defendant, Ritter, raised the eighth amendment issue in his federal habeas petition, arguing that the circumstances of Evans' execution constituted cruel and unusual punishment.

In Ritter [v. Smith, 568 F. Supp. 1499 (S.D. Ala. 1983)], the District Court found that execution in Alabama's electric chair did not violate the Eighth Amendment. Further, the Court specifically found that Evans' execution was not cruel and unusual punishment and did not violate the Eighth Amendment as there was no wanton infliction of pain, because Evans was unconscious after the first jolt, and consequently did not feel the other two. The court reached this conclusion after finding that electrocution involves "an instantaneous blocking of any sensory perceptions or instantaneously rendering the person unconscious so that he was unable to feel any pain." The Court expressly noted the possibility that the chair might not work at some point in the future, but ... that fact alone would not render the punishment unconstitutional. The Court noted that three separate jolts of electricity were unusual, but found no indication that any pain was involved. Neither did the burns on Evans body constitute cruel and unusual punishment....

After hearing the evidence, the Court considers that Thomas has not shown that his situation is materially different from Ritter's.... Lacking any credible evidence that painful executions are being carried out in Alabama, the Court finds no merit to Thomas' contention that his execution in Alabama's electric chair would violate the Eighth Amendment.

EXECUTION BY LETHAL GAS

The use of lethal gas as a method of execution is an early twentieth century Anglo-American jurisprudential phenomenon. The chemical agent used to carry out this method of execution is cyanide gas. Before 1983, no federal court had ever rendered an opinion on the constitutionality of execution by lethal gas.

Several state appellate courts had, before 1983, addressed the issue of whether execution by lethal gas was a cruel and unusual method of punishment. The first court to do so was the Nevada Supreme Court in 1923, in the case *State v. Gee Jon*.[27] This case involved two defendants,

Organ Transplants from Executed Prisoners

Gee Jon and Hughie Sing, who had been convicted and sentenced to death for committing the crime of murder. At the time of their crime, the state of Nevada had only recently changed its method of execution to lethal gas.

The defendants challenged the use of lethal gas as cruel and unusual punishment. The court in *Gee Jon* rejected this argument. In doing so, the court made the following observations:

> What has been the punishment for centuries for the crime of murder, of the character we know as murder in the first degree? It has been death. For the state to take the life of one who perpetrates a fiendish murder has from time immemorial been recognized as proper. The [statute] in question authorizes the taking of the life of a murderer as a penalty for the crime which he commits. It is the same penalty which has been exacted for ages—sanctioned in the old biblical law of "an eye for an eye and a tooth for a tooth." It is true that the penalty has been inflicted in different ways; for instance, by hanging, by shooting, and by electrocution; but in each case the method used has been to accomplish the same end, the death of the guilty party. Our statute inflicts no new punishment; it is the same old punishment, inflicted in a different manner, and we think it safe to say that in whatever way the death penalty is inflicted it must of necessity be more or less cruel.
>
> But we are not prepared to say that the infliction of the death penalty by the administration of lethal gas would of itself subject the victim to either pain or torture.... For many years animals have been put to death painlessly by the administration of poisonous gas.... No doubt gas may be administered so as to produce intense suffering. It is also true that one may be executed by hanging, shooting, or electrocution in such a bungling fashion as to produce the same result. But this is no argument against execution by either method.
>
> ... It may be said to be a scientific fact that a painless death may be caused by the administration of lethal gas.[28]

Since 1983, three federal appellate courts have addressed the issue of whether lethal gas is a cruel and unusual punishment. The federal appellate courts are split on this issue. Two courts concluded that lethal gas was not cruel and unusual punishment,[29] whereas the third court came to the opposite conclusion.[30] The case finding lethal gas cruel and unusual as a method of punishment was reversed by the Supreme Court. However, the reversal did not decide the issue of whether lethal gas was unconstitutional. The Supreme Court reversed the appellate court's ruling on

5. The Need for a New Method of Execution

the grounds that the jurisdiction involved, California, had changed its default method of execution from lethal gas to lethal injection.

Lethal Gas Jurisdictions. Only four capital punishment jurisdictions provide for the use of lethal gas to execute the death penalty. Two jurisdictions, California and Missouri, utilize lethal gas as an option for all capital felons. One jurisdiction, Arizona, utilizes lethal gas as an option for inmates sentenced before a specific date. The fourth jurisdiction, Wyoming, has designated lethal gas as the method of execution in the event its primary method is found unconstitutional.

Case Illustration. The 1983 case *Gray v. Lucas*,[31] provides the first federal opinion on the constitutionality of lethal gas as a method of execution.

> In October 1976 petitioner Jimmy Lee Gray was indicted by a grand jury of Jackson County, Mississippi, in the murder of a three-year-old girl. In a bifurcated jury trial, Gray was convicted and sentenced to death. On appeal, the Mississippi Supreme Court reversed the conviction and remanded the case for a new trial. On retrial, Gray was again convicted of capital murder and sentenced to death. The Mississippi Supreme Court affirmed both the conviction and the death sentence....
>
> The petitioner ... contends Mississippi's lethal gas method of execution constitutes cruel and unusual punishment. Gray contends that he is entitled to an evidentiary hearing upon the factual issue whether Mississippi's method of execution by lethal gas offends eighth amendment guarantees because it involves the unnecessary and wanton infliction of pain, in the nature of torture and a lingering death....
>
> In support of this claim Gray submits numerous affidavits, including three from individuals who have witnessed executions by lethal gas. Tad Dunbar, a television news anchorman, witnessed the 1979 Nevada execution of Jesse Walter Bishop by lethal gas. Dunbar attests that he was "shocked and horrified" that death came only after Bishop's protracted struggle with the lethal cyanide gas:
>
>> When the cyanide gas reached him, he gasped, and convulsed strenuously. He stiffened. His head lurched back. His eyes widened, and he strained as much as the straps that held him to the chair would allow. He unquestionably appeared to be in pain.
>>
>> Periodically now, perhaps at thirty second intervals, he would convulse, alternately straining and relaxing in the chair. I noticed he had urinated. The convulsions continued for approximately ten more minutes, and you could see his chest expand, and then contract, trying to take in fresh air. These movements became weaker as the minutes ticked away. You could not tell when Bishop finally lost consciousness.

Organ Transplants from Executed Prisoners

According to prison officials, Bishop died at 12:21 a.m., approximately 12 minutes after the cyanide pellets had dropped in the chamber. Death was pronounced after the shade on our observation window had been drawn, though there was still some slight movement in the body.

Howard Brodie, National News artist for CBS news, witnessed California's 1967 execution of Aaron Mitchell by lethal cyanide gas. Brodie had previously witnessed four executions, but he recalled that Mitchell's was particularly horrible:

> The pellets of cyanide were released by mechanical controls, and dropped into an acid jar beneath the chair. The gas rose, and seemed to hit him immediately. Within the first minute Mitchell slumped down. I thought to myself how quickly cyanide really worked.
>
> Within 30 seconds he lifted his head upwards again. He raised his entire body, arching, tugging at his straps. Saliva was oozing from his mouth. His eyes open, he turned his head to the right. He gazed through my window. His fingers were tightly gripping his thumbs. His chest was visibly heaving in sickening agony. Then he tilted his head higher, and rolled his eyes upward. Then he slumped forward. Still his heart was beating. It continued for another several minutes.
>
> He was pronounced dead, twelve minutes after the pellets were released, by the doctor who could hear his heart through the stethoscope....

The Reverend Myer Tobey witnessed four Maryland executions by lethal cyanide gas. Of the four, he remembered best the execution of Eddie Daniels in the late 1950's:

> In an instant, puffs of light white smoke began to rise. Daniels saw the smoke, and moved his head to try to avoid breathing it in. As the gas continued to rise he moved his head this way and that way, thrashing as much as his straps would allow still in an attempt to avoid breathing. He was like an animal in a trap, with no escape, all the time being watched by his fellow humans in the windows that lined the chamber. He could steal only glimpses of me in his panic, but I continued to repeat "My Jesus I Love You," and he too would try to mouth it.
>
> Then the convulsions began. His body strained as much as the straps would allow. He had inhaled the deadly gas, and it seemed as if every muscle in his body was straining in reaction. His eyes looked as if they were bulging, much as a choking man with a rope cutting off his windpipe. But he could get no air in the chamber.
>
> Then his head dropped forward. The doctor in the observation room said that that was it for Daniels. This was within the first few minutes after the pellets had dropped. His head was down for several seconds. Then, as we had thought it was over, he again lifted his head in another convulsion. His eyes were open, he strained and he looked at me. I said one more time, automatically, "My Jesus I Love You." And he went with me, mouthing the prayer. He was still alive after those several minutes, and I was horrified. He was in great agony. Then he strained and began the words with me again. I

5. The Need for a New Method of Execution

knew he was conscious, this was not an automatic response of an unconscious man. But he did not finish. His head fell forward again.

There were several more convulsions after this, but his eyes were closed. I could not tell if he were conscious or not at that point. Then he stopped moving, approximately ten minutes after the gas began to rise, and was officially pronounced dead.

Gray also submits scientific and medical evidence suggesting that the method of inducing death by cyanide gas causes painful asphyxiation. Dr. Richard Traystman, Director of the Anesthesiology and Critical Care Medicine Research Laboratories at Johns Hopkins Medical School, explained in his affidavit how cyanide causes asphyxiation:

Very simple, cyanide gas blocks the utilization of the oxygen in the body's cells. ...Gradually, depending on the rate and volume of inspiration, and on the concentration of the cyanide that is inhaled, the person exposed to cyanide gas will become anoxic. This is a condition defined by no oxygen. Death will follow through asphyxiation, when the heart and brain cease to receive oxygen.

The hypoxic state can continue for several minutes after the cyanide gas is released in the execution chamber. The person exposed to this gas remains conscious for a period of time, in some cases for several minutes, again depending on the rate and volume of the gas that is inhaled. During this time the person is unquestionably experiencing pain and extreme anxiety. The pain begins immediately, and is felt in the arms, shoulders, back, and chest. The sensation is similar to the pain felt by a person during a heart attack, where essentially, the heart is being deprived of oxygen. The severity of the pain varies directly with the diminishing oxygen reaching the tissues.

The agitation and anxiety a person experiences in the hypoxic state will stimulate the autonomic nervous system.... [The person] ... may begin to drool, urinate, defecate, or vomit. There will be muscular contractions. These responses can occur both while the person is conscious, or when he becomes unconscious.

When anoxia sets in, the brain remains alive for from two to five minutes. The heart will continue to beat for a period of time after that, perhaps five to seven minutes, or longer, though at a very low cardiac output. Death can occur ten to twelve minutes after the gas is released in the chamber.

Dr. Traystman concluded by stating that asphyxiation of animals for research purposes is disfavored in the scientific community. "We would not use asphyxiation, by cyanide gas or by any other substance, in our laboratory to kill animals that have been used in experiments—nor would most medical research laboratories in this country use it."

It is Gray's position that recent scientific evidence rebuts the fallacy, once commonly accepted, that death via lethal cyanide gas is painless. Gray submits that "[a] substantial body of authority now confirms that death by the administration of lethal gas is lingering, painful and terrifying, and involves substantial physical pain." While commentators have voiced this view, there has been as yet no thorough and definitive study on the precise issue Gray raises.

Gray stresses that neither the Supreme Court nor any federal court has addressed the issue whether the gas chamber constitutes cruel and unusual punishment....

Gray argues strongly that he has produced a factual predicate clearly demonstrating that death by cyanide gas, causing asphyxiation at the cost of protracted pain over a period that may exceed seven minutes, may offend an indicated eighth amendment prohibition against the unnecessary and wanton infliction of pain. He contends that, therefore, he is entitled to an evidentiary hearing to prove the facts indicated in order to vindicate his constitutional claim in that regard.

Accepting Gray's proffered facts as proven, we ultimately conclude that they do not as a matter of law establish the eighth amendment claim asserted by him and, therefore, no evidentiary hearing is required. Traditional deaths by execution, such as by hanging, have always involved the possibility of pain and terror for the convicted person. Although contemporary notions of civilized conduct may indeed cause some reassessment of what degree or length is acceptable, we are not persuaded that under the present jurisprudential standards the showing made by Gray justifies this intermediate appellate court holding that, as a matter of law or fact, the pain and terror resulting from death by cyanide gas is so different in degree or nature from that resulting from other traditional modes of execution as to implicate the eighth amendment right....

Having examined each of the contentions presented, we find no basis for federal habeas relief. Accordingly, the judgment of the district court is affirmed.

Inefficiency of Present Execution Methods

All of the current methods of execution are wasteful and inefficient. None of the methods permit harvesting healthy transplantable organs from executed capital murderers. Current methods of execution destroy such organs. This section will review traditional criticisms of the current methods of execution and pinpoint how each method destroys the healthy transplantable organs of capital murderers.

5. The Need for a New Method of Execution

CRITICISM OF FIRING SQUADS

Several arguments have been advanced against using firing squads to carry out the death penalty. First, it has been said that death by firing squad is not a clean method of execution. Blood pours out profusely and uncontrollably when a firing squad performs its task. Second, it has been argued that firing squads do not usually bring about a swift death, thereby causing capital murderers to languish, unattended, in pain and blood. The final criticism involves the draping of a hood and circular target over the capital murderer. It is said that the hood depersonalizes the capital murderer's humanity, as does also, the circular target, which is draped over the torso of a capital murderer and is used to direct the aim of the firing squad.[32]

Death sentence organ removal statutes and firing squad executions are incompatible. Death by firing squad must be abandoned. This method of execution senselessly and needlessly destroys many transplantable organs as a result of piercing and ripping by bullets.

CRITICISM OF HANGING

There are two basic arguments against using hanging as a method of execution. First, hanging presents the risk that death will occur as a result of asphyxiation, which can occur if the execution is not properly done. Asphyxiation death is slow and painful. The second concerns the risk of decapitation. A hanging done improperly could cause the head of a capital murderer to be torn from its trunk.[33]

Death sentence organ removal statutes and hanging executions are incompatible. Death by hanging must be abandoned. This method of execution senselessly and needlessly destroys many transplantable organs as a result of the "prolonged deprivation of oxygen and the amount of time that elapses before death is pronounced."[34]

CRITICISM OF LETHAL INJECTION

Lethal injection has been criticized on three fronts as being an unacceptable method of execution. First, it is argued that using a needle to cause death can be painful and can require surgery to implant the needle. For example, it was reported that during a 1985 execution in Texas, 23 attempts, over a time of 40 minutes, were needed to inject the needle in a capital murderer. Second, it is argued that the drugs frequently do not induce a quick and painless death. When death comes slowly, capital murderers are said to endure psychological trauma and in some instances physical pain. The final argument against lethal injection is that the drugs have not been approved by the federal Food and Drug Administration for the purpose in which they are being used.[35]

Death sentence organ removal statutes and executions by lethal injection are incompatible. Death by lethal injection must be abandoned. This method of execution senselessly and needlessly destroys many transplantable organs. It is said that "[l]ethal injection causes cardiopulmonary cessation and immediately destroys the viability of both the heart and lungs. The kidneys, liver, and other internal organs are rendered useless immediately thereafter."[36]

CRITICISM OF ELECTROCUTION

For over 100 years, two primary arguments have been used against electrocution as a method of execution. First, death by electrocution is not always immediate. It can take several minutes before a capital murderer is put to death. Tremendous pain is endured during this process. The second argument against electrocution is that it unnecessarily and grotesquely disfigures the capital murderer's corpse. For example, it has been reported that the eyes of capital murderers hideously melt or burst out, their brains bake as solid as rock, flames burst through their skin, and their corpses are burned to charcoal.[37]

Death sentence organ removal statutes and electrocution executions are incompatible. Death by electrocution must be abandoned. This method of execution senselessly and needlessly destroys all transplantable organs. "It is said that all internal organs, as well as the flesh, are essentially cooked before death is achieved."[38]

5. The Need for a New Method of Execution

CRITICISM OF LETHAL GAS

Two arguments have been made against the use of lethal gas as a method of execution. First, it is contended that cyanide gas causes excruciating pain. Capital murderers have been known to urinate, defecate, vomit, and drool while dying from cyanide gas. Second, death by this method can take more than 10 minutes. It is argued that this long span of time amounts to pure torture.[39]

Death sentence organ removal statutes and executions by lethal gas are incompatible. Death by lethal gas must be abandoned. This method of execution senselessly and needlessly destroys many transplantable organs. "It has been observed that cyanide gas fatally deprives cells of oxygen. As a consequence, internal organs, dependent on such oxygen, die."[40]

Utilizing an Efficient Method of Execution

The current methods of execution allow macabre deaths and needless destruction of transplantable organs. For death sentence organ removal statutes to be meaningfully carried out, "the current methods of execution must be abolished and replaced with a method of execution that does not destroy transplantable organs."[41]

One efficient execution method that saves healthy transplantable organs involves anesthesia-induced brain death. Execution "by anesthesia-induced brain death would prevent destruction of transplantable organs."[42] To bring about anesthesia-induced brain death, a capital murderer would be given an injection of sodium pentothal. Next, a sufficient dose of anesthesia would be administered to render the capital murderer brain-dead. While the capital murderer is in a state of brain death, all healthy transplantable organs could then be efficiently removed. Once all such organs are removed, the corpse could then be disposed of as provided by law.

6

OTHER NECESSARY CHANGES IN CAPITAL PUNISHMENT LAWS

A sad and unfortunate commentary on America is that its poor are too often denied fairness in the nation's highest court. For the better part of the nation's history there has not been a voice on the Supreme Court to argue for and defend those that a Biblical prophet said would always be with us—the poor. America moves tragically through the 21st century with the greatest threat to its security and stability perched on the bench of the Supreme Court, attired in politically trimmed robes.

Chronicling the unbridled insensitivity and blatant disdain for the poor, as reflected in the decisions of the Supreme Court, is beyond the scope of this book. The focus here must necessarily be narrow. In the area of capital punishment, the Supreme Court has unleashed a satanic wrath upon the poor. Its decisions have unequivocally sanctioned totally arbitrary discrimination against the poor in the prosecution of capital murder. The promise of *Furman v. Georgia*[1] has been turned into a lie.

Now is not the time for politically correct words. Death sentence organ removal statutes cannot be implemented in the cancerous legal environment created and nurtured by the Supreme Court. That environment would make the poor the exclusive source of transplantable organs. America must never allow this. In one firm voice, the will of the nation must tear asunder the unholy edicts of the Supreme Court and, with Samson-like determination, remove the entrenched pillars of arbitrary discrimination from capital punishment. This can be done legislatively, notwithstanding the widespread infectious venom lavishly flowing from the Supreme Court into the life-stream of the poor.

6. Other Necessary Changes in Capital Punishment Laws

The intent of this chapter is twofold: first, to identify those capital punishment areas that must be legislatively changed so as to minimize arbitrary discrimination against the poor; and second, to isolate capital punishment areas that must be legislatively altered so as to expedite the death penalty.

Minimizing Discrimination in Capital Punishment

The decision in *Furman*, which imposed a temporary moratorium on capital punishment, did not envision the total absence of unlawful arbitrary discrimination in capital punishment. Utopia must bow to reality. *Furman* demanded a meaningful reduction in capital punishment discrimination. Before the unfortunate arrival of a twisted majority mind-set in the Supreme Court, the demand of *Furman* was coming to fruition. However, the Supreme Court has ripped up the *Furman* decision and denies it ever existed. With Supreme Court backing, the letter of the law is being applied to the capital murderer who is poor and is being erased when the capital murderer is not poor.

Two of the areas in capital punishment prosecution that are used, with Supreme Court approval, to ensure that only the poor are sentenced to death for capital murder are (1) prosecutorial discretion in charging capital murder and (2) jury discretion in sparing a capital murderer from the death sentence.

PROSECUTORIAL DISCRETION AND CAPITAL PUNISHMENT

In 1994 Susan Smith was charged with murdering her two young children. After formally charging Smith, the prosecutor publicly announced that the state would seek the death penalty in its prosecution of Smith.[2] In 1993 James Jordan, the father of professional basketball star Michael Jordan, was senselessly murdered by Larry Demery and Daniel Green.[3] The prosecutor in that case publicly announced that the state would seek the death penalty against both men.

Organ Transplants from Executed Prisoners

In 1995 O. J. Simpson was charged with the murder of Ronald Goldman and Nicole Brown-Simpson. After formal charges were brought against Simpson, the prosecutor publicly announced that the state would not seek the death penalty in its prosecution of Simpson.[4] In 1996 John Du Pont was charged with the murder of the Olympic wrestler Dave Schultz. In that case the prosecutor announced publicly that the state would not seek the death penalty against Du Pont.[5]

The common denominator in all four of the above cases was money—or the lack thereof. Demery, Green, and Smith did not have wealth. Du Pont and Simpson did have wealth. Is it possible that the defendants who were subjected to the pressure of being exposed to the death penalty were victims of arbitrary economic discrimination? Ultimately, the answer to this question is known only to the prosecutors in the respective cases. Speculation, however, clearly indicates that prosecutorial discretion was exercised along economic lines.

To grasp the nature of prosecutorial discretion in capital punishment, it is necessary to first examine the roots of this legal doctrine.

The Prosecutor Under Common Law. Although the English Parliament existed during the height of the common law era, the English Crown was the true sovereign authority. As the sovereign authority, the Crown had the duty and responsibility to maintain the peace and enforce the laws of the realm. This duty and responsibility meant apprehending and prosecuting law-breakers. The Crown delegated, in large part, both its arrest[6] and its prosecution duties to the "people." In other words, under the common law, both the Crown and common citizens carried out criminal prosecutorial duties.

The English Crown employed numerous legal advisors. Some of the legal offices created by the Crown included (1) King's advocate general, (2) King's attorney general, (3) King's solicitor general, and (4) King's serjeants.[7] Legal advisors employed by the Crown enjoyed the benefits of the inherent "prerogative" of the Crown, due to their association with it. This meant, in practice, that legal advisors of the Crown were viewed literally as being above all other attorneys and were treated with absolute deference in courts of law. One scholar noted that the Crown's attorney did not represent the Crown in court because the Crown was theoretically always present. The attorney merely followed

6. Other Necessary Changes in Capital Punishment Laws

a case on behalf of the Crown.[8] This framework of absolute deference to the Crown's attorneys laid the seeds of prosecutorial discretion that is present in Anglo-American jurisprudence today.

In fulfilling its duty of prosecuting criminal offenders, the Crown relied primarily on its attorney general. However, the attorney general did not prosecute all crimes, although it had the authority to do so. Instead, the attorney general limited its attention to major felony crimes like treason, murder, outlawry, and robbery. The crimes of murder and treason were of particular interest to the Crown because the real property of defendants convicted of either offense escheated to the Crown. Enormous fines, which went to the Crown, were appended to other major felony offenses.

The fact that the attorney general selected the cases it would prosecute (those bringing the greatest bounty to the Crown) was a prerogative act of discretion that could not be challenged by common law courts or anyone, save the Crown itself. The attorney general represented the Crown. Thus, as one court put it: "If the agent of the sovereign desired that a prosecution should [not occur], that was the end of the matter. The public subjects had no interest and could not be heard to complain."[9]

Additionally, if the attorney general began a prosecution and decided it did not want to proceed further, it could discontinue the case by filing a nolle prosequi. The nolle prosequi was "a statement by the [attorney general] that he would proceed no further in a criminal case.... The discretion to discontinue prosecution rested solely with the [attorney general] and it was unnecessary to obtain the permission of the court to give legal effect to this decision."[10] The underlying justification for permitting the attorney general to have absolute discretion in determining the fate of a prosecution anchored itself to the fact that the Crown, as sovereign authority, "was theoretically the only party interested in the prosecution."[11]

Early Criminal Prosecution in North America. The common law did not have a public prosecutor, as this term is understood today.[12] Instead, the common law tolerated gross selective prosecution by the Crown's attorney general and wholesale prosecution by private citizens. Unfortunately, this chaotic method of prosecuting criminals was transplanted to the American colonies. Fortunately, however, another method of prosecuting criminal defendants also took root in North America. When the Dutch founded the colony of New Netherland during the 17th century, they also brought with them their system of prosecuting criminal defendants; a system that was not founded on English common law.

In all of England's American colonies, the Crown appointed attorney generals. The first appointment was made in Virginia in 1643.[13] The primary task of colonial attorney generals was to promote and protect the financial interests of the Crown. This meant that the bulk of the legal work performed by the colonial attorney generals was civil in nature.

Colonial attorney generals were also responsible for prosecuting criminal defendants. However, this duty was neglected. Rarely did colonial attorney generals prosecute criminal defendants. They intervened in this area only when a "notorious" major felony occurred. A routine murder was not considered notorious, unless it affected a colonial aristocrat.[14]

The attitude of colonial attorney generals was the same as their brethren in England—that is, if the Crown did not obtain a substantial monetary benefit from criminal prosecutions, there would be no prosecution by the sovereign authority whose duty it was to prosecute all crimes. Colonial judges did not challenge the discretion exercised by colonial attorney generals.

Two factors caused colonial judges to defer to the prosecutorial discretion of colonial attorney generals. First, the judges followed the legal principles of the common law, which held that the Crown's prosecutors had absolute discretion in deciding what course, if any, to take regarding a criminal offense. Second, colonial judges bowed to the whim of colonial attorney generals because of the Crown's power. Colonial attorney generals were not ordinary attorneys. The Crown's prerogative was vested in colonial attorney generals when they carried out their legal duties. No colonial judge could muster the courage to tell the Crown when it should prosecute a criminal case.

The fact that colonial attorney generals rarely prosecuted criminal defendants did not mean that vigorous criminal prosecutions were nonexistent in the colonies. Crime was routinely prosecuted, but by the citizens of the colonies rather than the agents of the Crown.

6. Other Necessary Changes in Capital Punishment Laws

The chaotic private prosecutorial method that existed in England was allowed to flourish in the colonies. The inducement used to encourage colonists to prosecute criminals was the same carrot that was used in England. Private prosecutors reaped monetary rewards for successfully prosecuting criminals. They also reaped rewards by intimidating defendants into settling criminal charges, before trial, by paying the private prosecutors monetary sums.[15]

A different situation existed in the New Netherland colony, settled by the Dutch in the 17th century. (This colony comprised parts of present-day Delaware, New Jersey, New York, Pennsylvania, and Connecticut).[16] As would be expected, Dutch colonists brought with them the Dutch culture, social norms, and system of government.

One aspect of the Dutch system of government that was brought with the colonists had a profound effect on Anglo-American jurisprudence. The legal system of the Dutch had an office called the *schout*. Although legal scholars rarely acknowledge the point, the principles undergirding the office of schout shaped the prosecutorial system that America would eventually adopt and that it uses to this day.[17]

The schout was a public prosecutor. Instead of the chaotic system of prosecution tolerated by the common law, Dutch law entrusted the task of prosecuting criminals to a single office—the office of schout. Dutch colonists did not haul their neighbors into criminal courts on real or monetarily imagined charges. If a criminal offense occurred, the office of schout prosecuted the crime.[18]

When the English eventually took New Netherland from the Dutch, the term *schout* was buried. However, the idea of entrusting a public prosecutor with the responsibility for prosecuting all crimes took root and blossomed in America. The public prosecutor of today is a distant cousin of the common law and the first cousin of the schout.[19]

When the American colonists threw off the yoke of the Crown, they also tossed out the common law's ad hoc approach to prosecuting criminal defendants. The nation unanimously moved in the direction of imposing the duty of prosecuting criminal defendants on individual governmental jurisdictions. Neither the nation nor its legal system was prepared to continue depending on private citizens to prosecute criminals. Crime would be prosecuted, but under the schout model.

Organ Transplants from Executed Prisoners

Today all jurisdictions have schouts, though they go by various names: district attorney, county prosecutor, state attorney, attorney general, or simply public prosecutor. A majority of jurisdictions provide for the election of prosecutors on a local, usually county level.[20]

In spite of the rejection of the common law's prosecutorial method, the judiciary continues to adhere to the common-law principle that a prosecutor has broad discretion regarding the disposition of criminal cases. Although the nation is not governed by a "Crown," the judiciary continues to allow prosecutors to have "almost" unassailable prosecutorial power and authority.

Prosecutorial Discretion to Seek the Death Penalty. Traditionally the determination of what penalty a convicted defendant will receive is made by the presiding judge, based on the penalty range provided by statute.[21] For example, if a prosecutor obtains a conviction for rape and the penalty for the offense is from five to fifteen years of imprisonment, the prosecutor cannot absolve the defendant from being subject to this penalty. At most, a prosecutor may recommend to the trial judge that the defendant receive probation or some other disposition. The court can accept or reject the recommendation.[22] In other words, once a prosecutor charges a defendant with a crime, the penalty automatically attaches and the prosecutor cannot, *sua sponte*, remove the defendant from exposure to the penalty (short of dismissing the charge).

Tradition is abandoned, however, in capital murder prosecutions. In this context the prosecutor can invade the traditionally exclusive domain of the trial judge. All capital punishment jurisdictions give prosecutors statutory discretion to waive the death penalty, *sua sponte*, for any death eligible offense.[23] One appellate court noted that the exercise of this discretion does not "violate the separation of powers provision of [federal or state constitutions], in that the prosecutor is given power to exercise a part of the sentencing process, which should properly be a judicial function."[24]

Table 6.0 Number of Executions, 2000–2011

Year of Execution	Number of Prisoners Executed			
	All Races	White	Black	Other
2000	85	43	35	7
2001	66	45	17	4

6. Other Necessary Changes in Capital Punishment Laws

2002	71	47	18	6
2003	65	41	20	4
2004	59	36	19	4
2005	60	38	19	3
2006	53	25	20	8
2007	42	22	14	6
2008	37	17	17	3
2009	52	24	21	7
2010	46	28	13	5
2011	43	22	16	5
Total	679	388	229	62

SOURCE: U.S. Department of Justice, Capital Punishment 2011, Bureau of Justice Statistics Table 11 (July 2013).

In the infamous 1987 case *McCleskey v. Kemp*,[25] the defendant argued that the state of Georgia's capital punishment statute was unconstitutional because it gave unfettered discretion to prosecutors to determine when they would seek the death penalty for capital offenses. The defendant contended that the Constitution required that death penalty statutes set out guidelines to control the circumstances in which a prosecutor may seek, or decline to seek, the death penalty. The Supreme Court categorically disagreed with the defendant:

> [T]he policy considerations behind a prosecutor's traditionally wide discretion suggest the impropriety of our requiring prosecutors to defend their decisions to seek death penalties....
> ... Our refusal to require that the prosecutor provide an explanation for his decisions ... is completely consistent with this Court's longstanding precedents that hold that a prosecutor need not explain his decisions unless the criminal defendant presents a prima facie case of unconstitutional conduct with respect to his case....
> ... Similarly, the capacity of prosecutorial discretion to provide individualized justice is firmly entrenched in American law. As we have noted, a prosecutor can ... decline to seek a death sentence in any particular case. Of course, the power to be lenient [also] is the power to discriminate, but a capital punishment system that did not allow for discretionary acts of leniency would be totally alien to our notions of criminal justice[.]
> We have held that discretion in a capital punishment system is necessary to satisfy the Constitution.... Prosecutorial decisions necessarily involve both judgmental and factual decisions that vary from case to case. Thus, it is difficult to imagine guidelines that would produce ... predictability ... without sacrificing the discretion essential to a humane and fair system of criminal justice.[26]

Table 6.1 Characteristics of Death Row Inmates, 2011

Characteristic	Percentage
Male	98.0%
Female	2.0%
White	55.3%
Black	41.8%
Other races	3.0%
8th grade or less	13.6%
9th to 11th grade	35.3%
Diploma/GED	41.9%
Some college	9.2%
Married	22.3%
Divorced/separated	20.1%
Widowed	3.0
Never married	54.6
Total death row population	3,082

SOURCE: U.S. Department of Justice, *Capital Punishment* 2011, Bureau of Justice Statistics Table 5 (July 2013).

The decision in *McCleskey* will be remembered as one of the most unforgivable decisions ever rendered by any court in human history. No rational legal system can permit its prosecutors to approach capital punishment cases with the unbridled discretion that may be appropriate in routine drug or shoplifting cases. The death penalty symbolizes the apex of societal intolerance with a specific crime—capital murder. It is imperative that substantively restrictive guidelines be placed on prosecutors in addressing this crime on behalf of society. Execution death, notwithstanding the edicts of the Supreme Court, is not a child's game—it is a mature response to tragedy and should be accorded adult scrutiny.

The consequences of *McCleskey's* irrational and adolescent decision are reflected in Table 6.1. As Table 6.1 illustrates, in 2011 the only people waiting to be executed in the nation were the undereducated—the poor. The Supreme Court is satisfied with this outcome. The American public must never be satisfied with such blatant unlawful and immoral discrimination.

Prosecutors, with the Supreme Court's blessing, have systematically and politically targeted the poor and destitute for exclusive capital punishment prosecution. This is unconscionable, unacceptable, and simply wrong. The death penalty must punish equally or punish none at all. The poor do not have a patent on capital murder. However, the Supreme

6. Other Necessary Changes in Capital Punishment Laws

Court has taken out a patent on the death penalty for the poor. Prosecutors have recognized this patent on the poor and have entered into an unholy alliance with the Supreme Court to advance their careers by cannibalizing the poor.

The American public must renounce the wrong that was constitutionalized by *McCleskey*, before any jurisdiction enacts a death sentence organ removal statute. Strict guidelines must be put in place, in every capital punishment jurisdiction, to direct and control the course that prosecutors must take in capital murder cases. The Simpsons and the Du Ponts must face the same threat of capital punishment as do the Smiths, the Greens, the Demerys—and the Timothy McVeighs.

JURY DISCRETION AND THE DEATH PENALTY

The primary focus of the *Furman* decision was the arbitrariness that juries were allowed in determining whether to impose the sentence of death on capital murderers. Currently, the majority of capital punishment jurisdictions have *death discretionary* provisions, which permit jury arbitrariness to continue. The Supreme Court has approved of these death discretionary provisions.

Understanding the nature of death discretionary provisions requires some discussion of a slightly complicated area of death penalty law. To simplify this subject, the discussion will proceed as follows: (1) distinguishing guilt phase and penalty phase; (2) determination of aggravating and mitigating circumstances; (3) weighing and nonweighing determination; (4) death automatic and death discretionary jurisdictions; and (5) repealing death discretionary statutory provisions.

Distinguishing Guilt Phase and Penalty Phase. Capital prosecutions have two distinct phases. First, a capital defendant's guilt must be determined. This occurs at what is called the guilt phase. The guilt phase is nothing more than a capital defendant's jury trial (or trial before a judge). Once the guilt phase has ended and a verdict of guilty of capital murder is returned, the second stage of the prosecution will begin. The second stage is called the penalty phase. The purpose of the penalty phase is to determine whether a convicted capital murderer will be sentenced to death.[27]

Organ Transplants from Executed Prisoners

The penalty phase proceeds much the same as did the guilt phase trial. Witnesses are permitted to testify, and physical evidence may be introduced. Usually a jury will be the fact finder at the penalty phase. Based on the evidence presented at the penalty phase, the jury determines whether or not to impose the death penalty (a few jurisdictions allow the jury only to make a nonbinding recommendation to the judge).

Determination of Aggravating and Mitigating Circumstances. The evidence presented at the penalty phase will be of two types: aggravating and mitigating. The prosecutor presents evidence that it believes establishes a statutory aggravating circumstance. The Supreme Court has held that the death penalty cannot be imposed unless at least one statutory aggravating circumstance is proven to exist. (Examples of statutory aggravating circumstances include the following: the victim was tortured; the victim was a child; the victim was poisoned; the victim was a police officer; several victims were killed in one incident.)

The capital felon will present mitigating evidence. The Supreme Court has held that a capital felon must be permitted to present all relevant mitigating evidence. The purpose of mitigating evidence is to try to persuade the jury not to impose the death penalty.

Weighing and Nonweighing Determination. Once all the evidence has been submitted at the penalty phase, the jury retires to deliberate. The first stage of the deliberation is that of making a determination of how many statutory aggravating circumstances and mitigating circumstances were proven to exist. When the jury decides on the number of statutory aggravating circumstances and mitigating circumstances that were proven to exist, the second stage of deliberation is triggered. This stage requires the jury to compare the mitigating and statutory aggravating circumstances. The comparison process is carried out in one of two ways, depending on the requirement of the jurisdiction: (1) weighing or (2) nonweighing.

The Utah Supreme Court described the jury weighing process[28] in *State v. Wood*[29]:

> [This] standard require[s] that the sentencing body compare the totality of the mitigating against the totality of the aggravating factors, not in terms of the relative numbers of the aggravating and the mitigating factors, but in terms of their respective substantiality and persuasiveness. Basically,

6. Other Necessary Changes in Capital Punishment Laws

what the sentencing authority must decide is how ... persuasive the totality of the mitigating factors are when compared against the totality of the aggravating factors. The sentencing body [is] making the judgment that aggravating [or mitigating] factors "outweigh," or are more [persuasive] than, the mitigating [or aggravating] factors[.][30]

Wood points out that the weighing process does not involve determining if more mitigating circumstances exist than statutory aggravating circumstances. A mere tallying of numbers is not the purpose of the weighing process. It matters not, for example, that three statutory aggravating circumstances but only one mitigating circumstance was found to exist. The fact finder could still decide that the mitigating circumstance outweighed the three statutory aggravating circumstances.

The weighing process is carried out in four distinct ways. First, nine capital punishment jurisdictions require the jury to determine whether statutory aggravating circumstances outweigh mitigating circumstances.[31] Second, ten capital punishment jurisdictions require the jury to determine whether mitigating circumstances outweigh statutory aggravating circumstances.[32] Third, one capital punishment jurisdiction requires the jury to determine whether statutory aggravating circumstances outweigh mitigating circumstances by a preponderance of evidence.[33] Finally, four capital punishment jurisdictions require the jury to determine whether statutory aggravating circumstances outweigh mitigating circumstances beyond a reasonable doubt.[34]

What about nonweighing jurisdictions? These exist because the Supreme Court has held that the Constitution does not *require* weighing mitigating and statutory aggravating circumstances.[35] In nonweighing jurisdictions, juries are instructed merely to consider the sufficiency of mitigating and statutory aggravating circumstances. There are currently eight nonweighing capital punishment jurisdictions.[36]

The nonweighing process is carried out in two distinct ways.[37] First, seven capital-punishment jurisdictions require nothing more than that the penalty phase jury determine whether sufficient mitigating circumstances exist to warrant leniency.[38] Second, one capital-punishment jurisdiction requires the jury to determine whether sufficient mitigating circumstances do not exist beyond a reasonable doubt.[39]

Death Automatic and Death Discretionary Jurisdictions. Once the weighing and nonweighing processes end, a result must follow. The weighing or nonweighing process will be favorable to the capital felon or to the prosecutor. The focus here is on what happens when a weighing or nonweighing process determination is made that is favorable to the prosecutor.

A large minority of capital punishment jurisdictions are *death automatic jurisdictions*. They require death be imposed once a weighing or nonweighing determination is made that is favorable to the prosecutor. Thirteen weighing capital-punishment jurisdictions require the death penalty be imposed if the weighing process was favorable to the prosecutor.[40] Two nonweighing jurisdictions require the death penalty be imposed if the nonweighing process was favorable to the prosecutor.[41]

The remaining majority of capital punishment jurisdictions permit the jury to refuse to impose the death penalty even though the weighing or nonweighing process was favorable to the prosecutor.[42] These are called *death discretionary jurisdictions*. Twelve weighing capital-punishment jurisdictions permit the jury to arbitrarily decline to impose the death penalty even though the weighing process was favorable to the prosecutor.[43] Four nonweighing capital-punishment jurisdictions permit the jury to arbitrarily decline to impose the death penalty even though the nonweighing process was favorable to the prosecutor.[44]

Repealing Death Discretionary Statutory Provisions. The crux of what *Furman* opposed has now ironically been placed on a pedestal and embraced by the Supreme Court in its acceptance of death discretionary statutory provisions. *Furman* castigated the arbitrary imposition of the death penalty. The sine qua non of death discretionary statutory provisions is that of arbitrariness.

The purported rationale for permitting death discretionary statutory provisions to thrive is that those who are not given leniency by juries have nevertheless been processed through the constitutional standards for having the death penalty imposed. This type of rationale is typical of what a fox would say in defense of its right to be gatekeeper of a chicken coop. It is self-serving sophistry that is fraught with an inherent contradiction.

Furman did not say that so long as a particular capital murderer

6. Other Necessary Changes in Capital Punishment Laws

received a constitutionally fair prosecution, the Constitution permitted a similarly situated capital murderer to be given leniency. If *Furman* stood for such a proposition, there would have been no need for the decision's moratorium on capital punishment. Those who were sentenced to die before *Furman* were justly convicted of capital crimes. And too, before *Furman*, many defendants convicted of capital crimes were spared the death penalty for reasons known only to the arbitrary whim and fancy of juries. *Furman's* passionate plea called for the equalization of leniency.

Death discretionary statutory provisions are the antithesis of the cardinal principle of equalization of leniency. Such provisions instruct juries to return to their arbitrary whim and fancy to dole out leniency. This makes the methodical pre-leniency processes a sham, an exercise in constitutionally correct gymnastics that result in the unconstitutionally discriminatory flexing of biceps.

Death sentence organ removal statutes must not see the light of day in jurisdictions that embrace death discretionary statutory provisions. The Supreme Court would tolerate the existence of both in the same jurisdiction. So be it. The moral will and spirit of the people in death discretionary jurisdictions must descend upon their legislative halls to demand the repeal of death discretionary statutory provisions. This must and shall be done because it is the right thing to do—notwithstanding the probable unanimous dissent by the Supreme Court. When this massive tide of repeal has run its course, death sentence organ removal statutes should take their rightful place in all capital punishment jurisdictions.

Expediting Capital Punishment

Death-sentence organ-removal statutes will achieve maximum purpose and result through swift executions. Current death penalty appellate procedures retard this maximization of purpose and result. To understand the legislative changes required to expeditiously execute capital murderers under death sentence organ removal statutes, requires a review of court structures and death penalty appellate procedures.[45]

GENERAL STRUCTURE OF COURT SYSTEMS

Anglo-American jurisprudence has long rejected allowing a trial court to have the final word in criminal prosecutions. This rejection is manifested in appellate courts. Part of the function of appellate courts is to examine criminal convictions and sentences for prejudicial error.[46] All jurisdictions, capital and noncapital, have appellate courts. However, there is no constitutional right to have a conviction or sentence examined by an appellate court. Over 100 years ago, in the case *McKane v. Durston*,[47] the Supreme Court indicated, "[A] State is not required by the Federal Constitution to provide appellate courts or a right to appellate [examination of errors] at all."[48] Although *McKane* is still good law today, its pronouncement is meaningless because all jurisdictions do in fact provide appellate courts.

The judicial systems in the nation may be broken down into two categories: (1) two-tier systems and (2) three-tier systems. Jurisdictions that utilize a three-tier system have (1) a court of general jurisdiction, (2) an intermediate appellate court, and (3) a final appellate court. Two-tier system jurisdictions have (1) a court of general jurisdiction and (2) an appellate court. The majority of capital punishment jurisdictions use the three-tier system.[49]

Table 6.2 Court Systems

Type of System	Court of General Jurisdiction	Intermediate Appellate Court	Final Appellate Court
two-tier	yes	no	yes
three-tier	yes	yes	yes

SOURCE: Louis J. Palmer, Jr., *The Death Penalty in the United States: A Complete Guide to Federal and State Laws* 218, Box 21.0 (2013).

UNDERSTANDING DIRECT APPEAL AND DEATH SENTENCE REVIEW

Before capital punishment was abolished by *Furman*, all capital punishment jurisdictions allowed capital felons to bring their conviction and sentence to appellate courts by way of a *direct appeal* (or *writ of error*, as it was sometimes called). Under the pre–*Furman* protocol, cap-

6. Other Necessary Changes in Capital Punishment Laws

ital felons had to bring alleged conviction errors and sentencing errors together as one direct appeal.

When the Supreme Court resurrected the death penalty in *Gregg*, it did so by approving of a capital punishment scheme that allowed appellate death sentence review. In approving this new appellate death sentence review process, the Supreme Court did not hold that the Constitution required such a process. The Supreme Court indicated merely that the appellate death sentence review process was constitutionally acceptable.[50]

As it stands now, only one capital punishment jurisdictions does not utilize an appellate death sentence review process.[51] This jurisdiction continues to cling to the traditional direct appeal process.

Most appellate death sentence review jurisdictions provide by statute that the review of a death sentence is automatic.[52] That is, the capital felon does not have to request a review of the sentence. The review will occur as a matter of law, without a valid waiver by the capital felon.[53]

The appellate death sentence review process involves only penalty phase issues. What this means is that the question of whether a capital felon was erroneously found guilty of the offense is not being considered. The only issue at stake in the appellate death sentence review process is whether a capital felon was sentenced to die in accordance with the law.[54] The issue of a capital felon's guilt is brought to the appellate level by way of the traditional direct appeal. A minority of capital punishment jurisdictions that utilize appellate death sentence review provide by statute that if a capital felon prosecutes a guilt phase direct appeal, the direct appeal is to be consolidated with the penalty phase appellate death sentence review issues.[55]

IMPACT OF APPELLATE STAYS ON EXECUTION OF DEATH SENTENCE

The 679 capital murderers executed in the period 2000–2011 (see Table 6.0) spent an average of twelve years on death row.[56] The ability of a capital murderer to remain on death row for an average of twelve years is due to the Anglo-American appellate process. To shed some light on why the appellate process hinders expeditious executions, we will review the path taken by the average "state" capital murderer after receiving a sentence of death.[57]

The Meaning of Judicial Stay. A judicial stay involves the entry of an order by a court, stopping an event from occurring, until the court examines an allegation concerning the event. A judicial stay is temporary. In the context of capital punishment, a judicial stay is a court order halting the scheduled execution of a capital murderer, pending the court's examination of allegations that the death penalty should not be executed.

Stay During State Appellate Review and Appeal. The first judicial stay that surfaces when a capital murderer is sentenced to death occurs immediately after the sentence is imposed. This stay is necessary to allow the capital murderer to have the sentence and conviction examined by the state appellate court. The length of time involved at this stage depends on several factors.

If the state has a two-tier judicial system, the initial stay will be from six months to a year. If the state has a three-tier system, but the direct appeal and sentence review go directly to the final appellate court, then the initial stay in this system will also range from six months to a year. However, if the state is a three-tier system and the intermediate appellate court is permitted to hear the sentence review and direct appeal before the matter is brought to the final appellate court, then two stays of about one year to 18 months each will occur. That is, there will be a stay imposed for intermediate appellate court examination and a stay imposed for final appellate court examination.

Stay During Supreme Court Appeal. Assuming that a capital murderer did not obtain relief at the state appellate court level, the next step will usually be that of entering the federal system.[58] This initial journey in the federal system will usually move directly to the Supreme Court.[59] If the Supreme Court grants a writ of certiorari, a stay will be imposed by the Supreme Court pending its examination of the case. The proceedings in the Supreme Court can consume a year.

Stay During State Habeas Corpus Proceedings. If the capital murderer is denied relief by the Supreme Court, the capital murderer will usually begin an attack on the conviction and sentence, indirectly, by filing a petition for a writ of habeas corpus. A habeas corpus proceeding

6. Other Necessary Changes in Capital Punishment Laws

involves the capital murderer's allegations that the conviction and sentence were imposed in violation of constitutional rights.[60]

During this first round of habeas corpus proceedings, the capital murderer will usually start out at the state level, though this process can begin in the federal system. Depending on the requirements of the particular state, the habeas corpus petition will be filed in the trial court where the capital murderer was convicted and sentenced or in the state's highest court.

If the capital murderer is permitted to file the habeas corpus petition in the trial court, a stay will be entered pending review by the trial court. The case could linger in the trial court for over a year. If the trial court does not grant the capital murderer relief, there will be an appeal of the denial of the requested relief. If the state has a three-tier judicial system, this appeal will usually go initially to the intermediate appellate court. A stay will be entered pending disposition by the intermediate appellate court. This stay can last up to a year.

If the intermediate appellate court does not grant relief (or if the state has a two-tier judicial system), the capital murderer will appeal to the highest court in the state. While the state high court reviews the habeas corpus appeal, a stay will be imposed that can last up to a year.

Stay During Federal Habeas Corpus Proceedings. If the highest court in the state denies the capital murderer habeas corpus relief, the case will enter the federal system again, initially in the Supreme Court. If the Supreme Court grants a writ of certiorari for habeas corpus, a stay will be imposed by the Supreme Court pending its examination of the issues. This proceeding before the Supreme Court can consume a year.

If the Supreme Court denies the capital murderer relief on the state habeas corpus claim, the capital murderer will seek relief from the conviction and sentence under federal habeas corpus statutes. This time, however, the capital felon will start out in a federal district court. During this initial round of federal habeas corpus proceedings, the district court will stay execution of the death penalty. This stay can last a year.

Should the capital murderer not obtain relief in the federal district court, there will be an appeal to a federal court of appeals. This court will grant a stay that can last a year. If the court of appeals denies relief, the capital murderer will seek an appeal to the Supreme Court. If the

Supreme Court grants certiorari, a stay will be in place for usually up to a year.[61]

The Great Writ War. If the capital murderer fails to obtain federal habeas corpus relief from the Supreme Court, the great writ war begins. It is at this stage that a capital murderer has made all known legal reasons for vacating the conviction and sentence and has failed to obtain relief. To continue clinging to life, the capital murderer will begin filing tons of meritless petitions for writs of mandamus, coram nobis, prohibition, and habeas corpus, based on nothing more than an unwillingness to relinquish life. Statistics indicate that capital murderers are able to squeeze out years of life through judicial stays because of this great writ war.[62]

Consolidating Evidentiary and Constitutional Assignments of Error

The central reason for the unnecessary time gap between the imposition of the death sentence and the execution of the sentence is the separation of evidentiary issues from constitutional issues. Evidentiary issues are brought through the appellate process under direct appeal and death sentence review. Constitutional issues are brought through the appellate process by way of habeas corpus. To maximize the purpose and result of death sentence organ removal statutes, the separation of evidentiary and constitutional issues should be abolished .

It is imperative that a capital murderer be allowed to challenge the conviction and sentence on evidentiary grounds and on constitutional grounds. It is not, however, necessary for these issues to be brought in separate proceedings that occur years apart and that consume years in their own right. There is no constitutional requirement that death penalty evidentiary and constitutional issues be prosecuted separately in appellate courts. This is nothing more than a mere legal practice that has been written into the statutes. This practice must be written out of the statutes.

7

PRACTICAL CONSIDERATIONS

The final words of this book bring to the surface two important issues: the ownership rights to transplantable organs removed from capital felons; and the anonymity concerns of transplant patients and capital felons. Although these issues are merely touched on here, they will likely receive exhaustive legislative consideration.

Ownership of Body Parts

Transplantable organs taken from an executed capital murderer escheat to the jurisdiction that removed the organs under a death sentence organ removal statute. The jurisdiction's ownership rights to transplantable organs are, for a limited purpose, total and complete. Neither the executed capital murderer (through will or other conveyance) nor the relatives of the capital murderer have any ownership rights, in whole or in part, to the organs. Consequently, neither the executed capital felon nor the relatives have the authority to direct who ultimately obtains the organs through transplant.

The jurisdiction's ownership rights to transplantable organs removed from a capital felon under its execution laws are transitory. This is so because the jurisdiction's ownership is for a specific purpose: to preserve the transplantable organs in a healthy condition and make them available free of charge to needy transplant patients. The jurisdiction's ownership rights do not include the power or authority to do anything else with the organs. Of course, should healthy organs somehow become damaged after removal from an executed capital felon and thereby be nontransplantable, a jurisdiction would then have the authority to turn over such damaged organs for medical research.

Once an organ of a capital felon has been donated to and implanted in a transplant patient, the rights of the jurisdiction to the organ terminate. The transplant patient becomes the exclusive owner of the organ after implantation. This means that if the transplant patient should die shortly after receiving the organ, the jurisdiction has no authority to seek the return of the organ.

There is one optional exception to a jurisdiction's transitory rights in an executed capital felon's transplantable organs. A jurisdiction, through appropriate legislation, could require a transplant patient to return possession and ownership to the jurisdiction at the death of the patient—should the organ be healthy enough for recycling purposes.

Anonymity Issues

To spare transplant patients any stigmatism that may develop from transplantable organs of capital felons, jurisdictions are advised to institute measures that ensure anonymity of transplant patients who receive such organs. Of course, for practical reasons, total anonymity will not be possible. Specific medical professionals and institutions will be privy to the identity of the recipients of organs from capital felons. The physician-patient privilege, however, is sufficient to protect the medical privacy of transplant patients.

The hard issue of anonymity involves possibly revealing to a transplant patient the identity of the capital felon whose organ the patient received. This matter involves two decisions. First, should a transplant patient be told that the organ came from a capital felon? Second, if so, should the actual name and criminal history of the capital felon be revealed to the patient? The advisable course for jurisdictions to take on this issue is not to inform transplant patients that their organs came from capital felons. Of course, if a jurisdiction decides that it wants to have the freedom to retrieve organs from deceased patients for recycling purposes, it cannot preserve anonymity regarding the sources of organs.

Appendix: Model Death Sentence Organ Removal Statute

A. **Sentence.** Immediately on receipt by the court of a verdict of death for the defendant, the court shall

(1) sentence the defendant to anesthesia-induced brain death, and

(2) require removal of all healthy transplantable organs from the defendant on infliction of brain death.

B. **Method of Execution.** A defendant sentenced to death under this statute shall have death imposed as follows:

(1) a predetermined sufficient dosage of sodium pentothal, or other chemical substance rendering like results, shall be injected into the defendant;

(2) a predetermined quantity of anesthesia shall be administered to the defendant, resulting in immediate brain death; and

(3) immediately on infliction of brain death, the defendant's healthy transplantable organs shall be extracted from the corpse.

C. **Execution of Sentence.** (a) The execution of the defendant under this statute shall be carried out in two stages. The first stage will proceed as follows:

(1) The defendant shall be taken to the prison execution chamber, which shall have all necessary equipment, instruments, and the like for performing the method of execution required under this statute.

(2) Anesthesia-induced brain death shall be inflicted on the defendant by the method set out under this statute. In addition,

Appendix

    (i) brain death shall be inflicted only by a trained nonmedical professional, and

    (ii) brain death shall be determined and proclaimed to the witnesses present, by a physician attending the execution.

(3) Witnesses to the infliction of brain death shall be
- (i) an appropriate number of correctional officers,
- (ii) the commissioner of corrections,
- (iii) the attorney general for the state,
- (iv) the prison warden,
- (v) clergy member requested by the defendant,
- (vi) two members of the defendant's family requested by the defendant,
- (vii) two members of the victim's family chosen by the commissioner of corrections,
- (viii) two members of the general public chosen by the commissioner of corrections,
- (ix) five members of the media chosen by the commissioner of corrections
    - (aa) no visual cameras or audio recorders of any description shall be permitted in or near the execution chamber during any aspect of the execution under this statute
- (x) an appropriate number of physicians, chosen by the commissioner of corrections, to extract the defendant's healthy transplantable organs
    - (aa) each or any of said physicians shall be allowed to designate the attendance at the execution of any necessary medical professional assistant.

(b) The second stage of the execution under this statute shall be carried out as follows:

(1) Once the defendant's brain death has been proclaimed by a physician present, all witnesses, except the physicians and their designated assistants, shall immediately leave the execution chamber and shall not view in any manner the removal of the defendant's organs.

Model Death Sentence Organ Removal Statute

    (2) The physicians shall remove all healthy transplantable organs from the defendant,

    (3) The physicians shall reasonably suture all open wounds after all healthy transplantable organs have been removed from the corpse.

    (4) Under predetermined instructions from the commissioner of corrections, the physicians shall have all healthy transplantable organs transported to a medical facility for proper storage and disposition as outlined in other statutes.

  D. **Healthy Transplantable Organ Defined.** The phrase "healthy transplantable organ" shall mean

    (1) kidneys, liver, heart, lungs, pancreas, tendons, inner ear (hammers, anvils, and stirrups), bone marrow, corneas, eyes, glands, stomach, and blood vessels, and

    (2) those that will reasonably function after transplantation to another human body.

  E. **Disposal of Corpse.** After the defendant's healthy transplantable organs have been removed, and all open wounds caused therefrom reasonably sutured, the remains of the defendant's corpse shall be

    (1) turned over to a requesting spouse or relative,

    (2) turned over to a requesting friend, in the event no spouse or relative makes a request, or

    (3) disposed of in the manner provided by statute for the burial of paupers.

Chapter Notes

Chapter 1

1. *Louisville & Nashville Railroad Co. v. Wilson*, 123 Ga. 62 (1905).
2. *Beard v. Worrell*, 212 S.E.2d 598 (W.Va. 1974).
3. *Id.* at 601–2.
4. *Gilman v. Choi*, 406 S.E.2d 200, 213 (W.Va. 1990).
5. *Id.*
6. *Miranda v. Arizona*, 384 U.S. 436 (1966).
7. *Haynes' Case*, All E.R. Rep. 611 (1614).
8. *Id.* at 612.
9. Reported in 2 E. East, *A Treatise of the Pleas of the Crown* 652 (1803), *cited in* Roy Hardiman, *Toward the Right of Commerciality: Recognizing Property Rights in the Commercial Value of Human Tissue*, 34 UCLA L. Rev. 207, 225 n.92 (1986). Although East reported *Exelby* in 1803, the case actually occurred in 1749. *See* Paul Matthews, *Whose Body? People as Property*, 36 Current Legal Probs. 193, 209 (1983).
10. Hardiman, *supra* note 9.
11. *Williams v. Williams*, 20 Ch.D. 659 (1882).
12. *Id.* at 665.
13. *Id.*
14. *Id.*
15. *Louisville & Nashville Railroad Co. v. Wilson*, 123 Ga. 62 (1905), *reported in* 3 American & English Ann. Cases 128, 129 (1906).
16. *In re Beekman Street*, 4 Bradf. 503 (N.Y. 1857).
17. *Id.* at 519.
18. *Rex v. Lynn*, 100 E.R. 394 (1788).
19. *Id.*, *quoting* 3 Coke, *Institutes of the Laws of England* 203 (1671).
20. R. S. Guernsey, *The Ownership of a Corpse Before Burial*, 4 Redfield's Rep. 527, 532 (Appendix) (N.Y. 1881).
21. *Id.*
22. *Jones v. Ashburnham*, 4 East 460 (1804), *reported in* Guernsey, *supra* note 20, at 533.
23. *Id.*
24. *Regina v. Fox*, 114 E.R. 95 (1841).
25. *Regina v. Scott*, 114 E.R. 97 (1842).
26. *Id.*
27. *Rex v. Topham*, 4 Term. R. 127, *reported in* Guernsey, *supra* note 20, at 532.
28. *Regina v. Stewart*, 113 E.R. 1007 (1840).
29. *Id.* at 1009.
30. *Id.*
31. *Regina v. Vann*, 169 E.R. 523 (1851).
32. *Id.* at 523–24.
33. *Id.* at 525–26.
34. *Regina v. Price*, 12 Q.B.D. 247 (1884).
35. *Id.* at 253.
36. *Id.* at 255.
37. *Id.*, at 254–55. *But see Regina v. Stephenson*, 13 Q.B.D. 331 (1884) (upholding convictions for burning an infant corpse for the purpose of preventing an inquest into the cause of death).
38. *Ambrose v. Kerrison*, 138 E.R. 307 (1851).
39. Guernsey, *supra* note 20, at 529.
40. *Rex v. Lynn*, 100 E.R. 394 (1788).
41. *Id.* at 395.
42. *Id.*
43. *Regina v. Sharpe*, 169 E.R. 959 (1857).
44. Louis J. Palmer, Jr., *Capital Punishment: A Utilitarian Proposal for Recycling Transplantable Organs as Part of a Capital Felon's Death Sentence*, 29 U. West L.A. L. Rev. 1, 6 n.12 (1998), *quoting Regina v. Sharpe*, 169 E.R. 959 (1857).
45. *Regina v. Sharpe*, 169 E.R. 960 (1857).
46. *Regina v. Price*, 12 Q.B.D. 252 (1884).
47. *Gilbert v. Buzzard*, 161 E.R. 761 (1821).
48. *Id.* at 768.
49. *Regina v. Price*, 12 Q.B.D. 251 (1884).
50. *Id.* at 250–51.

Notes—Chapter 1

51. *Regina v. Feist*, 169 E.R. 1132 (1858).
52. *Id.* at 1135.
53. *Id.*
54. *Id.*
55. Guernsey, *supra* note 20, at 535.
56. *Rex v. Cundick*, 171 E.R. 900 (1822).
57. *Id.*
58. Jesse Root, 1 Conn. Rpts. iii (1798).
59. *Larson v. Chase*, 50 N.W. 238 (Minn. 1891).
60. *Griffith v. Charlotte, Columbia & Augusta R'd Co*, 55 Am. Rep. 1 (S.C. 1884).
61. Id. at 2–5.
62. Id. at 5–6.
63. *Long v. Chicago, Rock Island & Pac. R'y Co.*, 86 P. 289 (Okla. 1906).
64. *Id.*
65. *Id.* at 292.
66. *Id.* (internal quotations omitted).
67. *Meagher v. Driscoll*, 99 Mass. 281 (1868).
68. *Secord v. Secord*, 18 Abb. N.C. 78 (N.Y. 1870).
69. *State v. Wilson*, 94 N.C. 1015 (1886).
70. *Peters v. Peters*, 10 A. 742 (1887).
71. *Hackett v. Hackett*, 26 A. 42 (R.I. 1893).
72. *Thompson v. Deeds*, 61 N.W. 842 (Iowa 1895).
73. *Choppin v. Labranche*, 20 So. 681 (La. 1896).
74. *Keyes v. Konkel*, 78 N.W. 649 (Mich. 1899).
75. *Id.*
76. *Id.*
77. *Enos v. Snyder*, 63 P. 170 (Cal. 1900).
78. *Id.* at 171.
79. *Hockenhammer v. Lexington & Eastern R'y Co*, 74 S.W. 222 (Ky. 1903).
80. *Id.* at 223.
81. *Pierce v. Proprietors of Swan Point Cemetery*, 14 Am. Rep. 667 (R.I. 1872).
82. *Id.* at 676–77.
83. *In re Beekman Street*, 4 Bradf. 503 (N.Y. 1857).
84. *Id.* at 521.
85. *Id.* at 516–17.
86. *Id.* at 532.
87. *Bessemer Land & Improvement v. Jenkins*, 18 So. 565 (Ala. 1895).
88. *Jacobus v. Congregation of Children of Israel*, 33 S.E. 853 (Ga. 1899).
89. *Bessemer Land & Improvement v. Jenkins*, 18 So. 565 (Ala. 1895).
90. *Jacobus v. Congregation of Children of Israel*, 33 S.E. 853 (Ga. 1899).
91. *Kyles v. Southern Railway Co*, 61 S.E. 278 (N.C. 1908).
92. *Id.* at 279.
93. *Id.* at 281.
94. *Id.*, at 280. See *Ginsberg v. Manchester Memorial Hosp.*, 2010 WL 796841, 3 Conn. Super. 2010) ("Any interference with the legal right to the possession of a corpse for the purposes of preservation and burial, by mutilating or otherwise disturbing the body is an actionable wrong.").
95. *Foley v. Phelps*, 37 N.Y.S. 471 (1896).
96. *Id.*
97. *Id.*
98. *Id.* at 473–74. See *Boorman v. Nevada Mem'l Cremation Society*, 236 P.3d 4, 9 (Nev. 2010) ("A county coroner has a narrow limited duty to account for a deceased person's remains and may be held liable for emotional distress to the person with the right to dispose of the deceased's body for negligently handling a deceased person's remains.").
99. *Larson v. Chase*, 50 N.W. 238 (Minn. 1891).
100. *Id.*
101. *Id.* See *Benson v. Superior Court*, 111 Cal.Rptr.3d 27, 28 (Cal.App. 2010) ("A county coroner conducting an inquiry into cause of death has no duty to obtain consent from next of kin before retaining a part of the decedent's body to determine cause of death, or for scientific investigation or coroner training.").
102. *Koerber v. Patek*, 102 N.W. 40 (Wis. 1905).
103. *Id.* at 41.
104. *Id.*
105. *Id.* at 42–45. See *In re Human Tissue Litigation*, 955 N.Y.S.2d 721 (2012) (relatives of decedents whose bodies were cut open to remove tissue, organs, and bones without the consent of the decedents before their death or the consent of their next kin after death, brought action against tissue processors that redistributed the tissue, organs, and bones for use in the healthcare industry).
106. *Renihan v. Wright*, 25 N.E. 822 (Ind. 1890).
107. *Id.* at 823.
108. *Id.*
109. *Id.* at 824.
110. *Id.* See *Drakeford v. University of Chicago Hospitals*, 2013 WL 3296586, 3 Ill.App. 2013)("To state a cause of action based on the right of the next of kin to possession and preservation of the body of a decedent, plaintiffs must demonstrate by specific facts that defendant's conduct was wilful and wanton.").

Notes—Chapter 1

111. Palmer, *supra* note 44, at 12.
112. *Scott v. Riley*, 16 Phila. 106 (Pa. 1883). See *Seals v. H & F, Inc.*, 301 S.W.3d 237, 242 (Tenn. 2010) ("[W]e have determined that the decedent, as a general rule, has the primary entitlement to expressly elect the method of disposal of his or her body, or, in the alternative, to designate an individual to elect the method of disposal; if the decedent does not do so, however, the legal right to direct the disposal of remains descends to the following parties, in order of priority: (1) the spouse of the decedent; (2) adult children of the decedent; (3) parents of the decedent; (4) adult siblings of the decedent; (5) adult grandchildren of the decedent; (6) grandparents of the decedent; and (7) an adult who has exhibited special care and concern for the decedent.").
113. *Bogert v. City of Indianapolis*, 13 Ind. 134 (1859). See *Melfi v. Mount Sinai Hosp.*, 877 N.Y.S.2d 300, 304 (2009) ("It is well established that the common-law right of sepulcher gives the next of kin the absolute right to the immediate possession of a decedent's body for preservation and burial, and that damages will be awarded against any person who unlawfully interferes with that right or improperly deals with the decedent's body.").
114. *Garvey v. McCue*, 3 Redf. Sur. 313 (N.Y. 1877). See *Arkansas Bd. of Embalmers and Funeral Directors v. Reddick*, 233 S.W.3d 639, 644 (Ark. 2006) ("A quasi-property right in dead bodies vests in the nearest relatives of the deceased, arising out of their duty to bury their dead.").
115. *Fox v. Gordon*, 11 Wkly. Notes Cas. 302 (Pa. 1882). See *Marino v. Marino*, 981 A.2d 855 (N.J. 2009) (holding that widow did not have a right to disinter her husband's body for reburial in a place different from that chosen by executors of decedent's estate).
116. *State v. Little*, 1 Vt. 331 (1828); *Commonwealth v. Loring*, 25 Mass. 370 (1829); *Tate v. State*, 6 Blackf. 110 (Ind. 1837); *People v. Dalton*, 58 Cal. 226 (1881).
117. *Georgia Lions Eye Bank, Inc. v. Lavant*, 335 S.E.2d 127 (Ga. 1985).
118. *In re Moyer*, 577 P.2d 108 (Utah 1978).
119. *People v. Fitzgerald*, 43 Hun. 35 (N.Y. 1887).
120. *Weld v. Walker*, 130 Mass. 422 (1881).
121. *Hale v. Bonner*, 17 S.W. 605 (Tex. 1891).
122. *Lindh v. Great Northern R'y Co.*, 109 N.W. 823 (Minn. 1906).
123. *Bennett v. 3C Coal Co.*, 379 S.E.2d 388 (W.Va. 1989).
124. *Crocker v. Pleasant*, 778 So.2d 978 (Fla. 2001).
125. Section 1983 provides in pertinent part: "Every person who, under color of any statute, ordinance, regulation, custom, or usage of any State or Territory or the District of Columbia, subjects, or causes to be subjected, any citizen of the United States or other person within the jurisdiction thereof to the deprivation of any rights, privileges, or immunities secured by the Constitution and laws, shall be liable to the party injured in an action at law, suit in equity, or other proper proceeding for redress."
126. *Crocker v. Pleasant*, 778 So.2d 978, 982–988 (Fla. 2001). See *Taylor v. Jersey City Medical Center*, 2005 WL 3501877 N.J.Super. 2005) (mother sued hospital for failing to inform her that her daughter died).
127. *Akers v. Prime Succession of Tennessee, Inc.*, 387 S.W.3d 495 (Tenn. 2012).
128. *Id.* at 499.
129. *Id.* at 509–511. A class-action lawsuit that arose out of the crematorium's conduct was filed in a Georgia federal district court. See *In re Tri-State Crematory Litigation*, 215 F.R.D. 660 (N.D.Ga. 2003).
130. *Evanston Ins. Co. v. Legacy of Life, Inc.*, 370 S.W.3d 377 (Tex. 2012).
131. *Id.* at 385–387.
132. *Board of Regents v. Oglesby*, 591 S.E.2d 417 (Ga.App. 2003).
133. *Id.* at 419–420.
134. *Id.* 420–421.
135. The Court of Appeals relied on additional reasons for ordering the case dismissed.
136. *Board of Regents v. Oglesby*, 591 S.E.2d 417, 421–422 (Ga.App. 2003). The decision in *Oglesby* concluded with the following observations: "We note that any concern about the continued display of [Bessie's] remains should have been resolved by [the Medical College's] unconditional offer to return the remains to [Francis]. The offer stated its intention to begin the process of returning the remains to [Francis], stated [the Medical College's] intention to procure a casket for the remains, asked [Francis] to state her preferences regarding the casket, and asked her to identify the funeral home to which the casket should be transported for burial. Although [Francis] then declined the offer because she wished to display the remains to a jury, in

Notes—Chapter 2

view of our disposition of this case, she may wish to reconsider that decision, and we anticipate that [the Medical College] would honor its earlier unconditional offer." *Oglesby*, 591 S.E.2d at 423.

137. *Colavito v. New York Organ Donor Network, Inc.*, 356 F.Supp.2d 237 (E.D.N.Y. 2005).

138. *Id.* at 241–244.

139. *Mazur v. Woodson*, 191 F.Supp.2d 676 (E.D.Va. 2002).

140. The lawsuit also named other defendants.

141. *Mazur v. Woodson*, 191 F.Supp.2d 676, 679–682 (E.D.Va. 2002).

142. *Benson v. Superior Court*, 111 Cal. Rptr.3d 27 (Cal.App. 2010).

143. *Id.* at 28.

144. *Albrecht v. Treon*, 889 N.E.2d 120 (Ohio 2008).

145. *Id.* at 120.

146. *Crawford v. J. Avery Bryan Funeral Home, Inc.*, 253 S.W.3d 149 (Tenn.Ct.App. 2007).

147. The wife had settled the case against the defendants in a previously filed class action. See *In re Tri-State Crematory Litigation*, 215 F.R.D. 660 (N.D.Ga. 2003).

148. *Crawford v. J. Avery Bryan Funeral Home, Inc.*, 253 S.W.3d 149, 156–160 (Tenn. Ct.App. 2007). The court in *Crawford* was careful to note that it was "not holding that someone who does not have control over disposition of a decedent's body never can bring a tort claim for emotional distress and the like. For example, if the body was mutilated in the presence of a family member, then our holding in this case would not prevent that family member from filing a lawsuit, even if that family member did not have control over the body's disposition." *Id.* at 160.

149. *Akers v. Buckner-Rush Enterprises, Inc.*, 270 S.W.3d 67 (Tenn.Ct.App. 2007).

150. *Id.* at 73.

151. *Walker v. Firelands Community Hosp.*, 869 N.E.2d 66 (Ohio App. 2007).

152. *Id.* at 69.

153. Id. at 71–76.

154. *Janicki v. Hospital of St. Raphael*, 744 A.2d 963 (Conn.Super. 1999).

155. *Id.* at 964–974. See *Emeagwali v. Brooklyn Hosp. Center*, 2006 WL 435813, 5 (N.Y.Sup. 2006) ([T]hough a stillborn fetus does not have survivors in the same legal sense that a once living human has survivors, the mother nonetheless retains a quasi-property right in the body because fetuses, stillborn or not, have symbolic importance vastly different from that of ordinary tissue due to the physical presence mothers feel in their body and the hopes and dreams she had for its future.").

Chapter 2

1. Laura-Hill M. Patton, *A Call for Common Sense: Organ Donation and the Executed Prisoner*, 3 Va. J. Soc. Pol'y & L. 387, 389 (1996). Another commentary indicated that a healthy corpse could provide the following transplantable parts: 2 corneas; 2 inner ear hammers, anvils, and stirrups; 1 jaw bone; 1 heart; 1 heart pericardium; 4 heart valves; 2 lungs; 1 liver; 2 kidneys; 1 pancreas; 1 stomach; 206 separate bones; 2 hip joints; 27 ligaments and cartilages; 20 square feet of skin; 60,000 miles of blood vessels; and 90 ounces of bone marrow. Danielle M. Wagner, *Property Rights in the Human Body: The Commercialization of Organ Transplantation and Biotechnology*, 33 Duq. L. Rev. 931, 943 n.109 (1995). See David Hamilton, *A History of Organ Transplantation: Ancient Legends to Modern Practice* (University of Pittsburgh Press, 2012).

2. Louis J. Palmer, Jr., *Capital Punishment: A Utilitarian Proposal for Recycling Transplantable Organs as Part of a Capital Felon's Death Sentence*, 29 U. West L.A. L. Rev. 1, 14 (1998).

3. Joel D. Kallich and Jon F. Merz, *The Transplant Imperative: Protecting Living Donors from the Pressure to Donate*, 20 J. Corp. L. 139–40 (1994). On June 17, 1950, at the Little Company of Mary Hospital in Evergreen Park, Illinois, Dr. James W. West, Dr. Richard H. Lawler, and Dr. Raymond P. Murphy performed the first kidney transplant. The organ was transplanted in a 44-year-old woman named Ruth Tucker, who suffered from polycystic kidney disease. The kidney was taken from a cadaver. The transplanted kidney only functioned for about six weeks, which was enough time for Ms. Tucker's other kidney to begin working again. She was able to live another five years. Michelle Martin, *Making and Remembering Transplant History*, http://www.catholicnewworld.com/cnw/issue/2004/transplant_092604.html. See William Yardley, *Dr. James West, a Pioneer in Addiction Study and Care, Dies at 98* (2012). http://www.nytimes.com/2012/08/09/health/dr-

Notes—Chapter 2

james-west-pioneer-in-addiction-treatment-dies-at-98.html?_r=0.

4. Kallich and Merz, supra note 3, at 140.

5. *Id.*

6. Sheldon F. Kurtz and Michael J. Saks, *The Transplant Paradox: Overwhelming Public Support for Organ Donation vs. Under-Supply of Organs: The Iowa Organ Procurement Study*, 21 J. Corp. L. 767, 771 (1996).

7. *Id.* at 771 n.9.

8. Palmer, *supra* note 2, at 14 n.52.

9. Patton, *supra* note 1, at 390.

10. Andrew C. MacDonald, *Organ Donation: The Time Has Come to Refocus the Ethical Spotlight*, 8 Stan. L. & Pol'y Rev. 177, 179 (1997).

11. Monique C. Gorsline and Rachelle L. K. Johnson, *The United States System of Organ Donation, the International Solution, and the Cadaveric Organ Act: "And the Winner Is...,"* 20 J. Corp. L. 5, 6 (1994). In 1995 the FDA approved two new rejection factor drugs for use in transplant recipients. These are: CellCept (mycophenolate mofetil), and Neoral, a new formulation of cyclosporine. In 1999 the FDA approved Rapamune (sirolimus), a new rejection factor drug used to prevent rejection in patients receiving kidney transplants.

12. Palmer, *supra* note 2, at 14.

13. *Based on OPTN data (2013)*, United States Department of Health and Human Services. See also, Gregory S. Crespi, *Overcoming the Legal Obstacles to the Creation of Futures Market in Bodily Organs*, 55 Ohio S.L.J. 1, 8 n.27 (1994).

14. *Based on OPTN Data (2013)*, United States Department of Health and Human Services. See also, Fred H. Cate, *Human Organ Transplantation: The Role of Law*, 20 J. Corp. L. 69 (1994).

15. Melissa Wong, *Coverage for Kidneys: The Intersection of Insurance and Organ Transplantation*, 16 Conn. Ins. L.J. 535, 535 (2010).

16. Jennifer M. Smith, *Dirty Pretty Things and the Law: Curing the Organ Shortage & Health Care Crises in America*, 12 Chap. L. Rev. 361, 373 (2008).

17. Yosuke Shimazono, *The State of the International Organ Trade: A Provisional Picture based on Integration of Available Information*, 85 Bull. W.H.O. 955 (2007). This black market has been colorfully described as "a new international network of body Mafia ranging from the sleazy (and sometimes armed and dangerous) underworld 'kidney hunters' of Istanbul and Cesenau, Moldova to the sophisticated but clandestine 'medical tourism' bureaux of Tel Aviv and Manila to the medical intermediaries posing as religious or charitable trusts and 'patient's advocacy organizations' found in downtown Philadelphia, Brooklyn, and Chinatown, New York City." Nancy Scheper-Hughes, *Rotten Trade: Millennial Capitalism, Human Values and Global Justice in Organs Trafficking*, 2 J. Hum. Rights. 197, 214 (2003).

18. Yosuke Shimazono, *The State of the International Organ Trade: A Provisional Picture based on Integration of Available Information*, 85 Bull. W.H.O. 955, 956–957(2007). One commentator has described an irony caused by medical science in unlocking the secrets of organ transplantation as follows: "The irony lies in the fact that the most altruistic of endeavors, the regifting of life by generous donors and skilled surgeons can simultaneously be perverted into the most hideous form of crime where the poor are inveigled into parting with organs, usually kidneys, that are then sold at huge profits to those who can afford to buy themselves a new life. Worst of all is the alleged kidnapping and execution of people, who are then utilized for the harvesting of their organs." Ranee Khooshie Lal Panjabi, *The Sum of a Human's Parts: Global Organ Trafficking in the Twenty-First Century*, 28 Pace Envtl. L. Rev. 1, 8 (2010).

19. *China: Organ Transplant Program Will Phase Out Executed Inmates*, http://www.nytimes.com/2013/08/16/world/asia/china-organ-transplant-program-will-phase-out-executed-inmates.html?_r=0. See G. P. Westall, P. Komesaroff, M. W. Gorton, and G. I. Snell, *Ethics of Organ Donation and Transplantation Involving Prisoners: The Debate Extends Beyond Our Borders*, 38 Int. Med. J. 56 (2008).

20. For a good discussion of the international black market in human body parts, see Emily Kelley, *International Organ Trafficking Crisis: Solutions Addressing the Heart of the Matter*, 36 B.C. Int'l & Comp. L. Rev. 1317 (2013); Jason Altman, *Organ Transplantations: The Need for an International Open Organ Market*, 5 Touro Int'l L. Rev. 161 (1994).

21. *U.S. Government Information on Organ and Tissue Donation and Transplantation*, United States Department of Health & Human Services. http://organdonor.gov/about/data.html.

Notes—Chapter 2

22. *Id.*
23. *Based on OPTN data 2013, United States Department of Health and Human Services.*
24. John Sten, *Rethinking the National Organ Transplant Program: When Push Comes to Shove,* 11 J. Contemp. Health L. & Pol'y 197 (1994).
25. Theodore Silver, *The Case for a Post-Mortem Organ Draft and a Proposed Model Organ Draft Act,* 68 B.U.L. Rev. 681 (1988).
26. Palmer, *supra* note 2, at 17. Commentators have noted that with the exception of a few countries, trafficking in the sale of human organs is illegal across the globe. See I. Glenn Cohen, *Transplant Tourism: The Ethics and Regulation of International Markets for Organs,* 41 J.L. Med. & Ethics 269, 269 (2013).
27. National Organ Transplant Act, Pub. L. No. 98-507, 98 Stat. 2339 (1984) (codified as amended at 42 U.S.C. §§ 273-274 [1988]).
28. See 42 U.S.C.A. § 274 (1988).
29. *See Developments in the Law: Medical Technology and the Law,* 103 Harv. L. Rev. 1519, 1622-25 (1990). *See also* Note, *Antitrust Problems and Solutions to Meet the Demand for Transplantable Organs,* 1991 U. Ill. L. Rev. (1991); Note, *Regulating the Sale of Human Organs,* 71 Va. L. Rev. 1015 (1985); Note, *The Sale of Human Body Parts,* 72 Mich. L. Rev. 1182 (1974).
30. Palmer, *supra* note 2 at, 18. *See also* Roger D. Blair and David L. Kaserman, *The Economics and Ethics of Alternative Cadaveric Organ Procurement Policies,* 8 Yale J. on Reg. 403, 415-17 (1991). For a discussion about the black market in children's organs, see Maria N. Morelli, *Organ Trafficking: Legislative Proposals to Protect Minors,* 10 Am. U. J. Int'l L. & Pol'y 917 (1995); Gloria J. Banks, *Legal and Ethical Safeguards: Protection of Society's Most Vulnerable Participants in a Commercialized Organ Transplantation System,* 21 Am. J. L. & Med. 45, 72-75 (1995).
31. Crespi, *supra* note 13, at 15.
32. *Flynn v. Holder,* 684 F.3d 852 (9th Cir. 2012).
33. *Flynn,* 684 F.3d at 860-861. See Mary G. Vitale, *National Organ Transplant Act's Ban on Bone Marrow Donation Compensation: Legal Compensation to Create Life, but Not to Save a Life,* 85 St. John's L. Rev. 1221 (2011).
34. See Tracy Connor, *Brooklyn Black-Market Kidney Broker Pleads Guilty to Selling Israeli Organs to Desperate Americans,* http://www.nydailynews.com/news/crime/brooklyn-black-market-kidney-broker-pleads-guilty-selling-israeli-organs-desperate-americans-article-1.968040.
35. See Bridget J. Crawford, *Our Bodies, Our Selves,* 31 Va. Tax Rev. 695, 701-702 (2012).
36. Drew Griffin and David Fitzpatrick, *Donor Says He Got Thousands for His Kidney,* http://edition.cnn.com/2009/WORLD/meast/09/01/blackmarket.organs/.
37. *Commonwealth v. Garzone,* 993 A.2d 306 (Pa.Super. 2010).
38. See *Commonwealth v. Garzone,* 993 A.2d 1245 (Pa.Super. 2010) (the criminal case against Louis Garzone).
39. See *Commonwealth v. Mastromarino,* 2 A.3d 581 (Pa.Super. 2010) (criminal case against Mastromarino).
40. *Commonwealth v. Garzone,* 993 A.2d 306, 308-309 (Pa.Super. 2010).
41. *Specialty Nat. Ins. Co. v. English Bros. Funeral Home,* 606 F.Supp.2d 466 (S.D.N.Y. 2009).
42. *Specialty Nat. Ins.,* 606 F.Supp.2d at 469.
43. *See* Raymond Cotton and Andrew Sadler, *The Regulation of Organ Procurement and Transplantation in the United States,* 7 J. Legal Med. 55 (1986).
44. UAGA of 1968, 8A U.L.A. 63 (1993) (superseded by UAGA of 1987).
45. UAGA of 1987, 8A U.L.A. 29 (1993). For a discussion of the 1987 version of UAGA, see Ann McIntosh, *Regulating the "Gift of Life"—The 1987 Uniform Anatomical Gift Act,* 65 Wash. L. Rev. 171 (1990).
46. See Ala. Code § 22-19-160 et seq.; Alaska Stat. § 13.50.100 et seq. and § 13.52.173 et seq.; Ariz. Rev. Stat. Ann. § 36-841 et seq.; Ark. Code Ann. § 20-17-1201 et seq.; Cal. Health & Safety Code § 7150 et seq.; Colo. Rev. Stat. § 12-34-101 et seq.; Conn. Gen. Stat. Ann. § 19a-270 et seq.; Del. Code Ann. tit. 16, § 2710 et seq.; D.C. Code Ann. § 7-1501.01 et seq. and § 7-1531.01 et seq.; Fla. Stat. Ann. § 765.510 et seq.; Ga. Code Ann. § 44-5-140 et seq.; Hawaii Rev. Stat. § 327-1 et seq.; Idaho Code § 39-3401 et seq. (1993); Ill. Comp. Stat. Ann. ch. 755, § 50/1-1 et seq.; Ind. Code § 29-2-16.1-1 et seq.; Iowa Code § 142C.1 et seq.; Kan. Stat. Ann. § 65-3220 et seq.; Ky. Rev. Stat. Ann. § 311.1911 et seq.; La. Rev. Stat. Ann. § 17:2351 et seq.; Me. Rev. Stat. Ann. tit. 22, § 2941 et seq.; Md. Code Ann. Est. & Trusts §

Notes—Chapter 2

4-501; Mass. Gen. L. ch. 113A, § 1 et seq.; Mich. Comp. Laws Ann. § 333.10101 et seq.; Minn. Stat. § 525A.01 et seq.; Miss. Code Ann. § 41-39-101 et seq.; Mo. Rev. Stat. § 194.210 et seq.; Mont. Code Ann. § 72-17-101 et seq.; Neb. Rev. Stat. § 71-4824 et seq.; Nev. Rev. Stat. § 451.500 et seq.; N.H. Rev. Stat. Ann. § 291-A:1 et seq.; N.J. Stat. Ann. § 26:6-77 et seq.; N.M. Stat. Ann. § 24-6B-1 et seq.; N.Y. Pub. Health Law § 4300 et seq.; N.C. Gen. Stat. § 130A-412.3 et seq.; N.D. Cent. Code § 23-06.6-01 et seq.; Ohio Rev. Code Ann. § 2108.01 et seq.; Okla. Stat. Ann. tit. 63, § 2200.1A et seq.; Or. Rev. Stat. § 97.951; Pa. Stat. Ann. tit. 20, § 8601 et seq.; R.I. Gen Laws § 23-18.6.1-1 et seq.; S.C. Code Ann. § 44-43-300 et seq.; S.D. Codified Laws Ann. § 34-26-49 et seq.; Tenn. Code Ann. § 68-30-101 et seq.; Tex. Health & Safety Code Ann. § 692A.001 et seq.; Utah Code Ann. § 26-28-101 et seq.; Vt. Stat. Ann. tit. 18, § 5250a et seq.; Va. Code Ann. § 32.1-291.1 et seq.; Wash. Rev. Code § 68.64.010 et seq.; W.Va. Code § 16-19-1 et seq.; Wis. Stat. § 157.06; Wyo. Stat. Ann. § 35-5-201 et seq.

47. Sara Naomi Rodriguez, *No Means No, but Silence Means Yes? The Policy and Constitutionality of the Recent State Proposals for Opt-Out Organ Donation Laws*, 7 FIU L. Rev. 149, 154–155 (2011).

48. The material in this part is taken, with express permission of the author, from Palmer, *supra* note 2, at 21–24.

49. For a discussion of other market-like proposals, see James F. Blumstein, *The Use of Financial Incentives in Medical Care: The Case of Commerce in Transplantable Organs*, 3 Health Matrix 1 (1993); David E. Chapman, *Retaining Human Organs Under the Uniform Commercial Code*, 16 J. Marshall L. Rev. 393 (1983); December. T. Freier, *Organ Selling for Transplantation*, 38 Prog. Clin. & Biol. Res. 141 (1980); Marvin Brams, *Transplantable Human Organs: Should Their Sale Be Authorized by State Statutes?* 3 Am. J.L. & Med. 183 (1977).

50. *See* Richard Schwindt and Aidan R. Vining, *Proposal for a Future Delivery Market for Transplant Organs*, 11 J. Health Pol., Pol'y & L. 483 (1986).

51. *See* Henry Hansmann, *The Economics and Ethics of Markets for Human Organs*, 14 J. Health Pol., Pol'y & L. 57 (1989).

52. *See* Lloyd Cohen, *Increasing the Supply of Transplant Organs: The Virtues of a Futures Market*, 58 Geo. Wash. L. Rev. 1 (1989).

53. *See* Crespi, *supra* note 13.

54. See Jonathan G. August, *Modern Models of Organ Donation: Challenging Increases of Federal Power to Save Lives*, 40 Hastings Const. L.Q. 393 (2013); Amber Rithalia, et al., *Impact of Presumed Consent for Organ Donation on Donation Rates: A Systematic Review*, BMJ (2009).

55. See Michael B. Gill, *Presumed Consent, Autonomy, and Organ Donation*, 29 J. Med. & Phy. 37 (2004).

56. *Presumed Consent Organ Donation: Why the Authorities Find It Easier to Nudge Us Toward Their Policies*, http://www.wales online.co.uk/news/health/presumed-consent-organ-donation-authorities-6066895.

57. Alberto Abadie and Sebastien Gay, *The Impact of Presumed Consent Legislation on Cadaveric Organ Donation: A Cross Country Study*, 25 J. Health Eco. 599 (2006).

58. See Arthur Caplan, *Organ Transplantation* http://www.thehastingscenter.org/Pub lications/BriefingBook/Detail.aspx?id=2198.

59. See Sara Naomi Rodriguez, *No Means No, but Silence Means Yes? The Policy and Constitutionality of the Recent State Proposals for Opt-Out Organ Donation Laws*, 7 FIU L. Rev. 149 (2011).

60. Thomas S. Ulen, *A Behavioral View of Investor Protection*, 44 Loy. U. Chi. L.J. 1357, 1363–1364 (2013).

61. Fred H. Cate, *Human Organ Transplantation: The Role of Law*, 20 J. Corp. L. 69, 84 (1995). See Alexander Powhida, *Forced Organ Donation: The Presumed Consent to Organ Donation Laws of the Various States and the United States Constitution*, 9 Alb. L.J. Sci. & Tech. 349 (1999).

62. *Tillman v. Detroit Receiving Hosp.*, 360 N.W.2d 275 (Mich.App. 1984).

63. *Tillman*, 360 N.W.2d at 277–279.

64. *State v. Powell*, 497 So.2d 1188 (Fla. 1986).

65. *Powell*, 497 So.2d at 1190—1191.

66. Aron Heller, *In Israel, a Radical Way to Boost Organ Supply*, http://www.nbcnews. com/id/35842049/ns/health-health_care/t/ israel-radical-way-boost-organ-supply/.

67. Kiran Sheffrin, *Establishing an International Organ Exchange Through the General Agreement on Trade in Services*, 38 Brook. J. Int'l L. 829, 838 (2013).

68. See Jonathan G. August, *Modern Models of Organ Donation: Challenging Increases of Federal Power to Save Lives*, 40 Hastings Const. L.Q. 393, 411–412 (2013);

Danielle Ofri, *In Israel, a New Approach to Organ Donation*, http://well.blogs.nytimes.com/2012/02/16/in-israel-a-new-approach-to-organ-donation/?_r=0.

69. See Judd Kessler and Al Roth, *Deceased Organ Donation and Allocation: 3 Experiments in Market Design*, http://www.stanford.edu/~niederle/Deceased%20Organ%20Donation%20Experiments.Kessler%20Roth.pdf; Muireann Quigley, Linda Wright, and Vardit Ravitsky, *Organ Donation and Priority Points in Israel: An Ethical Analysis*, http://www.academia.edu/1540311/Organ_Donation_and_Priority_Points_in_Israel_An_Ethical_Analysis-Transplantation-2012.

70. Dan Even, *Family Consent for Organ Donations in Israel Declines After Surprise Spike in 2011*, http://www.haaretz.com/news/national/family-consent-for-organ-donations-in-israel-declines-after-surprise-spike-in-2011.premium-1.501941.

71. See Haley Cotter, *Increasing Consent for Organ Donation: Mandated Choice, Individual Autonomy, and Informed Consent*, 21 Health Matrix 599 (2011); *Presumed Consent and Mandated Choice for Organs from Deceased Donors*, http://www.ama-assn.org/ama/pub/physician-resources/medical-ethics/code-medical-ethics/opinion2155.page.

72. Texas and Virginia had milder forms of mandated choice statutes. See Jonathan G. August, *Modern Models of Organ Donation: Challenging Increases of Federal Power to Save Lives*, 40 Hastings Const. L.Q. 393, 402–403 (2013).

Chapter 3

1. See generally Louis J. Palmer, Jr., *The Death Penalty in the United States: A Complete Guide to Federal and State Laws* (McFarland, 2013).

2. Mass. Gen. L. ch. 113, § 6 (1996). The statute is now repealed.

3. R. S. Guernsey, *The Ownership of a Corpse Before Burial*, 4 Redfield's Rep. 527, 536 (Appendix) (N.Y. 1881).

4. See 18 U.S.C.A. § 3567 (1985) (repealed as of November 1, 1986, Pub. L. No. 98-473, § 212(a)(2), 98 Stat. 1987 (1984)). For a discussion of the dissection-enhanced statutes, see Louis J. Palmer, Jr., *Capital Punishment: A Utilitarian Proposal for Recycling Transplantable Organs as Part of a Capital Felon's Death Sentence*, 29 U. West L.A. L. Rev. 1, 39–40 (1998).

5. The material in this part is taken, with express permission of the author, from *id.* at 35–36.

6. Ala. Code § 15-18-85(a); Ga. Code Ann. § 17-10-43; Ky. Rev. Stat. Ann. § 431.270; Miss. Code Ann. § 99-19-55(4); N.C. Gen. Stat. § 15-196; Ohio Rev. Code Ann. § 2949.26; Pa. Stat. Ann. tit. 61, § 4307; S.C. Code Ann. § 24-3-570 (1989); S.D. Codified Laws Ann. § 23A-27A-39; Tex. Criminal Procedure Code Ann. § 43.25; Va. Code Ann. § 53.1-236; Wyo. Stat. Ann. § 7-13-915 .

7. Ala. Code § 15-18-85(b); Ga. Code Ann. § 17-10-43; Ky. Rev. Stat. Ann. § 431.270; Ohio Rev. Code Ann. § 2949.26; S.C. Code Ann. § 24-3-570 .

8. Ala. Code § 15-18-85(a); Ga. Code Ann. § 17-10-43; Ky. Rev. Stat. Ann. § 431.270; Miss. Code Ann. § 99-19-55(4); N.C. Gen. Stat. § 15-196; Ohio Rev. Code Ann. § 2949.26; Tex. Criminal Procedure Code Ann. § 43.25; Wyo. Stat. Ann. § 7-13-915 .

9. Ala. Code § 15-18-85(a) .

10. Miss. Code Ann. § 99-19-55(4); Tex. Criminal Procedure Code Ann. § 43.20 .

11. Fla. Stat. Ann. § 922.11(3) .

12. Ala. Code § 15-18-85(a); Ga. Code Ann. § 17-10-43 *(1990)*; Ky. Rev. Stat. Ann. § 431.270; Miss. Code Ann. § 99-19-55(4); N.C. Gen. Stat. § 15-196; Ohio Rev. Code Ann. § 2949.26; Pa. Stat. Ann. tit. 61, § 4307; S.C. Code Ann. § 24-3-570; S.D. Codified Laws Ann. § 23A-27A-39; Tex. Criminal Procedure Code Ann. § 43.25; Wyo. Stat. Ann. § 7-13-915 .

13. *Furman v. Georgia*, 408 U.S. 238 (1972).

14. *Id.* at 241–57.

15. *Gregg v. Georgia*, 428 U.S. 153 (1976).

16. Id. at 162–207.

17. *See generally* Palmer, *supra* note 1, at 10–28 .

18. *See* Palmer, *supra* note 4, at 41.

19. For a general discussion of the need to educate the public about organ transplantation, see Lisa E. Douglass, *Organ Donation, Procurement, and Transplantation: The Process, the Problems, the Law*, 65 UMKC L. Rev. 201 (1996); Melissa N. Kurnit, *Organ Donation in the United States: Can We Learn from Successes Abroad?* 17 B.C. Int'l & Comp. L. Rev. 405 (1994).

20. *Reprinted in* Ian C. Pilarczyk, *Organ Donor Trusts and Durable Powers of Attorney for Organ Donation: New Twists on the Living Trust and Living Will*, 13 Prob. L.J. 29, 37 (1995).

21. For a general discussion of principles of justification for capital punishment, see Jonathan S. Abernethy, *The Methodology of Death: Reexamining the Deterrence Rationale*, 27 Colum. Hum. Rts. L. Rev. 379 (1996); James R. Acker, *When the Cheering Stopped: An Overview and Analysis of New York's Death Penalty Legislation*, 17 Pace L. Rev. 41 (1996); Brian P. Hill, *Judicial Response to Changing Societal Values on the Death Penalty: Must the Method Chosen Be the Most Humane?* 7 St. Thomas L. Rev. 409 (1995).
22. *See* Palmer, *supra* note 4, at 4.
23. *Commonwealth v. Edmiston*, 634 A. 2d 1078 (Pa. 1993).
24. *Id.*
25. *Maynard v. Cartwright*, 486 U.S. 356 (1988).
26. *Id.*
27. *See* Palmer, *supra* note 4, at 38.
28. *Blystone v. Pennsylvania*, 494 U.S. 299 (1990).
29. *Id.*
30. *Walton v. Arizona*, 497 U.S. 639 (1990).
31. *Id.*
32. *See* Palmer, *supra* note 4, at 39.
33. *State v. Simpson*, 462 S.E.2d 191 (N.C. 1995).
34. *Id.*
35. *Payne v. Tennessee* 501 U.S. 808 (1991).
36. *Id.*
37. *See* Palmer, *supra* note 4, at 39.
38. *Tison v. Arizona*, 481 U.S. 137 (1987).
39. *Id.*
40. *Ford v. State* 360 S.E.2d 258 (Ga. 1987).
41. *Id.*

Chapter 4

1. For a general discussion of the Free Exercise Clause, see Herbert W. Titus, *The Free Exercise Clause: Past, Present, and Future*, 6 Regent U. L. Rev. 7 (1995); Bernard Roberts, *The Common Law Sovereignty of Religious Lawfinders and the Free Exercise Clause*, 101 Yale L.J. 211 (1991); Douglas W. Kmiec, *The Original Understanding of the Free Exercise Clause and Religious Diversity*, 59 UMKC L. Rev. 591 (1991); Russell W. Galloway, Jr., *Basic Free Exercise Clause Analysis*, 29 Santa Clara L. Rev. 865 (1989); Jesse H. Choper, *The Free Exercise Clause: A Structural Overview and an Appraisal of Recent Developments*, 27 Wm. & Mary L. Rev. 943 (1985).
2. *Thomas v. Review Bd. of Indiana Employment Security Div.*, 450 U.S. 707, 714 (1981). See P. Bruzzone, *Religious Aspects of Organ Transplantation*, 40 Trans. Proc. 1064 (2008).
3. *See Braunfeld v. Brown*, 366 U.S. 599 (1961).
4. *Gillette v. United States*, 401 U.S. 437, 452 (1971).
5. *Church of the Lukumi Babalu Aye, Inc. v. City of Hialeah*, 508 U.S. 520, 546 (1993).
6. For a general discussion of the Establishment Clause, see Akhil Reed Amar, *Some Notes on the Establishment Clause*, 2 Roger Williams U. L. Rev. 1 (1996); Michael J. Mannheimer, *Equal Protection Principles and the Establishment Clause: Equal Participation in the Community as the Central Link*, 69 Temp. L. Rev. 95 (1996); Anastasia P. Winslow, *Sacred Standards: Honoring the Establishment Clause in Protecting Native American Sacred Sites*, 38 Ariz. L. Rev. 1291 (1996).
7. *Lemon v. Kurtzman*, 403 U.S. 602 (1971).
8. *Id.* at 612–13.
9. *See* John E. Joiner, *A Page of History or a Volume of Logic? Reassessing the Supreme Court's Establishment Clause Jurisprudence*, 73 Den. U. L. Rev. 507 (1996).
10. *Agostini v. Felton*, 117 S. Ct. 1997, 2015 (1997).
11. *Roemer v. Board of Public Works of Md.*, 426 U.S. 736 (1976).
12. *Butler v. Perry*, 240 U.S. 328, 332 (1916).
13. *United States v. Kozminski*, 487 U.S. 931 (1988).
14. *Id.* at 942.
15. *Id.*
16. *Id.*
17. Additionally, the Supreme Court has recognized that the prohibition against involuntary servitude does not prevent governments from compelling individuals, by the threat of criminal sanction, to perform certain civic duties. *See Hurtado v. United States*, 410 U.S. 578 (1973) (jury service); *Selective Draft Law Cases*, 245 U.S. 366 (1918) (military service).
18. *Civil Rights Cases*, 109 U.S. 3, 20 (1883).
19. *Armstrong v. United States*, 364 U.S. 40 (1960).
20. *Id.* at 49.
21. Louis J. Palmer, Jr., *Capital Punishment: A Utilitarian Proposal for Recycling Transplantable Organs as Part of a Capital Felon's Death Sentence*, 29 U. West L.A. L. Rev. 1, 5 n.9 (1998).
22. *Id.* at 212 (emphasis in original).

Notes—Chapter 5

23. *Kaiser v. United States*, 444 U.S. 164, 176 (1979).
24. *Bennis v. Michigan*, 116 S. Ct. 994, 1001 (1996).
25. *Soldal v. Cook County*, 506 U.S. 56, 66 (1992).
26. *United States v. Jacobsen*, 466 U.S. 109 (1984).
27. *Id*. at 113.
28. *Soldal v. Cook County*, 506 U.S. 56 (1992).
29. *Id*. at 63 n.7.
30. *Hudson v. Palmer*, 468 U.S. 517 (1984).
31. The Supreme Court has held that there is an "equal protection component of the Due Process Clause of the Fifth Amendment." *United States v. Armstrong*, 116 S. Ct. 1480, 1486 (1996).
32. *Jones v. Helms*, 452 U.S. 412 (1981).
33. *Id*. at 423–24.
34. *See generally* Louis J. Palmer, Jr., *The Death Penalty in the United States: A Complete Guide to Federal and State Laws* 5–9 (2013).
35. *Id*. at 18.
36. *Id*.
37. *Coker v. Georgia*, 433 U.S. 584 (1977).
38. *Id*.
39. *Id*.
40. *Kennedy v. Louisiana*, 554 U.S. 407 (2008).
41. In *Graham v. Florida*, 130 S.Ct 2011 (2010) the Supreme Court held that "[t]he Constitution prohibits the imposition of a life without parole sentence on a juvenile offender who did not commit homicide."
42. *Kennedy v. Louisiana*, 554 U.S. 407, 437 (2008).
43. *Jurek v. Texas*, 428 U.S. 262 (1976).
44. *See generally* Palmer, *supra* note 34, at 91–106.
45. *Id*.
46. *Jurek v. Texas*, 428 U.S. 262 (1976).
47. *Id*.
48. The Fifth Amendment also contains a Due Process Clause.
49. *See Loving v. Virginia*, 388 U.S. 1 (1967).
50. *See Skinner v. Oklahoma ex rel. Williamson*, 316 U.S. 535 (1942).
51. *See Meyer v. Nebraska*, 262 U.S. 390 (1923).
52. *See Griswold v. Connecticut*, 381 U.S. 479 (1965).
53. *See Eisenstadt v. Baird*, 405 U.S. 438 (1972).
54. *See Rochin v. California*, 342 U.S. 165 (1952).
55. *See Planned Parenthood v. Casey*, 505 U.S. 833 (1992).
56. *Washington v. Glucksberg*, 117 S. Ct. 2258 (1997).
57. *Id*. at 2265.
58. *Id*.
59. *Id*. at 2265–66.
60. *Id*. at 2269.
61. *Id*.
62. *Id*. at 2271.
63. *Id*.
64. *Furman v. Georgia*, 408 U.S. 238 (1972).
65. *Id*.
66. For a discussion of the historical development of the first ten amendments to the Constitution, see R. Rutland, *The Birth of the Bill of Rights, 1776-1791* (1955).
67. *Furman v. Georgia*, 408 U.S. 238 (1972).
68. *Id*.
69. *Id*.
70. *Id*. Other states adopted similar clauses: Delaware Declaration of Rights (1776); Maryland Declaration of Rights (1776); Massachusetts Declaration of Rights (1780); and New Hampshire Bill of Rights (1783).
71. Anthony F. Granucci, *Nor Cruel and Unusual Punishments Inflicted: The Original Meaning*, 57 Cal. L. Rev. 839 (1969).
72. *Trop v. Dulles*, 356 U.S. 86 (1958).
73. *Furman v. Georgia*, 408 U.S. 238 (1972).
74. *See generally* Palmer, *supra* note 34, at 177–89.
75. *Id*. at 187.
76. *Furman v. Georgia*, 408 U.S. 238 (1972).
77. Kim Moon, *Organ Transplantation*, http://rxethics.org/Kim%20Moon%20Organ%20Donation%20paper.pdf.
78. *Furman v. Georgia*, 408 U.S. 238 (1972).
79. *State ex rel. Cooper v. Board of Educ. of Summers County*, 478 S.E.2d 341, 347 (W.Va. 1996).
80. *Gregg v. Georgia*, 428 U.S. 153 (1976).
81. *Id*.

Chapter 5

1. Alabama, California, Florida, Missouri, South Carolina, Virginia, and Washington.
2. Arkansas (if unconstitutional), Delaware (if unconstitutional), New Hampshire (for any reason), Oklahoma (if unconstitutional), Utah (if unconstitutional), and Wyoming (if unconstitutional).

Notes—Chapter 6

3. Arizona, Kentucky and Utah.
4. Tennessee.
5. *Campbell v. Wood*, 18 F.3d 662 (9th Cir. 1994).
6. *See* Louis J. Palmer, Jr., *Capital Punishment: A Utilitarian Proposal for Recycling Transplantable Organs as Part of a Capital Felon's Death Sentence*, 29 U. West L.A. L. Rev. 1, 28 (1998).
7. *Id.*
8. *Gilmore v. Utah*, 429 U.S. 1012 (1976).
9. *Id.*
10. *Furman v. Georgia*, 408 U.S. 238 (1972).
11. *Gregg v. Georgia*, 428 U.S. 153 (1976).
12. *Gilmore v. Utah*, 429 U.S. 1012 (1976).
13. *Andrew v. Shulsen*, 802 F.2d 1256 (10th Cir. 1986).
14. *Wilkerson v. Utah*, 99 U.S. 130 (1878).
15. *See* V. A. C. Gatrell, *The Hanging Tree: Execution and the English People, 1770–1868* (1994).
16. *Rupe v. Wood*, 863 F. Supp. 1307 (W.D. Wash 1994).
17. *Ex parte Granviel*, 561 S.W.2d 503 (Tex. 1978).
18. *Id.*
19. *Woolls v. McCotter*, 798 F.2d 695 (5th Cir. 1986).
20. *In re Kemmler*, 136 U.S. 436 (1890).
21. *Id.*
22. *Id.*
23. *Id.*
24. *Id.*
25. *Francis v. Resweber*, 329 U.S. 459 (1947).
26. *Thomas v. Jones*, 742 F. Supp. 598 (S.D. Ala. 1990).
27. *State v. Gee Jon*, 211 P. 676 (Nev. 1923). *See also Duisen v. State*, 441 S.W.2d 688 (Mo. 1969) (holding that lethal gas was not cruel and unusual); *People v. Daugherty*, 256 P.2d 911 (Cal. 1953) (holding that lethal gas was not cruel and unusual). In accord, *Calhoun v. State*, 468 A.2d 45 (Md. 1983).
28. *State v. Gee Jon*, 211 P. 676 (Nev. 1923).
29. *Gray v. Lucas*, 710 F.2d 1048 (5th Cir. 1983); *Hunt v. Nuth*, 57 F.3d 1327 (4th Cir. 1995).
30. *Fierro v. Gomez*, 77 F.3d 301 (9th Cir. 1996), *rev'd*, 117 S. Ct. 285 (1996).
31. *Gray v. Lucas*, 710 F.2d 1048 (5th Cir. 1983).
32. Palmer, *supra* note 6, at 28.
33. *Id.* at 29.
34. *Id.*
35. *Id.* at 30.
36. *Id.* at 31.
37. *Id.* at 32.
38. *Id.*
39. *Id.* at 34.
40. *Id.*
41. *Id.* at 36.
42. *Id.*

Chapter 6

1. Furman v. Georgia, 408 U.S. 238 (1972).
2. Smith was eventually convicted of both murders; however, the death penalty was not imposed on her.
3. Demery entered a plea of guilty, and Green was found guilty by a jury. Both men escaped the death penalty and were sentenced to life in prison.
4. Simpson was ultimately acquitted of all charges stemming from both homicides.
5. Du Pont was eventually convicted of second-degree murder and sentenced to prison.
6. The ordinary citizen was required to assist in the arrest of felons and misdemeanants. During the thirteenth century, communities were fined if they failed to apprehend a homicide suspect. 2 William Holdsworth, *A History of English Law* 598–607 (reprint 1973).
7. 7 William Holdsworth, *A History of English Law* 4 (reprint 1973).
8. 6 William Holdsworth, *A History of English Law* 466–81 (reprint 1971).
9. *Skinner v. Dostert*, 278 S.E.2d 624 (W.Va. 1981).
10. *Id.*
11. *Id.*
12. England did not utilize a public prosecutor until 1879, when it created the Director of Public Prosecutions Office. W. Scott Van Alstyne, Jr., *The District Attorney—A Historical Puzzle*, 1952 Wis. L. Rev. 125 (1952).
13. 3 Sanford H. Kadish, *Encyclopedia of Crime and Justice* 1286 (1983).
14. *Id.*
15. *Id.*
16. Van Alstyne, *supra* note 12.
17. *Id.*
18. *Id.*
19. *Id.* England conquered New Netherland in 1664.
20. Connecticut (criminal justice commission appoints prosecutors); Delaware (attorney general appoints prosecutors); Florida (attorney general appoints prosecutors); New Jersey (governor appoints prosecutors);

Notes—Chapter 6

Rhode Island (attorney general appoints prosecutors); federal system (president appoints prosecutors).

21. For a general discussion of a trial judge's ability to prevent the prosecutor from seeking the death penalty, see Margaret T. Stopp, *The Power of the Judiciary to Preclude the Death Penalty Before Trial*, 68 Fla. B.J. 116 (1994).

22. Some jurisdictions provide for binding punishment recommendations that judges must follow, if accepted by the court—e.g., Rule 11(1)(e)(C) of the Federal Rules of Criminal Procedure. "Type C" agreements, as they are called, are rare because they do in fact invade the province of the judiciary in determining the sentence.

23. *See* Louis J. Palmer, Jr., *The Death Penalty in the United States: A Complete Guide to Federal and State Laws* 63 (McFarland, 2013).

24. *People ex rel. Carey v. Cousins*, 397 N.E.2d 809, 812 (Ill. 1979).

25. *McCleskey v. Kemp*, 481 U.S. 279 (1987).

26. *Id.*

27. *See generally* Palmer, *supra* note 23, at 160–165.

28. For a critique of the weighing process, see Marcia A. Widder, *Hanging Life in the Balance: The Supreme Court and the Metaphor of Weighing in the Penalty Phase of the Capital Trial*, 68 Tul. L. Rev. 1341 (1994).

29. *State v. Wood*, 648 P.2d 71 (Utah 1981).

30. *Id.*

31. Alabama, California, Indiana, Louisiana, Montana, Nebraska, New Hampshire, Pennsylvania, and the federal system.

32. Arizona, Colorado, Florida, Idaho, Kansas, Kentucky, Mississippi, Nevada, North Carolina, and Oklahoma.

33. Delaware.

34. Arkansas, Ohio, Tennessee, and Utah.

35. For further discussion of the distinction between weighing and nonweighing, see Srikanth Srinivasan, *Capital Sentencing Doctrine and the Weighing-Nonweighing Distinction*, 47 Stan. L. Rev. 1347 (1995).

36. Georgia, Montana, Oregon, South Carolina, South Dakota, Virginia, Washington, and Wyoming.

37. There was a third nonweighing process used by the state of Connecticut. That process is no longer used because that state abolished the death penalty in 2012.

38. Georgia, Missouri, Oregon, South Carolina, South Dakota, Virginia, and Wyoming.

39. Washington.

40. Alabama, Arizona, California, Delaware, Idaho, Indiana, Kansas, Ohio, Oklahoma, Pennsylvania, Tennessee, Texas and Wyoming.

41. Oregon and Washington.

42. For a discussion along these lines, see John W. Poulos, *The Supreme Court, Capital Punishment, and the Substantive Criminal Law: The Rise and Fall of Mandatory Capital Punishment*, 28 Ariz. L. Rev. 143 (1986).

43. Colorado, Florida, Kentucky, Louisiana, Mississippi, Missouri, Montana, Nebraska, Nevada, New Hampshire, North Carolina, and the federal system.

44. Georgia, South Carolina, South Dakota, and Virginia.

45. *See generally* Palmer, *supra* note 23, at 167–183, 209–224.

46. For a discussion of "harmless" error analysis in death-penalty cases, see C. Elliot Kessler, *Death and Harmlessness: Application of the Harmless Error Rule by the Bird and Lucas Courts in Death Penalty Cases—A Comparison and Critique*, 26 U.S.F. L. Rev. 41 (1991).

47. *McKane v. Durston*, 153 U.S. 684 (1894). *See Franz v. State*, 754 S.W.2d 839 (Ark. 1988).

48. *McKane v. Durston*, 153 U.S. 684 (1894).

49. Alabama, Arizona, California, Colorado, Florida, Georgia, Indiana, Louisiana, Missouri, North Carolina, Ohio, Oklahoma, Oregon, Pennsylvania, Tennessee, Texas, Washington, and the federal system.

50. For a general discussion of appellate review, see Ira P. Robbins, *Toward a More Just and Effective System of Review in State Death Penalty Cases*, 40 Am. U. L. Rev. 1 (1990).

51. Utah.

52. Alabama, California, Delaware, Idaho, Indiana, Kansas, Kentucky, Mississippi, Missouri, Montana, Nevada, North Carolina, Oklahoma, Oregon, Virginia, Washington, and Wyoming.

53. For a discussion of the waiver issue, see Tim Kaine, *Capital Punishment and the Waiver of Sentence Review*, 18 Harv. C.R. C.L. L. Rev. 483 (1983).

54. For further discussion of the harmless error doctrine, see Linda E. Carter, *Harmless Error in the Penalty Phase of a Capital Case: A Doctrine Misunderstood and Misapplied*, 28 Ga. L. Rev. 125 (1993).

55. Georgia, Idaho, Maryland, Missouri, Nevada, Oklahoma, South Carolina, South Dakota, Virginia, Washington, and the federal system.

Notes—Chapter 6

56. U.S. Department of Justice, *Capital Punishment 2011*, Bureau of Justice Statistics Table 10 (July 2013).

57. For further discussion, see Gerald Kirven, *Capital Crime and Punishment: Shortening the Time Between Them*, 42 Fed. Law. 20 (1995).

58. The defendant could remain in the state system by starting state habeas corpus proceedings.

59. The defendant can begin by filing a federal habeas corpus petition in a federal district court.

60. For a critical discussion of habeas corpus, see Alan W. Clarke, *Procedural Labyrinths and the Injustice of Death: A Critique of Death Penalty Habeas Corpus*, 30 U. Rich. L. Rev. 303 (1996).

61. For a discussion of federal habeas corpus issues, see Joseph L. Hoffman, *Is Innocent Sufficient? An Essay on the U.S. Supreme Court's Continuing Problems with Federal Habeas Corpus and the Death Penalty*, 68 Ind. L.J. 817 (1993); Stephanie O. Joy, *A Claim of Newly Discovered Evidence of Actual Innocence Does Not Entitle Death Penalty Claimant to Federal Habeas Corpus Relief*, 4 Seton Hall Const. L.J. 361 (1993); Joseph L. Hoffman, *Starting from Scratch: Rethinking Federal Habeas Review of Death Penalty Cases*, 20 Fla. St. U. L. Rev. 133 (1992); Karl N. Metzner, *Retroactivity, Habeas Corpus, and the Death Penalty: An Unholy Alliance*, 41 Duke L.J. 160 (1991); Vivian Berger, *Justice Delayed or Justice Denied? A Comment on Recent Proposals to Reform Death Penalty Habeas Corpus*, 90 Colum. L. Rev. 1665 (1990); Diane Wells, *Federal Habeas Corpus and the Death Penalty: A Need for a Return to the Principles of Furman*, 80 J. Crim. L. & Criminology 427 (1989).

62. One of the Supreme Court decisions limiting habeas corpus petitions in federal court is *McCleskey v. Zant*, 111 S. Ct. 1454 (1991). For a discussion of this case and its impact, see Cheryl R. Sweeney, *McCleskey v. Zant: The Cause and Prejudice Standard in Capital Punishment Cases*, 24 U. Tol. L. Rev. 231 (1992); Martha Hallisey, *To Habe or Not to Habe: Curtailing the Writ of Habeas Corpus in McCleskey v. Zant*, 19 New Eng. J. on Crim. & Civ. Confinement 397 (1993); David D. Kammer, *Restricting New-Claim Successive Applications for Federal Writs of Habeas Corpus: McCleskey v. Zant*, 60 U. Cin. L. Rev. 1405 (1992); Philip A. Bower, *Setting New Standards for Successive Different-Claim Habeas Corpus Petitions: McCleskey v. Zant*, 19 Ohio N.U. L. Rev. 139 (1992); Paul C. Gluckow, *Habeas Corpus—Abuse of the Writ—Petitioner Raising Claim in Second or Subsequent Federal Habeas Corpus Petition Not Advanced in Prior Petition Must Show Cause for Failing to Bring Claim Previously and Prejudice Therefrom—McCleskey v. Zant*, 22 Seton Hall L. Rev. 467 (1992); Thomas S. Hall, *McCleskey v. Zant: A Stricter Standard of Review for Abuse of the Writ of Habeas Corpus Involving Successive Federal Petitions*, 25 Creighton L. Rev. 233 (1991).

INDEX

aggravating circumstances 67–68, 102–103, 152–153
Akers v. Buckner-Rush Enterprises, Inc. 40
Akers v. Prime Succession of Tennessee, Inc. 33
Albrecht v. Treon 39
Alzheimer's 38
Amaker v. King County 40
Ambrose v. Kerrison 17
American Academy of Orthopedic Surgery 36
American Bar Association 70
American Medical Association 127
Anatomical Gift Act 35, 52, 60
Anatomy Act 18–19
Andrew v. Shulsen 120
Andrews v. McGowan 39
anesthesia-induced brain death 141
Anesthesiology and Critical Care Medicine Research Laboratories 137
Anglo-American jurisprudence 97, 101, 122, 130, 133, 145, 147, 156
anonymity 4, 161–162
arbitrary 32, 65–66, 68, 99, 102, 108, 113, 141–143, 154–155
Armstrong v. United States 96
asphyxiation 137–139
atheist 88
Australia 46
Austria 57

barbiturate 125
Barnard, Christian 44
Beard v. Worrell 6
Becker, Donald P. 124
Becket, Thomas 6
Belgium 57

Benson v. Superior Court 39
bereaved 24, 31
Bessemer Land & Improvement v. Jenkins 26
bifurcated trial 67, 135
Biomedical Tissue Services 50
Bishop, Jesse Walter 135
black market *see* body part market
Blackstone, William 122
blood vessels 44
Blystone, Scott Wayne *see Blystone v. Pennsylvania*
Blystone v. Pennsylvania 75
Board of Regents v. Oglesby 35
body part market 44–45, 52–53; black market 49, 53; commercial proposals 53; demand for 45–47; method of obtaining 52–53; sale of 47–52
Bolivia 46
bone marrow 44, 48–49
Boxter, William 120
Brazil 46
Brennan, William 107–111, 113
Brodie, Howard 136
Brooks, Charlie 126
Brooks, James, Jr. 132
Bulgaria 57
Burger, Warren 119

cadaver 1–3, 9–10, 13–15, 17–18, 43–44, 50–51, 53, 55, 57, 63, 97, 107
Campbell, Charles 124; *see also Campbell v. Wood*
Campbell v. Wood 117
Canada 46
capricious 65, 68
Casscells, Ward 127
CBS News 136

181

Index

Chapman, Lisa 83
China 46
Choppin v. Labranche 23
Christian 6, 15–16, 28
Christopher, Charisse *see Payne v. Tennessee*
Christopher, Lacie *see Payne v. Tennessee*
Christopher, Nicholas *see Payne v. Tennessee*
civil liberty 29, 85
civilian law 119
Clark, Ramsey 65
Coke, Lord 12, 17
Coker v. Georgia 100
Colavito v. New York Organ Donor Network, Inc. 37
common law, origin and meaning 5–7
Commonwealth v. Edmiston 72–73
Commonwealth v. Garzone 50
Congress 7, 47, 49–50, 86, 120, 127
Constitutional Convention 109
Constitutions of Clarendon 6
Consumer Protection Act 33
coram nobis 160
cornea 44, 48, 53, 57–59
corpse: arresting of 13–14; compensation for disinterment of 25–27; compensation for failing turn over 30; compensation for mutilation of 27–28; compensation for unauthorized autopsy of 28–29; compensation for unauthorized removal of body part 29–30; digging up of 17–18, 22–23; disposing of by will 10–11, 24; dissection of 18–19; duty to bury 15–17; holding for payment of debt 23; inanimate object 8; libeling of 14–15; lump of earth 8–9; mutilation of 20–22; no-property rule 9–30; quasi-property rule 24–42, 97–98; statutory disposal of 63–64
court systems, general structure of 156
Craft, David 132
Crawford v. J. Avery Bryan Funeral Home, Inc. 39
cremate 9–10, 33, 40–41, 51, 85
crematory 33
Croatia 57
Crocker v. Pleasant 31
Cruel and Unusual Punishment Clause 65, 107–114

cyanide gas 133, 135–138, 141
cyclosporine 44
Cyprus 57
Czech Republic 57

Darragh, Martina 1
Darter, Jean *see State v. Simpson*
death: automatic sentence 153–154; death row 1–2, 94, 111, 150; discretionary sentence 153–154; eligible murders 102, 148; sentence review 156–160
default method of execution 123, 135
DeLora, Pablo 1
Demery, Larry 143–144, 151
Denmark 57
direct appeal 156–158, 160
discrimination 4, 65, 141–144, 149
dissection-enhanced punishment 62–63
Dodd, Westley Allen 124
donation-based organ supply system 52–53
donor card 53, 59–60
Douglas, William 65, 108
Dryden, John 13
Due Process Clause 103–106; liberty interest 104–105; personal choice 105–106; procedural due process 31–32, 103; substantive due process 32, 104–105
Dunbar, Tad 135
Dunkins, Horace, Jr. 132
Du Pont, John 143, 150

ecclesiastical courts 5–6, 9, 11–13, 17, 20, 24
Edmiston, Stephen Rex *see Commonwealth v. Edmiston*
Eighth Amendment 65–66, 107–109, 118, 121–122, 125–128, 131–133, 135, 138
electric chair 130–133
electrocution 111, 115–116, 128–134, 140
Ellenborough, Lord 13–14
England 3–9, 12, 15, 18, 20, 24, 108, 146–147
English Bill of Rights 65, 108–109
English jurisprudence 5, 20
Enos v. Snyder 24
Equal Protection Clause 49, 99, 103, 108
Establishment Clause 86, 91, 93; law cannot advance nor inhibit religion 92–93; no excessive entanglement with religion 93–94; secular purpose of law 91–92

Index

Estonia 57
Eury, Stephanie *see State v. Simpson*
Evans, John Louis 133
Evanston Ins. Co. v. Legacy of Life, Inc. 34
Ex parte Granviel 98
execution methods 115–117; electrocution 128–133, 140; firing squad 118–122, 138; hanging 122–126, 138; lethal gas 133–138, 140; lethal injection 126–128, 139–140; new method of 141
execution option jurisdictions 116
Exelby v. Handyside 9–11, 17
exhume 10
expediting capital punishment 155–160

fetus 40–42, 48
Fifth Amendment 96, 99
Finland 57
First Amendment 86, 118
First Person Consent Act 60
FK-506 44
Flamholz, David I. 1
Flynn v. Holder 49
Foley v. Phelps 28
Food and Drug Administration 126–127, 140
Ford, Melbert Ray, Jr. *see Ford v. State*
Ford v. State 82
Foster, Henry 14
Fourteenth Amendment 31–32, 99, 104–105, 130
Fourth Amendment 98
France 57
Francis, Willie *see Francis v. Resweber*
Francis v. Resweber 129
Free Exercise Clause 86–90, 118; compelling governmental interest 89–90; general applicability 88–89; neutrality requirement 87–88
Furman v. Georgia 64–70, 107–109, 111, 113, 119, 131–132, 142–143, 151, 154–156
futures-market organ supply system 54; Cohen model 54–55; Crespi model 54, 56; Hansmann model 54; Schwindt-Vining model 54

Garzone, Gerald 50–51
Garzone, Louis 50–51
Germany 57
Gilbert v. Buzzard 18
Gilmore, Gary *see Gilmore v. Utah*

Gilmore v. Utah 119
glands 44, 165
Goldman, Ronald 143
Gray, Jimmy Lee *see Gray v. Lucas*
Gray v. Lucas 135
great writ 160
Greece 57
Green, Daniel 143–144, 151
Greenawalt, Randy *see Tison v. Arizona*
Gregg v. Georgia 66, 69, 113–114, 119, 157
Griffith v. Charlotte, Columbia & Augusta R'd Co 20
guillotine 125
guilt phase 67, 151–152, 157

habeas corpus 123, 126, 133, 138, 158–160
Hackett v. Hackett 23
Haynes' Case 8–10
heart 27, 44–47, 136–137, 140, 165
Hendrickson, Barbara *see Campbell v. Wood*
Hill v. Travelers' Ins. Co. 39
Hindu (Hindoos) 16, 66
Hockenhammer v. Lexington & Eastern R'y Co 24
Hodes, Richard S. 127
Hoover, Robert *see Walton v. Arizona*
Hudson v. Palmer 98
human body part market *see* body part market
Hungary 57

immunosuppressive drug 44
In re Beekman Street 12, 25–26
In re Kemmler 128–129
India 46
international organ trade 45
intravenous injection 123, 126
Involuntary Servitude Clause 94–96
Iran 46
Iraq 46
Israel 27, 46, 50, 58–60
Israeli organ-for-organ law 59–60
Italy 57

Jacobus v. Congregation of Children of Israel 26–27
Janicki v. Hospital of St. Raphael 41
Japan 46
Jews 16
Johns Hopkins Medical School 137
Jon, Gee *see State v. Gee Jon*

Index

Jones v. Ashburnham 13
Jones v. Helms 99
Jordan, James 143
Jordan, Michael 143
judicial stay of execution 157–160
Jurek v. Texas 102
jury discretion 151–155
justification for removing organs 71; deterrent 74–77; moral 71–74; restitution 81–84; retributive 77–81

Kellam, Brandi L. 1
Kennedy v. Louisiana 101
Kester, Tracie M. 1
Ketchum, Black Jack 124
Keyes v. Konkel 23
kidney 37, 44–46, 48, 50, 59, 140
Koerber v. Patek 29
Kyles v. Southern Railway Co 27–28

Larson v. Chase 28
Latvia 57
Lemon v. Kurtzman 91
Leuchter, Fred A. 132
liver 44–46, 48, 59, 73, 140
long drop method of hanging 123, 125
Long v. Chicago, Rock Island & Pacific R'y Co. 21–22
Longo, Christian 2
lungs 45–46, 48, 59, 73, 140
Luxemburg 57
Lyons, Donnelda 82
Lyons, John 82

mandamus 160
mandated choice 60–61
Marshall, Thurgood 108
Mason, George 109
Mastromarino, Michael 50–51
Matich, Martha Chapman 83
Maynard v. Cartwright 73–74
Mazur, Betty *see Mazur v. Woodson*
Mazur, Paul *see Mazur v. Woodson*
Mazur v. Woodson 38–39
McCafferty, James 50–51
McCarrick, Pat M. 1
McCleskey v. Kemp 149–151
McKane v. Durston 156
McVeigh, Timothy 151
Meagher v. Driscoll 22
Medical College of Georgia 35–37
Miranda v. Arizona 7

miscarriage 40
Mitchell, Aaron 136
mitigating circumstances 67, 151–153
Moldova 46
moratorium 143, 155

National Conference of Commissioners on Uniform State Laws 52
National Organ Procurement and Transplantation Network 47
National Organ Transplant Act 47–49, 52
National Organ Transplant Registry 45
Nepal 46
nerves 44
Netherlands 57
no-property rule *see* corpse
nolle prosequi 145
nonbinding recommendation by jury 152
nonweighing process jurisdictions 151–154
Norway 57

Oglesby, Francis 35
Oman 46
opt in system 53
opt out system *see* presumed consent
organ removal: informing public 69–70; justification 71; part of sentence 62–64

Pakistan 46
pancreas 45–46, 48
paralytic agent 126–127
Parliament 7, 66, 144
Payne, Pervis Tyrone *see Payne v. Tennessee*
Payne v. Tennessee 79–81
penalty phase 67, 151–153, 157
Perales, Donny J. 1
Peru 46
Peter Bent Brigham Hospital 44
Peters v. Peters 23
Philippines 46
physician-assisted suicide 105
Pierce v. Proprietors of Swan Point Cemetery 25
poisonous gas 134
Poland 57
Portugal 57
Powell, Thomas 76
prejudice 19, 65–66, 68

Index

presumed consent 57–58
prisoners executed for organs *see* China
prohibition, writ of 160
prosecutor: Colonial America 145–148; common law 144–145; death penalty discretion 148–151; discretion 143; New Netherland colony 146–147; schout 147–148
Protestant 18

quasi-property rule *see* corpse

Ramsey, Sharold *see* Walton v. Arizona
Ravani, Bahram 124
Regina v. Feist 19
Regina v. Fox 13–14
Regina v. Price 16, 18
Regina v. Scott 14
Regina v. Sharpe 18
Regina v. Stewart 15
Regina v. Vann 15
rejection factor 44
Renihan v. Wright 30
Rex v. Cundick 19
Rex v. Lynn 12, 17
Rex v. Topham 14
Richardson, Ruth 1
Richter scale 64
Riddle, Charma 73
Riddle, Hugh 73
Ritter v. Smith 133
Roe v. Wade 40–41
Roemer v. Board of Public Works of Md. 93
Rosen, Nick 50
Rosenbaum, Levy Izhak 50
Rupe, Mitchell *see* Rupe v. Wood
Rupe v. Wood 123–126

Saudi Arabia 46
Schultz, Dave 144
Secord v. Secord 22
Seizure Clause 98–99, 104
Shkrum, Michael James 79
Simpson, Nicole Brown 144
Simpson, O.J. 144, 151
Sing, Hughie 134
skin 36, 44, 48, 51, 140
Skipper, Robert 132
Slavery Clause 94–96
Slovak Republic 57
Slovenia 57

Smith, Susan 143–144, 150
Smithburger, Dalton Charles, Jr. 75–76
sodium pentothal 141
sodium thiopental 127
Soldal v. Cook County 98
South Africa 44, 46
Spain 57
Specialty Nat. Ins. Co. v. English Bros. Funeral Home 51
Staiano-Ross, Kathryn 1
State v. Gee Jon 133–134
State v. Powell 58
State v. Simpson 78, 80
State v. Wilson 23
State v. Wood 152–153
stay *see* judicial stay of execution
Stewart, Potter 67
stillborn 40–42
strict scrutiny 89
Sweden 57

Takings Clause 96–98, 104
temporal court 5–7, 13, 20
Tencer, Alan 124
tendons 44, 51
Thirteenth Amendment 94–96
Thomas, Bobbie 79
Thomas v. Jones 131
Thompson v. Deeds 23
three-tier judicial system 156, 158–159
Tillman v. Detroit Receiving Hosp. 58
Tison, Donald *see* Tison v. Arizona
Tison, Gary *see* Tison v. Arizona
Tison, Raymond *see* Tison v. Arizona
Tison, Ricky *see* Tison v. Arizona
Tison v. Arizona 81, 84
Tobey, Myer 136
Tomasits v. Cochise Memory Gardens, Inc. 39
transplant tourism 46
Traystman, Richard 137
Trop v. Dulles 109
Turkey 46, 57
Turner, Barnard 13
Turner, Roger 83
two-tier judicial system 156, 158–159

Uniform Anatomical Gift Act *see* Anatomical Gift Act
United Kingdom 57
United States v. Jacobsen 98
United States v. Kozminski 95

Index

Vandam, Leroy David 127
Vann, William 15
Virginia's Declaration of Rights 109

Wales 57
Walker v. Firelands Community Hosp. 40
Walser v. Resthaven Memorial Gardens, Inc. 39
Walton v. Arizona 76–77
Washington v. Glucksberg 104–105
weighing process jurisdictions 152–154
Whaley v. County of Saginaw 39
Wicklund, Renae *see Campbell v. Wood*
Wicklund, Shannah *see Campbell v. Wood*

Wilborn, Bessie 35–36
Wilkerson v. Utah 120, 122
Willes, Lord 19
Williams v. Williams 10–11
Wood, Tana 124
Woodson, Victor 38
Woolls, Randy Lynn see *Woolls v. McCotter*
Woolls v. McCotter 126
Wright, Peter B. 36
writ of certiorari 129, 158–160
writ of error 120, 156

Zeigler-Hort, Matilda 128

www.ingramcontent.com/pod-product-compliance
Ingram Content Group UK Ltd.
Pitfield, Milton Keynes, MK11 3LW, UK
UKHW042013140426
5217IPUK00015B/1140